L'avventura

L'avventura

Michelangelo

Antonioni, director

Seymour Chatman and

Guido Fink, editors

Rutgers University Press

New Brunswick and London

L'avventura is volume 12 in the Rutgers Films in Print Series.

Copyright © 1989 by Rutgers,
The State University
All rights reserved
Manufactured in the United States of America

Library of Congress Cataloging-in-Publication Data

L'Avventura / Michelangelo Antonioni, director ;
Seymour Chatman and Guido Fink, editors.
   p. cm.—(Rutgers films in print ; v. 12)
   Filmography: p.
   Bibliography: p.
   ISBN 0-8135-1334-0 (cloth)
   ISBN 0-8135-1335-9 (pbk.)
   1. Avventura (Motion picture) I. Antonioni,
Michelangelo. II. Chatman, Seymour Benjamin, 1928–   III. Fink, Guido, 1935–
IV. Avventura (Motion picture) V. Series.
PN1997.A953A94 1988
791.43'72—dc19   88-18249
                                  CIP

British Cataloging-in-Publication information available

This continuity script is based, in part, on the screenplay L'avventura, by Michelangelo Antonioni, by arrangement with Grove Press.

The illustrations on pages 72, 137, and 157 are reproduced courtesy of the Museum of Modern Art/Film Stills Archive.

"A Talk with Michelangel Antonioni on His Work," Film Culture, no. 24 (Spring 1962): 50–51; originally published in Bianco e nero 22, nos. 2–3 (February/March 1961):69–95. "Vi parlo di me per raccontarvi un film" from Cinema nuovo 32, no. 284/5 (August/October 1983):4–6, translated by Seymour Chatman. Review of L'avventura by Marie-Claire Ropars-Wuilleumier, Espirit 12 (December 1960): 2080–2084, copyright © Editions du Seuil, 1970; translated by Seymour Chatman and Renée Morel; used by permission of Editions du Seuil and Marie-Claire Ropars-Wuilleumier. Remarks on L'avventura by Italo Calvino, "Quattro domande sul cinema italiano," Cinema nuovo, no. 149 (January/February 1961):33–34; translated by Alessandra Calanchi; used by permission of Cinema nuovo and Mrs. Esther Calvino. "A Shape Around a Black Point" by Geoffrey Nowell-Smith, Sight and Sound 33, no. 1 (Winter 1963/64):15–20; used by permission of Sight and Sound. "L'Avventura: A Closer Look" by Simon O. Lesser, Yale Review 54 (October 1964):41–50, © Yale University. "Dear Antonioni" by Roland Barthes, XL Mostra Internazionale del Cinema, 1979; translated by Nora Hoppe; used by permission of General Secretary of the Biennale of Venice. "Il concetto di scomparsa" by Pascal Bonitzer, in Michelangelo Antonioni: Identification di un autore, ed. Giorgio Tinazzi (Parma: Società Produzioni Editoriali, 1985); translated by Chris Breyer, Gavriel Moses, and Seymour Chatman; used by permission. "Antonioni, L'avventura, and Waiting" by Gianni Celati, Cinema & Cinema 14, no. 49 (June 1987):5–6; translated by Guido Fink.

Acknowledgments

The editors wish to express their thanks to Mirto Stone, Judith Rosen, Renée Morel, Gavriel Moses, Chris Breyer, Bertrand Augst, Leslie Mitchner, and Alessandra Calanchi.

We are especially grateful to Mirella Affron for help far beyond the normal duties of a general editor. To Charles Affron goes our fervent thanks for the preparation of the frame enlargements and the collection of the production stills.

Contents

Introduction

All the Adventures

Seymour Chatman

On a visit to New York, Antonioni asked if he could meet the painter Mark Rothko, whose work he admired. After looking closely at the paintings around the studio, he remarked that his films, like Rothko's paintings, were about "nothing." To take the remark literally would obviously miss Antonioni's point, a point clarified by Richard Gilman, who first recounted the incident, and went on to a fine assessment of Antonioni's place in modern art:

> Antonioni's films are indeed about nothing, which is not the same thing as being about nothingness.
>
> *L'avventura* and *La notte* are movies without a traditional subject. . . . They are about nothing we could have known without them, nothing to which we had already attached meanings or surveyed in other ways. They are, without being abstract, about nothing *in particular,* being instead, like most recent paintings, self-contained and absolute, an action and not the description of an action.
>
> They are part of that next step in our feelings which art is continually eliciting and recording. We have been taking that step for a long time, most clearly in painting, but also in music, in certain areas of fiction, in anti-theatre. It might be described as accession through reduction, the coming into truer forms through the cutting away of created encumbrances: all the replicas we have made of ourselves, all the misleading because logical or

only psychological narratives, the whole apparatus of reflected wisdom, the clichés, the inherited sensations, the received ideas.[1]

It is easy to suspect that Antonioni was punning, that "nothing" was meant both to echo, ironically, the proverbial Philistine reaction to modernist fiction ("Why, nothing happens in this story!") and, more seriously, to redefine the word: as Gilman puts it, Antonioni meant "nothing *in particular,*" that is, nothing except the spectacle of human lives simply being lived out. Narratives about "nothing" are not concerned with moments of eloquent closure on landmark events in ordinary life—marriage, coming into an inheritance, winning a war, solving a crime—in short, any of the resolutions or wrappings-up that nineteenth-century fictions lead us to expect.

"Accession through reduction" is a good way to describe cinema's rediscovered trust in the capacity of visual images to speak for themselves. With *L'avventura* Antonioni joined the tiny company of filmmakers in the sound era with sufficient inventiveness, courage, and respect for the medium to offer scenes of great psychological complexity with little or no dialogue. Or even more innovatively, scenes whose meanings are clearly unrelated to what the characters, if they could speak directly to us, might have us believe they mean. In the case of Antonioni, the effect is not one of irony. Rather, we are made to feel that the truth about people is more available in their faces, in the postures of their bodies, in their placement in the environment, than in their conversations. For the banality of conversation tends to opacify rather than clarify feelings.[2] Instead of turning us off, this way of revealing the characters' inner dilemmas inspires us, by some kind of aesthetic magic, to empathize, even to feel compassion for them, despite their shortcomings.

In recognizing that the cinema is a particularly appropriate medium to communicate such subtle effects, Antonioni pointed it in a new direction that has been called, perhaps a bit confusingly, "de-dramatized."[3] The term does not mean *un*dramatic in the sense of "without conflict or tension." It means, rather, "not theatrical, not pointedly controlled, focused, or manipulated to achieve height-

1. Richard Gilman, "About Nothing—with Precision," *Theater Arts* 46, no. 7 (July 1962), 11.

2. Among the early critics to appreciate Antonioni's retreat from sound was Parker Tyler: see the chapter entitled "Maze of the Modern Sensibility: An Antonioni Trilogy," in *Sex Psyche Etcetera in the Film* (New York: Horizon Press, 1969), especially pp. 83–88.

3. The term arose first, I think, in French criticism. It appears in the title of an early interview with Antonioni by Joseph Morgenstern called "How De-Dramatizer Works," *New York Herald Tribune* (April 2, 1961).

ened moments and effects." Because of cinema's capacity to reveal so much and on so large a screen,[4] Antonioni came to feel that he could eliminate more and more of the traditional auditory and visual enhancements inherited from the theater. These enhancements, of course, had evolved in the theater because of the considerable physical distance of the proscenium stage from the audience. In a way, Antonioni was only extending what stage actors had already learned when they went to Hollywood (often to their chagrin): that they had to tone down their delivery and gestures, that "projection" did not make sense in a medium that would record and even amplify the tiniest vocal and visual nuance. Beginning with *L'avventura*, Antonioni extended the "de-theatricalizing" or "de-histrionicizing" of cinema into areas other than acting, for instance, reducing and ultimately eliminating commentative music, using editing that did not reinforce or even deflected closure or dramatic intensity, promoting landscape and sets for their own sakes quite independently of their role as background, and so on.

Like any other stylistic approach to cinema, Antonioni's visual minimalism works best with certain kinds of themes and milieus. Central to his films of the early Sixties was the plight of the emotional life, the life that lies behind the visual façade that we present to the world. That plight, he thought, is most acutely displayed by the affluent because only they have the time and leisure to be preoccupied by it. As John Kenneth Galbraith observes, "The poor man has always a precise view of his problem and its remedy: he hasn't enough and he needs more. The rich man can assume or imagine a much greater variety of ills and he will be correspondingly less certain of their remedy."[5] Though Antonioni was interested in the emotional problems of the idle rich even in his first film, *Cronaca di un amore*, it took him ten years and four more feature films to perfect the means for representing them. In *Le amiche* (*The Girlfriends*, 1955), based on a novella of Cesare Pavese, the characters, though for the most part *haut bourgeois*, still said too much, still demonstrated too much verbal competence in expressing their feelings. Antonioni was first able to utilize silence and reticence as a powerfully characterizing tool in *Il grido* (*The Cry*, 1956) because the hero is a baffled proletarian, who sees his world crumble about him and responds by hitting the road. With such a protagonist, it made sense to present a sequence of picaresque scenes in relative silence. The character's appearance and the

4. It is not an accident that *L'avventura*, Antonioni's breakthrough film, should be his first in widescreen format.
5. John Kenneth Galbraith, *The Affluent Society*, 3rd ed. (New York: Signet, 1976), p. 1.

mournful winter background of the Po Valley say all that needs to be said about his plight.

But what Antonioni was struggling toward, and what he finally found in the company on Patrizia's yacht, on Lisca Bianca, at the villa of the Montaltos, and at the luxurious Hotel San Domenico, were intelligent and well-educated characters who would express their true feelings verbally if they *could,* but whose emotional situation was so confusing, fragile, and tenuous that they were reduced to chatter, in a feeble attempt to conceal their sense of futility. The silence that finally falls on them represents not a constitutional or social inarticulateness but an ultimate existential dilemma which robs them of the capacity to say what they feel.

From its earliest reviews, *L'avventura* was recognized as heavily influenced by existentialism—not in what Stanley Kauffmann has called its "cheapened" sense, but as a serious *modus vivendi,* a "belief that human beings can find a rationale, a morality, *in the living of their lives,* rather than huddling under a canopy of doctrine constructed to reassure." [6] Now this may seem to be what Sandro tries to get Claudia to believe when, in Noto (shot 362), she protests that "it's not right, it can't be right" that they should fall in love so soon after Anna's disappearance. "It's absurd," she cries. Sandro responds "Good. It's better if it's absurd. It just means there's nothing we can do about it. Do you understand?"

"Absurdity" may sound appropriate for the era, but how good an existentialist is Sandro? His refusal to accept traditional morality may seem endorsed by Antonioni's famous statement at a press conference at the 1960 Cannes Film Festival. Antonioni spoke of the "serious split between a science that is totally and consciously projected into the future, and a rigid and stereotyped morality which all of us recognize as such and yet sustain out of cowardice or sheer laziness." [7] People, he argued, find themselves "burdened with a heavy baggage

6. Stanley Kauffmann, "Michelangelo Antonioni's *L'avventura,*" *Horizon* 14, no. 4 (Autumn 1972), 52. The article was reprinted in *Living Images: Film Comment and Criticism* (New York: Harper & Row, 1975), pp. 332–340. Kauffmann had previously published one of the best early American reviews of the film: "Arrival of an Artist," *The New Republic* (April 10, 1961), 26–27, reprinted in *A World on Film* (New York: Dell, 1967), pp. 299–302.

7. This statement appears in "Contexts," below; it is excerpted from a translation of a discussion held on March 16, 1961, at the Centro Sperimentale di Cinema in Rome which appeared in "A Talk with Michelangelo Antonioni on His Work," *Film Culture,* no. 24 (Spring 1962), 50–51 (originally published in *Bianco e nero* 22, nos. 2–3 [February-March 1961], 69–95). A slightly different version of the Cannes statement appeared under the title "Eroticism—The Disease of Our Age," *Films and Filming* 7, no. 4 (January 1961), 7.

of emotional traits which . . . [are] unsuited and inadequate. They condition us without offering us any help, they create problems without suggesting any possible solutions."

Clearly, the statement particularly addresses the question of sexual morality from something like an existentialist perspective. It is easy to assume that Antonioni, like Sandro, is questioning received ideas about the institution of monogamy, personal loyalty, and the like. But he is far from endorsing Sandro's defense of erotic ambivalence. For one thing, the artist expressly disclaims moralistic intentions: "Naturally, I don't care to, nor can I, resolve it [the split between modern science and our inadequate morality] myself; I am not a moralist, and my film is neither a denunciation nor a sermon. It is a story told in images whereby, I hope, it may be possible to perceive not the birth of a mistaken attitude but the manner in which attitudes and feelings are misunderstood today."

For another, the film hardly shows us a man gaining real moral strength from his dismissal of conventional morality. When Sandro is discovered with the prostitute Gloria Perkins on a couch in the deserted hotel lounge (shots 452–474), he hides his head in shame. Then, as much in disgust with himself as with Perkins, he flings money contemptuously at her, and later weeps unrestrainedly on the piazza in front of the ruined San Domenico church tower. It is not clear that even the pity of Claudia, become more a maternal figure than a mistress, will help him solve his problems.

Clearly there is a self-serving element in Sandro's "existentialist" protest; *it* is of the "cheapened" rather than the authentic variety. It is the kind of argument one would expect from people in the Fifties who called themselves "existentialists" but were only bohemians (the name, but not the feeling, was to change in the Sixties to "hippies" or "flower children"). Sandro is being what the genuine existentialist most deplores, namely, "inauthentic." Existentialism would hardly excuse a sense of helplessness, whether from uxorious or any other need. Sandro's argument—"We can't help ourselves so let's let it all happen"—would be seen as a confession of weakness, not of moral strength. His behavior could hardly satisfy a philosophy which argues that the smallest of our acts affects the entire terrestrial, indeed, the universal order of things. He remains very much a victim of a "rigid and stereotyped morality."

Of course, Sandro's behavior is neither criticized nor condoned by the film; it is, rather, examined as under a microscope. Antonioni promoted the clinical metaphor by speaking, in the same interview, of the "*malattia dei sentimenti,*" the emotional sickness that afflicts modern man: "Eros is sick; man is uneasy, something is bothering him. And whenever something bothers him, man reacts, but he reacts badly, only on erotic impulse, and he is unhappy." ("Man" is ostensibly synonymous with "human being" here, but the fact is that Antonioni's men have considerably more trouble with eros than do his women.) In Sandro's case, there is a clear connection between excessive erotic preoccupation and an inability to practice the art that he loves and was trained to do. He has "sold out" as an architect and is now a cost-estimator.

Not only Sandro, but most of the other characters in the film suffer from psychological malaise connected in one way or another with eros: Anna's tormented ambivalence about when, how long, or even whether to be with her lover; Giulia's masochistic acceptance of Corrado's cold contempt and her childish revenge in the arms of the seventeen-year-old *principe*, Goffredo; Raimondo's tedious attachment to Patrizia, who remains monogamous out of sheer laziness. And, as if in choral reinforcement of the theme, there is the mass hysteria of the crowd in Messina about the split in Gloria Perkins's dress, the obsessive hovering about Claudia by the men of Noto, and the wretched marriage and roving eye of the druggist in Troina. Sandro shows visible disdain for these more proletarian sexual obsessions, but who is he to judge?

Sandro and the other characters are not existentialists, but they do suffer from what some psychoanalysts call "existential anxiety." Two psychoanalysts help us understand the emotional malaise portrayed in the film.[8] They attest to the prevalence of the condition, to the many patients who sought help for the problem in the Fifties and Sixties.[9] One praises the aptness of Antonioni's decision to cast the malaise in terms of a *search:*

> You go into a room to find something and realize you have forgotten what you were looking for. Then you remember, but perhaps feel some vague sense of dissatisfaction: "Was that really it?" This sense of bafflement is likely to be keener when you plan a day, a month, a career. . . . In the erotic life of man the situation seems, if anything, more difficult. How can you possibly find her whom you seek? Her image is blurred. At one time it may seem impossible to find her because there are so many women among whom

8. Simon O. Lesser, "*L'avventura:* A Closer Look," *Yale Review* 54, no. 1 (October 1964), 41–50, and Piero Amerio, "Antonioni: appunti per una psicologia dell' irrelevant," in *Michelangelo Antonioni,* ed. Carlo di Carlo (Rome: Edizioni di bianco e nero, 1964), pp. 45–66.
9. There is no reason to believe that the condition has ceased to afflict yuppies and others today. Indeed, it seems harder than ever for people to form satisfying erotic relationships.

to choose. At other times it may seem impossible because there are so few. Either way, the essential difficulty remains the same: how can you recognize your long-sought beloved when her image and her qualities are so indefinite and indistinct? How can you know love itself and distinguish it from its innumerable partial embodiments and counterfeits? After a time the hope of success may all but disappear. Because of need, the search may continue, but be pursued with a growing sense of futility and disillusionment.[10]

Especially, one might add, when the erotic pursuit is carried out *instead of* meaningful and dignifying work, which, if we are to believe Freud, necessarily constitutes the other half of life's necessary dyad.

Antonioni called *L'avventura* a *giallo alla rovescia,* a " 'yellow' in reverse." ("Yellows" are Italian murder mysteries, so-called because their covers are that color, just as French murder mysteries are *noirs.*) But "reverse" here does not mean that the ending comes before the beginning. Rather, there *is* no "ending": the "reversal" is a frustration of the expectation of any sort of solution. In the psychoanalytic context, Anna's physical disappearance does not matter. It is simply not what the film is about. Consider the ease with which we share Sandro's quick acceptance of Anna's disappearance:

> . . . we intuitively realize that Sandro has no real desire to find Anna. Before her disappearance, we sense, the relationship was played out. Anna had already been exposed as a surrogate, one of a long succession of women who had to be possessed and then renounced because none was the one for whom Sandro was searching. . . . Psychologically it is better that Anna's fate should be left in doubt: the search for her is at bottom a pseudosearch. It is engaged in to save face and to relieve guilt rather than to find Anna.[11]

Claudia, of course, is more sincere in her desire to find her friend, but even she succumbs to the distraction of eros, however guilty it may make her feel. (Guilt arises not because she is a woman, but because, as a member of the class below Anna's and Sandro's, she still adheres to conventional beliefs about personal loyalty.)

The other psychoanalyst's interpretation of the film, precisely because it comes

---

10. Lesser, "L'avventura," pp. 44–45. Even if we go beyond the orthodox Freudian patriarchal bias, and substitute "woman and man" and "he and she" at the appropriate places, this statement continues to seem fairly valid.

11. Ibid., p. 48.

out of a quite different tradition, corroborates these conclusions. The search for Anna is seen as an "irrelevant drive":

> An action is called irrelevant when its result is "not pertinent," not tied . . . to the series of motivations and "drives" in respect to which it claims to be situated. . . . The irrelevant action is . . . in essence a flight [*azione fuga*], intended to conceal a more insupportable state of mind: an action, that is, intended to blur anxiety and to avoid graver manifestations of psychosocial or psychosomatic discomfort.[12]

The flight or "fugue" amounts to a kind of emotional vagabondage. "The 'adventure,' of love or whatever, can be in itself a motive for flight from reality, for whitewashing, or for defensiveness." But as the ending of the film demonstrates so clearly, "vagabondage does not result in real happiness; on the contrary, at the moment of contact with reality, it crumbles in a banal and painful way. It is a species of neurotic compensation which works only up to a point, but when confronted with reality it evaporates, leaving the individual alone again with his secret anguish."[13]

The film, of course, contains themes other than the erotic, though these are distinctly less prominent. The theme of art versus commerce has been sufficiently discussed already. One other is worth noting since it was to be picked up again in a later film by Antonioni. It is the theme of the *Doppelgänger*. There is a rather clear suggestion that Anna is consciously choosing Claudia as her successor when she gives her the black blouse (shot 75) and that Claudia, however unconsciously, soon begins to act in some ways as Anna's surrogate (the primping and agitated waiting for Sandro at the Montalto villa and the "modeling" with the black wig under Patrizia's indulgent gaze, shots 296–302). The ease with which Sandro takes Claudia as a new Anna exemplifies, from his perspective, the "sex-as-anodyne" theme I have discussed. But the motif of the double

---

12. Amerio, "Antonioni," p. 47. My translation. Amerio's term "irrelevant drive" derives from the work of the American behaviorist Clark Hull.

13. Ibid., p. 48. In later films, Antonioni continued to find distraction a peculiarly representative modern state of mind. It is one of the themes of *Blow-Up,* for example. But Thomas, the hero of the later film, suffers from a psychic imbalance which in a way is opposite to Sandro's. He pursues his work—photography—so relentlessly that there is room for nothing else. He seems totally incapable of love and has no sense of his responsibilities as a human being in society. All that matters to him is to get the photo. But what is at stake in *Blow-Up* is no mere neurotic depression: like his prototype in Cortázar's story, Thomas sees his very sanity called into question. See *Michelangelo Antonioni, or the Surface of the World* (Berkeley and Los Angeles: University of California Press, 1985), chap. 7.

has independent interest. Antonioni was clearly intrigued by the idea of the trans-
fer of identity and was to find in Mark Peploe's scenario for *The Passenger*
(1975) an opportunity to examine it more extensively. Whereas the protagonist of
that film, David Locke, takes up the identity of a dead man because he is fed up
with his own, Anna gives *over* her identity (at least her sexual identity) for
motives that we shall never discover. In both cases, there is an allusion to the
motif of how it feels to walk "the road not taken." Switching identity, of course,
is simply one more kind of distraction and escapism, a theme very prevalent in
Antonioni's films, especially *Blow-Up*. Antonioni may well have been working
out a personal problem in his art: he has said that he himself often feels distracted, that as soon as he embarks on a project he finds his mind flooded with
other stories that beg to be pursued.

We do not go to art for its themes but for the way they are expressed. And
Antonioni is as much a formal as a thematic innovator. Narratively, he brings to
the cinema the newer attitudes of twentieth-century fiction, particularly with respect to what constitutes "tellability" and closure. He purposefully downplays
traditional reliance on causality as the spring driving the narrative machine, pre-
ferring what I have elsewhere called "contingency." In contingent plots event *x*
does not cause event *y;* rather *y* vaguely "depends for its existence, occurrence,
character, etc. on something not yet certain." [14] Not that the contingency leads to
a "plotless" narrative, as is sometimes claimed. On the contrary,

> a narrative without a plot is a logical impossibility [since "narrative" is
> precisely defined as a coherent series of events, that is, as "plotted"]. It is
> not that there is no plot, but rather that the plot is not an intricate puzzle, that
> its events are 'of no great importance,' that 'nothing changes.' In the tradi-
> tional narrative of resolution, there is a sense of problem-solving, of things
> being worked out in some way, of a kind of ratiocinative or emotional
> teleology. . . . 'What will happen?' is the basic question. In the modern plot
> of revelation, however, the emphasis is elsewhere; the function of the dis-
> course is not to answer that question nor even to pose it. . . . Things . . .
> stay pretty much the same. It is not that events are resolved (happily or
> tragically), but rather that a state of affairs is revealed. . . . Development
> in the first instance is an unraveling; in the second, a displaying. [15]

14. *Story and Discourse* (Ithaca: Cornell University Press, 1978), pp. 45–48. The quotation is from
the entry for "contingent" in *The American College Dictionary*.
15. *Story and Discourse*, pp. 47–48.

Clearly a contingent plot of revelation is well-suited to an art which is concerned with existence as such. A preoccupation with contingency, further, helps explain Antonioni's unusual (for the cinema) narrative pacing. Since what counts is a prevailing state of affairs, not privileged "dramatic" moments, narrative tactics like ellipsis can perform new functions. Instead of using a sudden straight cut, for instance, for "dramatic" impact, as in a conventional *film noir* or horror movie, Antonioni can use it to suggest the uncertainty of motives. (A good example occurs in the cut from the desolate Casa del Mezzogiorno town, shot 346, to the lovemaking scene al fresco, near the railroad, shot 347.)

We have already considered the thematic implications of Antonioni's *giallo alla rovescia*. Let us return to its formal implications. Remember Alfred Hitchcock's formula for suspense: it is quite the opposite of surprise. It depends on a drawing out of a dangerous situation rather than a sudden onset of unexpected occurrences. Hitchcock insisted that the filmmaker must supply viewers with all the information necessary about the pending catastrophe and then let them stew in anticipation of its occurrence. Still, no matter how long it took, no matter whether the result was death for the villain or salvation for the innocent, *something* had to eventuate. *L'avventura* stands that convention quite on its head: what starts out seeming to be suspense is extended too far and allowed to dissipate. No resolution occurs, and we join the characters' distraction from what by convention should be their chief preoccupation—solving the mystery.

This seemingly purposeless extension occurs not only at the global but at the local or stylistic level as well. At the end of the temporal spectrum opposite to narrative ellipsis, Antonioni is fond of what can be called "stretch," the dragging out in screen time of moments that seem to have no consequence to the plot. Typical of the latter is what French critics dubbed the *temps mort* or "dead time" effect: a noticeable hold on the background after the actors have gone offscreen. Far from being an editing mistake, as early viewers might have assumed, the technique is one of great deliberation. It was recognized as the cinematic equivalent of the *nouveau roman*'s "microrealistic" preoccupation with background description. By dwelling on the background, Antonioni's films underline the omnipresence of the environment, whether natural or synthetic, both its impact on and its indifference to the plight of the characters scurrying through it. It is not new, of course, to provide tempestuous characters and events (Anna's disappearance) with a tempestuous background (Lisca Bianca). What is new, in the cinema at least, is to endow that background with an integrity of its own. *Temps mort* is one of the chief devices by which Antonioni achieves a revelation of the sheer wonder of the world's surface.[16] "The film says not that 'this is such-and-such a place, in which plot event x occurs' but rather that 'this place is important quite independently of the immediate exigencies of plot, and you will sense (if not understand) its odd value if you scrutinize it carefully. That is why I give you time to do so.'"[17] Treating the environment as something apart, indeed as an aspect of visual design rather than of plot, does not seem to attenuate Antonioni's narrative line. On the contrary, it adds an unexpressed but powerful sense of disquiet, of portent, a sense, as we shall see, that is intensified by the mise-en-scène.

Another typically Antonionesque stylistic feature contributing to the audience's discomfort is a disregard for the conventional rules of continuity, in particular, the "axis of action" or "180°" rule. The axis of action is an imaginary line connecting two characters which is not supposed to be crossed by the camera, since to do so would confuse the audience's sense of the space and direction of the action.[18] To the extent that moral and psychological confusion constitutes Antonioni's principal thematic intention, however, the "violation" of the axis becomes a precise formal tool by which the audience can be made to feel that confusion. (A good example occurs in the scene early in *L'avventura* when Anna goes up to Sandro's apartment: the line is crossed in shot 19. Another occurs in Sandro's morning encounter with the old man on Lisca Bianca, shot 171.)

Confusion of motive and identity is also formally enhanced by choices in the mise-en-scène. Perhaps the most spectacular involves the use of deceiving mirrors. In the sequence in which Patrizia and Claudia try on wigs (shots 300–301), there are two mirrors, a vanity mirror on Patrizia's dressing table and a standing mirror elsewhere in the room. But only the first is revealed as such from the outset. The very existence of the standing mirror, which reflects Claudia's appearance in the dark wig, is concealed for most of the scene, and the audience is made to feel uneasy (if only subliminally) by the discovery that it has not been looking, as it imagined, at the real Claudia but rather at her reflection. Claudia's confusion of identity with Anna is underlined by our confusion about how to read her image and where in the diegetic world it is coming from.

16. Hence the subtitle of my book on Antonioni: *The Surface of the World*. See, especially, pp. 79, 87–98, and 125–131.
17. Ibid., pp. 125–126.
18. For a good discussion, see David Bordwell and Kristen Thompson, *Film Art: An Introduction,* 2nd ed. (New York: Knopf, 1986), pp. 210–218.

But perhaps the most brilliant achievement of Antonioni's mise-en-scène—and hence of his form as a whole—lies in the way it evokes a haunting sense of portent. This portent is kept deliberately vague and, again, involves the audience subliminally: Sandro's and Claudia's struggles get intensified by our struggles to grasp the film and the constant apprehension that it is slipping through our fingers. Even if our own marriages are happy, we keenly feel the general sense of being at a loss among choices, and, in the atomic era, of the poignant uncertainty of the future. Antonioni's genius is to render that sense in a purely visual way. Much has been said about his great visual powers, and he can be numbered not only in the company of the great filmmakers of particularly keen visual sense—Sergei Eisenstein, Carl Dreyer, Joseph von Sternberg—but also in that of painters and photographers of the twentieth century whose compositional practices he has obviously studied. Limiting the discussion to only one painter (and without arguing that there is a direct influence), we can recognize in the work of Giorgio De Chirico, the founder of "metaphysical" surrealism, a mood close to that of Antonioni's films of the early Sixties. Like De Chirico, Antonioni places figures against architectural and natural background which is somehow portentous and even ominous. There is a prose poem by De Chirico which captures, as do the paintings of his metaphysical period, this sense of environmental portent:

> Late in the afternoon, when the evening light was beginning slowly to obscure the mountains to the east of the city, and when the cliffs beneath the citadel were turning mauve, one could feel that SOMETHING WAS GATHERING, as the nurses would say while gossiping on the benches of the public square.[19]

Like De Chirico's paintings, Antonioni's films ask the question "Who can deny the troubling connection that exists between perspective and metaphysics?"[20] To describe the shot (346) in which Claudia and Sandro flee the abandoned neo-classical (or pseudo-classical) town whose architecture is made strange by the absence of human beings, a critic could scarcely improve on De Chirico's statement of what he intended in his own paintings:

> The whole nostalgia of the infinite is revealed to us behind the geometrical precision of the square. We experience the most unforgettable moments when certain aspects of the world, whose existence we completely ignore,

19. Quoted in J. T. Soby, *Giorgio De Chirico* (New York: Museum of Modern Art, 1955), p. 34.
20. De Chirico, as quoted in ibid., p. 33. The film that succeeds *L'avventura, La notte* (The Night), of 1961, is the most architectural of Antonioni's films.

suddenly confront us with the revelation of mysteries lying all the time within our reach.[21]

Of all the great filmmakers, Antonioni alone knows how to evoke, as did De Chirico, "an overwhelming silence made visually evident." And like De Chirico's paintings his films get much of their power from our sense of being "haunted by the past, disturbed by the present, terrified of the future." [22]

21. As quoted by Vernon Young in his excellent essay, "Nostalgia of the Infinite: Notes on Chirico, Antonioni, and Resnais," *Arts* 37, no. 4 (January 1963), 14–21. Reprinted in *On Film: Unpopular Essays on a Popular Art* (New York: Quadrangle/The New York Times Book Co., 1972), p. 189. Young's principal source for De Chirico's writings is Marcel Jean, *Histoire de la Peinture Surréaliste* (Paris: Editions du Seuil, 1959).
22. Young, "Nostalgia," in *On Film,* p. 185.

Michelangelo Antonioni

A Biographical Sketch

Guido Fink

Michelangelo Antonioni was born September 29, 1912, in Ferrara, a small town in the plains of the Po river valley, northern Italy.

Even though Antonioni has frequently denied feeling any particular attachment to his home town, where he spent the first twenty-seven years of his life, Italian critics have detected a "Ferrarese" quality in his cinematic style—a sense of isolation and "secret aristocracy," of silent, wide, empty streets, of a flat landscape with only an occasional vertical, of a strong moral attitude which, especially at the beginning of his career, could easily betray a "provincial" harshness.

The Po river and the flat, often misty, somewhat desolate countryside around Ferrara are the scenery of Antonioni's first documentary (*Gente del Po; People of the Po*, 1943–1947) as well as of his 1957 film, *Il grido (The Cry)*; Ferrara itself is the setting of the opening scenes in his first feature film, *Cronaca di un amore (Story of a Love Affair*, 1950). Even in his latest film, *Identificazione di una donna (Identification of a Woman*, 1982), largely set in Rome, one of the key sequences is clouded by a thick fog, suggesting Ferrarese, not Roman weather. Antonioni's personal reminiscences of his youth, of the color, the odors, the atmosphere of his home town may be found in his preface to *Sei film* (1964). With Federico Fellini—born in Rimini, not far from Ferrara—Antonioni belongs to what has been called the second or "provincial" wave of Italian neo-realist filmmakers, the generation after that of metropolitan first-wave directors like Roberto Rossellini and Vittorio De Sica (Rome) and Luchino Visconti (Milan).

The second son of working-class parents, Antonioni could not afford an exclusive *liceo* (college preparatory school), and attended a technical secondary school where students were trained to become clerks or accountants. In his teenage years, he showed a particular interest in music and drawing (the latter he has never abandoned), and, of course, he was a regular filmgoer. Above all, he was an excellent tennis player, which allowed him to mix with *la crème* of Ferrarese youth at the elegant club Marfisa (briefly visible in *Cronaca di un amore*). His literary education he owed mainly to his friends Lanfranco Caretti—later to become a critic and philologist—and the future novelist Giorgio Bassani. "We met at Bassani's house," Professor Caretti recalled during a 1982 symposium.

> Bassani was the most eager and passionate in trying to stir our intellectual indolence. The Ferrarese bourgeoisie was sleepy, conservative, reactionary. We were the first to read Joyce's *Ulysses,* in Larbaud's French translation. . . . We loved form, we were formalistic in our taste, form being something that could fill our ideological vacuum. . . . Bassani read some poetry; I was the hapless critic; another friend, Giuliani, expressed the antibourgeois viewpoint. . . . As for Michelangelo, he mostly kept silent. . . . Words were not his medium; he was waiting for other forms of expression. The image of Antonioni I remember from those days is one of silence and style—evident in his clothes as well. Form, style, eagerness, silence—even in his private life.[1]

When Antonioni enrolled at the University of Bologna (its School of Economics was one of the few at the time which did not require a *liceo* diploma), he continued to live in nearby Ferrara. In college he developed a strong interest in the theater, joining various amateur groups as actor, art director, even playwright. (He wrote a play called *Il vento, The Wind,* in 1935.) All of his dramatic efforts remain unpublished.

Between 1936 and 1938, Antonioni wrote film criticism for the Ferrara daily paper, *Corriere padano.* His many film reviews reveal what the cinema could mean to a young provincial Italian intellectual in the late Thirties. Decidedly hostile to the routine Italian production of the period, Antonioni did not seem

---

1. See Cesare Biarese and Aldo Tassone, *I film di Michelangelo Antonioni* (Rome: Gremese, 1985), pp. 26–27.

fond of the widespread American myth either. He never missed a chance of exposing the "bad taste" of Hollywood producers or of genre movies. He regularly sided with European *auteurs* like G. W. Pabst or Julien Duvivier whenever he felt that their integrity was being threatened by the commercialism of the industry. Remaining indifferent to the political content of the picture (he could praise both Nazi German and Soviet Russian films), the young critic was obviously influenced by foreign theoretists whose books were circulating in Italy at the time (Béla Bálász, V. I. Pudovkin), as well as by certain Idealistic philosophers (G. W. F. Hegel, Benedetto Croce). He advocated what he called *la sospensione figurativa,* a sort of suspension of meaning and "content" in pure form or visual expression. In any case, Antonioni's ideas about film can be better seen in his later critical work, when he had gotten beyond the narrow limits of daily reviewing—in his contributions to the magazines *Cinema* (1939–1941), *Film d'oggi* (1945), and *Bianco e nero* (1948–1950); of particular value are his essays on Marcel Carné and on Visconti's *La terra trema.* His critical interest was to show up, in a "self-reflexive" way, in films like *La signora senza camelie,* "Il provino," *Blow-Up,* and *Identificazione di una donna.*

Introduced during the 1938 Venice Film Festival to Count Vittorio Cini, a prominent personality in the cultural establishment of the period, Antonioni left for Rome as one of Cini's secretaries, with the particular assignment of organizing an international exhibition to be held in the Italian capital. Disliking this clerical job, he quit and accepted at a smaller salary a job as editorial secretary of *Cinema,* a bimonthly magazine edited by Mussolini's son, Vittorio. Though nominally Fascist, this magazine often published sharply polemical articles, written by covert or open anti-Fascists. It was published in a political atmosphere that permitted Visconti to create the first Italian neorealist film, *Ossessione* (1942). Antonioni's *Cinema* essays reveal a strong interest in art, form, and technique (he often discusses the use of color in the movies). They do not share the enthusiastic appeal of other *Cinema* contributors for more reality in Italian cinema, and for realistic stories and settings. Antonioni briefly attended the State Film School, Centro Sperimentale di Cinematografia. He had just three months' training before being drafted for military service. But it was enough to give him his first chance to use a camera. (A previous attempt, in the insane asylum of Ferrara with a sixteen-millimeter camera had failed miserably: uneasy in front of the inmates, he had abandoned the set.) His first effort was much appreciated by the Centro faculty. It pictured the embarrassed visit of a society lady to a poor tenement where a prostitute has summoned her by some sort of blackmail. At the end of a single long take, the screen revealed the face of the prostitute—who is a mirror-image of the lady (and is played by the same actress). This is a foreshadowing of Antonioni's celebrated long takes, for instance, the technically ingenious ending of *Professione: reporter* (*The Passenger,* 1974).[2]

In 1942, after being drafted, Antonioni became a signaller in the army, a job which allowed him to work as a scriptwriter in his spare time. He was one of the collaborators of *I due Foscari,* a Venetian-Renaissance adventure film, vaguely adapted from one of Lord Byron's verse tragedies. Antonioni also collaborated on *Un pilota ritorna* (*The Return of a Pilot*), from an original story by "Tito Silvio Mursino," none other than Mussolini's son, Vittorio. This film, though intended as anti-British propaganda, was transformed by cool dialogue, restrained acting, and Roberto Rossellini's low-key direction into something quite different (and still worth seeing). Thanks to a leave of absence, Antonioni was also allowed to work on the set of *I due Foscari* as assistant director. Then he obtained an extraordinary leave of absence—and of Italy—to work with Marcel Carné, the most famous European director of the time, on his medieval romance, *Les visiteurs du soir,* then in production in Fascist-occupied Nice. Carné was highly suspicious of this young Italian, and though he was working with one of his idols, Antonioni was quite disappointed. Despite other job offers in France, as an assistant to Jean Cocteau and Jean Grémillon, he had to return to Italy at the expiration of his leave.

Back in the Rome of 1943, Antonioni found the film industry in complete chaos. Somehow, even with a small crew, he succeeded in making his first documentary film in the valley of the Po river, not far from where Visconti was shooting *Ossessione.* Antonioni wrote in 1964 that he was trying to work out his own kind of neorealism. "It was 1943. Visconti was making his *Ossessione* on the banks of the Po river, and a few kilometers away I was doing my first documentary. . . . All I did later on, good or bad, stems from *Gente del Po*" ("Preface" to *Sei Film,* 1964). The war situation prevented Antonioni from editing his film, and a good deal of footage was lost or destroyed. As an officer, he was supposed to report to his superiors in the Nazi-controlled Repubblica di Salò, but he escaped to Abruzzo. Later, in the summer, he secretly reentered Rome and joined the clandestine radical group "Partito d'Azione."

Admitted to the narrow circle of Visconti's devotees, Antonioni spent the first months in liberated Rome co-scripting two pictures which would never be shot.

2. See ibid., p. 30.

Then, he spent part of 1946 looking for the footage of his Po river documentary. He learned that most of it had disappeared, perhaps not by chance, in transit from the studio in Rome to the Fascist North. Of the final section—showing a storm and a flood in the delta of the river—only a few shots remain.

> It is a pity, because the rest was really impressive. The land became mud and swamp. Inside the thatched huts, children were placed on tables so that they could be saved from drowning, and bed sheets were hung to the ceiling to collect falling water. Italian films avoided such subjects in those days, and the Fascist regime forbade them. I hope not to sound conceited, but I happened to be the first to deal with such things.[3]

On September 2, 1947, at the reborn Venice Film Festival, a nine-minute version of *Gente del Po* was shown for the first time as a "curtain-raiser" before the much-awaited Hitchcock film, *Spellbound*. A few reviewers found space in their reports to give modest praise to this "deeply human" documentary, which, however, appeared to be "heavily cut."

Antonioni's reputation as a documentary filmmaker was firmly established after his second effort, *N.U.* (for *Nettezza urbana, Municipal Sanitation*), a nine-minute film, made in 1948, depicting a day in the life of the invisible but omnipresent Roman street-cleaners. Though much appreciated, *N.U.* was mistakenly linked with neorealistic *reportages* and the social protest mood prevailing at the time. But Antonioni seemed more interested in having the audience *look* at things in a different way. ("Street-cleaners are a part of the city life, as inanimate objects," says the voice-over of the narrator. "Yet they do participate in the life of the city. How do they *see* it?"). The urban landscape was already typically Antonionesque,[4] and the Bach and jazz motifs played on a saxophone suggest an unconventional approach to the filmic material. *N.U.* was the first collaboration of Antonioni with Giovanni Fusco, the composer for all of his films through *L'avventura* (as well as of the first pictures directed by one of Antonioni's admirers, Alain Resnais).

Antonioni continued making documentaries: *L'amorosa menzogna,* his third documentary, is a mildly satiric glance at the world of *fumetti* or photoromances,

3. See ibid., p. 32.
4. Its "tonality resembles that of the cityscapes of *Cronaca di un amore* and *La signora senza camelie* . . . already, too, we get a sense of Antonioni's compositional ability, particularly in his placement of figures against their grounds." Seymour Chatman, *Antonioni, or the Surface of the World* (Berkeley and Los Angeles: University of California Press, 1985), p. 9.

popular soap operas "acted" by live models and published in cheap weeklies. Hoping to graduate to feature films, Antonioni submitted to various producers the story *Lo sceicco bianco* (*The White Sheik,* a development of *L'amorosa menzogna*), but it was rejected (only to be purchased later by Carlo Ponti and shot, with many modifications, by Federico Fellini). After the sweeping Democratic Christian victory of 1948 and the defeat of the Left, the newly reconstructed Italian film industry seemed to prefer routine comedies and genre films, films that avoided controversial issues. Throughout the Fifties, even the masters of *neorealismo,* who should have been credited for reopening the international markets to Italian film, were practically blacklisted (De Sica went back to acting, Rossellini and Visconti had very few directorial opportunities). For a young unknown director with aesthetic ambitions, it was even more difficult to get a break: Antonioni, at thirty-seven, was still a newcomer according to the cautious standards of the time, as was Fellini, eight years his junior. Both were waiting in the wings, despite long apprentice work. Apparently, Antonioni's only option was to continue as a documentary-maker (and as a critic). But documentaries have their problems as well: *Superstizione,* his fourth, about folkloric rituals and superstitious practices in a Central Italian village, was savagely cut by the producers, probably because its subject matter seemed unappealing and unpatriotic. What he had the opportunity to shoot was often of no interest to him at all (*Sette canne, un vestito,* a routine description of the processing of synthetic fibers).

In 1950, after two more uninteresting documentaries, *La funivia del Faloria* (about a funicular) and *La villa dei mostri* (about the Tivoli Gardens, near Rome), Antonioni realized his long-cherished possibility of making a feature film when he was introduced to Franco Villani, a Turin theater owner willing to invest some of his money in the production of a movie. He made *Cronaca di un amore* with a budget which was ridiculously insufficient, even in those days. With the exception of the popular male Italian star Massimo Girotti, the cast was practically unknown. For the complex role of a rich neurotic woman in her late twenties (and unable to have his first choice, Gene Tierney), Antonioni signed a nineteen-year-old Milanese shop assistant, Lucia Bosé, recently proclaimed Miss Italy, but inexperienced as an actress. Even before its release, there was excited anticipation about Antonioni's new techniques; for instance, having the camera shadow the actors in long, fluent takes and refusing to cut even when the action was finished, in order to capture their nervous embarrassment. Daily papers and popular magazines carried rumors about this movie, which promised "psychology in fur coats" and referred to certain recent scandals in Milanese high society. But the film was rejected by the Venice Film Festival, and shown there only semi-privately. *Cronaca* opened on November 25 in Rome: reviewers found it slow, cold, detached, uneventful. But *Cronaca di un amore* was enthusiastically appreciated by *cinéphiles* and leading film quarterlies.

Antonioni immediately announced two new projects—*Le allegre ragazze del '24,* about the rise of Fascism in a northern provincial town, and *La signora senza camelie,* the story of a beauty queen who rises to stardom without having any talent. But he was only able to get financing for an episodic film on juvenile delinquency and the "crisis" among the new postwar generation, a much-discussed issue in those days. The film was tentatively entitled "I nostri figli" ("Our Children").

Even as he struggled with "I nostri figli," another Italian producer offered to back *La signora senza camelie* (*The Lady without Camellias*), as a vehicle for Gina Lollobrigida. An increasingly popular Italian star of the day, Lollobrigida's rags-to-riches life-story and career, like Bosé's, reflected that of the film's heroine. Although she signed and approved the script, Lollobrigida did not appear on the set, claiming that the film was a vulgar insult to herself, to all her colleagues, and to the Italian film industry. Bosé took over the role.

Along with Visconti's *Bellissima* (1951), Lattuada and Fellini's *Luci del varietà* (*Variety Lights,* 1951), and Fellini's *Lo sceicco bianco* (1953), *La signora senza camelie* shows a self-reflexive trend in the Italian cinema of the early Fifties, though only Visconti's and Antonioni's films actually dealt with the movie world. None of these movies, though later revived and revalued, had any success at the time of their showing. *La signora* had perhaps the worst reception of all. Even the Italian critics who admired and supported Antonioni were somewhat dismayed by the "pessimism" and the mood of emptiness and despair pervading the movie. The picture was a commercial failure. It would only come to be appreciated in France, but not until 1959.

If Antonioni was disappointed by the failure of his third film, he probably felt even worse about the second, which finally opened with a new title, *I vinti, The Vanquished.* The Catholic producers had prefaced the film with a moralistic sermon and completely altered the dialogue and the editing of the central, Roman episode. They changed it from a story of right-wing terrorists into a banal plot about cigarette smuggling.

Antonioni's next assignment was an episode in *Amore in città* (*Love in the*

City). Antonioni was asked to confront the problem of attempted suicides provoked by disappointments in love. Antonioni's contribution was an experiment in cinéma-vérité. He shot a series of interviews, visually striking in their spareness. The film opened in Rome to tepid critical approval.

In 1955, Antonioni persuaded a young and rather inexperienced producer, Franco Cancellieri, to join him on an adaptation of Cesare Pavese's novella, *Tra donne sole* (*Among Women Only*). The work is one of the last and best works by Pavese, who killed himself in 1950, at the peak of his professional success. The film was retitled *Le amiche* (*The Girlfriends*). Sharing with two other films the second prize, or Silver Lion, at the Venice Film Festival, *Le amiche* was immediately distributed all over Italy, in a slightly shortened version, and for the first time Antonioni had a box-office success.

The unexpected success of *Le amiche* prompted Antonioni to attempt his most difficult and challenging film to date—*Il grido* (*The Cry*, 1956). In the fall of 1956, in a gloomy period full of the premonition of war (Russia invaded Hungary, shaking many Italian communists), Antonioni, back in Ferrara, started work on the saddest and bleakest of his films. His camera followed his hero's aimless drifting along the Po river, with or without his little daughter, in the vain attempt to forget his common-law wife and to find a new reason to live. This was his first attempt at exploring the working-class milieu, thus contradicting the myth that he was only interested in elegant upper-class women. At the same time, it is an intensely personal, even covertly autobiographical film. It seems more imbued with Pavese's true spirit than does *Le amiche*. *Il grido* won a special award in July 1957 at the Locarno Film Festival, but the Italian critics were far from enthusiastic. When it finally appeared in Italian theaters, it flopped miserably. Once again, it was the French who saw merit in the film's premise— that even an industrial worker could suffer after being deserted by his woman, and that such suffering was quite unrelated to the class struggle.

While dubbing *Il grido* (a standard procedure in Italian cinema, in this case all the more necessary because of the American actors in the cast), Antonioni met Monica Vitti, who spoke the lines of Virginia, an energetic proprietress of a gas station in the middle of nowhere. Vitti was to play a critical role in Antonioni's personal life and career.

For the time being, however, and despite his growing reputation, the author of *Il grido* was unable to continue his film career. His scripts were regularly rejected. In order to survive, he accepted a couple of jobs as second-unit director, shooting some scenes for Alberto Lattuada's blockbuster, *La tempesta,* and taking over Guido Brignone's *Nel segno di Roma.*

With Vitti and other young stage actors like Virna Lisi, Antonioni formed a theatrical company in 1958 which performed in the Teatro Eliseo in Rome and toured a few Italian cities.

In the meantime, he had begun work on a new story for the screen, dealing with the unexplained disappearance of a girl during a cruise. The working title was "L'isola," or "L'isola nuda" ("The Island," or "The Naked Island"). Ultimately entitled *L'avventura,* it was to prove the turning point in his career—and a turning point in modern filmmaking as well. After winning a special award at the 1960 Cannes Film Festival, it went on to become a critical and commercial success.[5]

The first half of the Sixties was an intensely creative period for Antonioni; he completed the great tetralogy begun by *L'avventura* with *La notte* (*The Night,* 1964), *L'eclisse* (*The Eclipse,* 1962), and *Deserto rosso* (*Red Desert,* 1964). Antonioni was now working under more favorable conditions, without the pressures and the difficulties he had confronted in his earlier career. This was due not only to the international prestige of *L'avventura,* but to a general change in the policy of the Italian film industry and in Italian society at large. In the climate of international détente (the so-called Kennedy-Khrushchev-Pope John era), a Center-Left coalition took over the government of Italy after a long period of Center-Right domination, often with neo-Fascist support. The new government ended unofficial blacklisting and political censorship of the industry. Also, the unpredicted success of controversial and "uncommercial" pictures produced by the French New Wave, Ingmar Bergman, and the British Free Cinema prompted the executives of the Italian film industry to offer new possibilities to directors who had been considered unreliable or "difficult." Fellini, who had just completed *La dolce vita* despite many problems, was given big budgets for such daring films as *8½* and *Juliet of the Spirits;* Visconti obtained even larger funds, as well as an international distribution, for *The Leopard;* new filmmakers had a chance to make their first feature films (among them were Pier Paolo Pasolini, Enmanno Olmi, the Taviani brothers, Bernardo Bertolucci, and Antonioni's old friend Marco Ferreri).

With *L'avventura* showing all over Europe, Antonioni signed for a new film

---

5. For the production history of *L'avventura,* see "Contexts," below.

to be shot entirely in Milan, *La notte*. The two main roles went to Marcello Mastroianni and Jeanne Moreau. Monica Vitti was assigned the chief supporting role. *La notte* opened in Milan on January 24, 1961. It was awarded the first prize at the Berlin Film Festival. In Italy, the film won the David di Donatello award for best direction, and three Silver Ribbons for best film, best music (Giorgio Gaslini), and best supporting actress (Monica Vitti).

In April, while driving with Vitti on the Autostrada del Sole, Antonioni was able to shoot a few meters of film during a total eclipse of the sun. Although the footage has never been shown, it was the original seed of *L'eclisse* (a story set in Rome, where no literal eclipse would occur). *L'eclisse* was shot in Rome during the fall, in a French-Italian coproduction, starring Vitti and Alain Delon. It opened in Milan on April 4, 1962, then at the Cannes Film Festival, where once again the audience seemed puzzled, especially by the "abstract" final scene. The film shared a "special award" of the Jury, together with Robert Bresson's *Le procès de Jeanne d'Arc*.

In October 1963, in Ravenna, Antonioni began work on *Deserto rosso,* his first color film. Newspapers titillated their readers with news that he had had entire settings and even pine trees painted white or silver. It won three awards at the Venice Film Festival. Its use of color is still considered to be one of the finest in film history.

In 1964, Dino De Laurentiis asked Antonioni to shoot a brief introduction to former Empress Soraya's first (and last) experience in film acting, *I tre volti* (*The Three Faces*). He agreed to make a short called "Il provino" ("The Screen Test"), showing the protagonist during makeup and preparations for her debut. Heavily cut by the producer, *I tre volti* opened on February 11, 1965, in Milan, but like many omnibus films, it was an immediate failure.

Blow-Up was Antonioni's first film with an all-English cast and crew. This was the beginning of the third, "international" phase for the director, who signed on with Carlo Ponti and M.G.M. for two more films. Shown in May 1967 at the Cannes Film Festival where it received the first prize, *Blow-Up* was a great success everywhere except in Italy, where, quite unexpectedly, it ran into censorship trouble because of the scene with the two teenagers who visit the protagonist's studio. Unwilling to cut this scene, Antonioni premiered his new film for the Italian press in the independent Republic of San Marino. Only in October was the movie approved for distribution in Italy. The box-office returns worldwide were the largest of Antonioni's career.

In 1968, invited to make a film in Japan (where *L'eclisse,* perhaps his most difficult work, had been a great success), Antonioni visited the West Coast of the United States. Enormously impressed by the country and by the spread of revolutionary feelings among students and young people at large, he changed his mind and decided to devote his next film to the American scene. The script was largely inspired by contemporary episodes of student unrest in California. As the second of his three-film contract with M.G.M., Antonioni completed *Zabriskie Point* in 1969. It was to be his most expensive film and his worst financial failure.

In 1971, Antonioni agreed to prepare a four-hour documentary on China for Italian television. Filming in China proved very difficult because of continuous control by local authorities and officials of Chinese television. *Chung Kuo Cina* was broadcast by Italian television in 1973 and was initially approved by some Chinese observers as well. But in 1974, one among many victims of the Chinese Cultural Revolution, *Chung Kuo Cina* was violently attacked as a slanderous libel against China and part of an international "imperialistic" conspiracy against the country. Even though there was wide interest in the China film, Italian television executives decided against releasing it commercially.

Antonioni's last film for M.G.M. was *Professione: reporter* (in English, *The Passenger*). This was to become one of his most personal films. Despite the elimination by the studio of ten minutes that Antonioni considered essential, the film was released with considerable critical success both in Europe and the United States.

Antonioni did not go back to filmmaking until 1978, when Italian television offered Monica Vitti, who had not worked with Antonioni since *Deserto rosso,* the starring role in Jean Cocteau's solo play *La voix humaine* (*The Human Voice*) and allowed her the right to choose her own director. She invited Antonioni to join the project. The text, however, was replaced by another Cocteau melodrama, *L'aigle à deux têtes* (*The Eagle with Two Heads*), because Antonioni was unwilling to compete with Roberto Rossellini's Forties film based on *La voix humaine,* starring Anna Magnani. Antonioni was not very interested in the tragic and turgid work of Cocteau. He saw the film mostly as an opportunity to experiment with color mixing, high-definition film, and the total visual control permitted by video production. The premiere of the Cocteau film, retitled *Il mistero di Oberwald,* took place at the Venice Film Festival in September 1980, where it was granted a Silver Ribbon for the best visual effects.

In 1981, Antonioni made *Identificazione di una donna* (*Identification of a*

Woman). The film gave Antonioni a chance to return to the Roman scene and to the chronicle of contemporary malaise and sexual mores. Released in 1982, *Identificazione di una donna* was more appreciated in France and England than in Italy, where it was reviewed with respect but some embarrassment. (This, however, has been the case with all of Antonioni's films except *Professione: reporter,* which the Italians liked better than the French did.)

In 1983, Italian television asked Antonioni to go back to Lisca Bianca, the islet where *L'avventura* had been shot twenty-three years before. Lingering on the rocks where Sandro, Claudia, and the others passed two days, Antonioni shot a nine-minute film called *Ritorno a Lisca Bianca* (or *Insert Shot at Lisca Bianca*). It was shown on television (and again in 1985).

That was Antonioni's last film to date. In 1983, he published a collection of minimalist prose narratives under the title *Quel bowling sul Tevere* (it was translated under the title *That Bowling Alley on the Tiber* by William Arrowsmith). In the same year, an exhibition opened in St. Mark's Square, Venice, of what Antonioni calls his *montagne incantate* ("magic mountains"), miniature paintings generally inspired by blown-up photographic details (also exhibited).

In 1985, Antonioni suffered a stroke. As of this writing, he seems to be better and is working on a new project, *The Crew.*

L'avventura

L'avventura

Antonioni had a long career as a critic and writer on the cinema before he made his first movie. He has continued to publish incisive observations about the cinema and the filmmaking process, and has published an interesting volume of stories that were to have been made into films.[1] In Italy he is associated with the literati no less than with the cinema. Given this commitment to literature it is all the more striking to read his disclaimers about the merits of published shooting scripts. In the introduction to his *Screenplays* (1963), he complains:

> Arranging scenes is a truly wearisome job. You have to describe

images with provisional words which later will no longer have any use, and this in itself is unnatural. What is more, the description can only be general or even false because the images are in the mind without any concrete point of reference. You sometimes end up describing weather conditions. 'The sky is clear, but large clouds block the horizon. As though coming out of these clouds, X's car appears on the horizon.' Isn't it absurd? . . .

As far as I'm concerned, it's only when I press my eye against the camera and begin to move the actors that I get an exact idea of the scene; it's only when I hear dialogue from the actor's mouth itself that I realize whether the lines are correct or not.

Besides, if it were not so, pictures would be clumsy illustrations

1. *Quel bowling sul Tevere* (Turin: Einaudi, 1983). Translated by William Arrowsmith as *That Bowling Alley on the Tiber* (New York: Oxford University Press, 1985).

of a script. It often happens, but I disapprove of making movies that way.[2]

On another occasion, Antonioni describes how he tries to be a "virgin" when he first gets to a location, hours before the rest of the crew and cast have arrived. Obviously, the work which trusts so much to on-the-scene spontaneity will result in a great deal of variation between the finished film and the shooting script. Indeed, Antonioni refers to the latter as nothing more than "sheets of notes for those who, at the camera, will write the film themselves."[3]

The shooting script of *L'avventura* was first published in 1960 in an edition by Tommaso Chiaretti for the Cappelli publishing house. It was reprinted in a second edition in 1977. The first edition formed the basis of the first English translation, by Louis Brigante, and published by Orion Press in 1963 (the volume also contained translations of *Il grido, La notte,* and *L'eclisse*). A slightly different version of the shooting script was included in an anthology of six films (*Sei Film,* published by Einaudi in 1964). This later version seems to reflect a closer approximation to the actual film, though there remain several differences.

The first continuity script—that is, actual transcription of what can be seen and heard in the film itself—was published by the Grove Press in 1969, in the Film Book series. David Denby transcribed the visuals, and the dialogue was translated by Jon Swan.

The present edition of the continuity script is based entirely on the American print of the film. It was compared with an unsubtitled Italian print, but the latter proved practically identical, except for the deletion of a few shots, and changes in a few words of dialogue. We have described the visuals anew and have revised the translation of the dialogue. Though the Grove Press edition was our constant point of departure, we felt the need to provide more information about camera angles, lighting, mise-en-scène, positioning of actors, and the like. One thing that we do not include, however, is the duration in seconds of each shot. This information can be found in the Grove Press edition.

We use the following abbreviations to indicate camera distance:

ELS   Extreme long shot
LS   Long shot
MLS   Medium long shot
MS   Medium shot
MCU   Medium close-up
CU   Close-up
ECU   Extreme close-up

2. In *Screenplays of Michelangelo Antonioni,* trans. Roger J. Moore and Louis Brigante (New York: Orion Press, 1963), pp. xiv–xvii.
3. *Ibid.,* p. xviii.

Credits

Director
Michelangelo Antonioni

Production Company
A Cino del Duca Co-Production
(Amato Pennasilico): Produzioni
Cinematografiche Europee (Rome)
and Société Cinématographique Lyre
(Paris)

Screenplay
Michelangelo Antonioni, Elio
Bartolini, and Tonino Guerra, based
on a story by Michelangelo Antonioni

Photography
Aldo Scavarda

Sets
Piero Poletto

Costumes
Adriana Berselli

Music
Giovanni Fusco

Sound
Claudio Maielli

Editor
Eraldo da Roma

Assistant Directors
Franco Indovina, Gianni Arduini,
Jack O'Connell

Director of Production
Luciano Perugia

Organization
Angelo Corso

Locations
Rome and Sicily (Lipari or Aeolian
Islands, Milazzo, Catania, Taormina)

Shooting Schedule
September 1959 through January 1960

Distribution
Mondial (Europe), Janus Films (U.S.)

Premieres
Cannes Film Festival, May 1960
Italy: September 25, 1960 (Bologna);
October 18, 1960 (Milan); November
2, 1960 (Rome)
France: September 13, 1960 (Paris)
U.S.: April 4, 1961 (New York)

Running Time
145 minutes

Prizes
Special Jury Prize and Prix des
Ecrivains de Cinéma et de Télévision,
Cannes Festival, 1960; The British
Film Institute's Sutherland Trophy
for the Best Foreign Film, 1960;
the *Nastro d'argento,* 1961 (for
Giovanni Fusco's music); The Foreign
Press Prize (for Monica Vitti's
performance); *Saraceno d'oro* (for
the film and for Monica Vitti's and
Gabriele Ferzetti's performances);
Crystal Star (for Monica Vitti's
performance).

Cast

Sandro
Gabriele Ferzetti

Claudia
Monica Vitti

Anna
Lea Massari

Giulia
Dominique Blanchar

Anna's Father
Renzo Ricci

Corrado
James Addams

Gloria Perkins
Dorothy De Poliolo

Raimondo
Lelio Luttazzi

Goffredo
Giovanni Petrucci

Patrizia
Esmeralda Ruspoli

Old Man on the Island
Joe, fisherman from Panarea

Ettore
Prof. Cucco
with Enrico Bologna,
Franco Cimino, Giovanni Danesi,
Rita Molè, Renato Pinciroli, Princess
Angela Tomasi di Lampedusa,
Vincenzo Tranchina

The Continuity Script

1. *A sunny summer day. Anna, a young brunette woman in a white dress, walks forward in* LS *between a row of hedges along a driveway in front of a country villa. The camera tracks back as Anna turns into the road and then comes into* MCU. *She stops, looks to the left, and, hearing her father's voice, moves toward him.*

   FATHER (*off*): It won't be long before this poor villa will be completely surrounded. And to think that this was once all woods.

   Anna moves out of the frame left.

2. LS: *Anna's father standing and talking to a worker. Behind them lie fields and a gravel road. The panorama of Rome and the Vatican is visible, but will soon be blotted out by the construction of new apartment buildings.*

   WORKER (*gesturing toward the fields*): There will be houses all over there soon.

   FATHER (*gesturing with his newspaper and then turning away*): Well, I suppose it's inevitable.

   WORKER: Yes, you're right. Goodbye, Excellency. (*He walks down the gravel road.*)

   FATHER: Goodbye.

   ANNA (*off, then entering right*): Oh, you're here, Papa? I was looking for you upstairs.

   FATHER: I thought you would be on the high seas by now.

   ANNA (*slightly irritated*): Not yet, Papa.

   FATHER (*looking her up and down a bit ironically*): Isn't it the fashion to wear a sailor's cap with the name of the yacht on it?

   ANNA (*crossing in front of him, then turning back toward him*): No, Papa, it's not the fashion.

   As camera tracks in to MS *and moves left with her, we see workers crossing the fields. Beyond them are more buildings, some of which are under construction.*

   FATHER: How long will you be gone?

   ANNA: Four or five days.

   FATHER (*turning away from her*): I see. That means I'll be all by myself this weekend. I'll get some rest. (*He taps his folded newspaper on the*

palm of his hand. Pan left follows him crossing in front of and away from Anna, his back to her. They are separated by the ugly apartment buildings in the background.) I should be used to it by now.

ANNA: Used to what, Papa?

FATHER (MCU, *with his back to Anna*): To being retired, not only as a diplomat but also as a father.

ANNA (*with a gesture of protest*): Why do you say such things?

FATHER (*turning slightly, but not enough to face her*): Because it's true. I trust that after thirty years of not telling the truth to anyone, I may at least be permitted to speak it to my own daughter. (*Turns completely to face her.*)

Pan follows Anna as she walks right, leaving her father offscreen; then she stops and turns toward him.

ANNA: Do you have any other truths to tell me?

3. MCU: *Father, looking down.*

FATHER: You know.

4. MCU: *Anna, as in 2.*
   ANNA: I really wish you'd spare me that one. (*A pause. She begins to move toward him.*) Goodbye, Papa. (*She exits left.*)
5. *Entering right in* MS, *she kisses him on the cheek, but he doesn't move. A chauffeur passes from right to left behind them carrying bags; Claudia follows. She is blond, about the same age as Anna, and wears a dark sweater.*
   FATHER: That fellow will never marry you, child.
   ANNA: So far, I've been the one who won't marry him. (*She crosses left in front of her father.*)
   FATHER: It's all the same. (*Camera tracks left with him as he walks behind Anna.*) Goodbye, my dear.
   CLAUDIA (*off*): Hello, good morning.
   Father continues moving left, passing Claudia, who smiles at him. He nods curtly to her without turning his head, and moves offscreen. Claudia moves right to greet Anna, who crosses distractedly in front of her.
   CLAUDIA: Have you been waiting long? I'm sorry, but . . .
   Anna passes in front of her, not answering; she stops and gazes intently in her father's direction.
6. MS: *the two women from the back. Between them, the figure of Anna's father can be seen in* LS, *walking toward the gate of the villa. Anna exits right. Claudia watches Anna's father enter the gate. Camera pans right and tracks with Claudia as she approaches and gets into a convertible. The chauffeur moves behind and to her left to hold the door, taking off his hat. Claudia sits down in the back seat and Anna joins her on the right. The car pulls away.*
   ANNA (*to chauffeur*): Alvaro, hurry up, it's late.
   Dissolve.
7. MS *from the back of the open car. Scenery and archways pass by quickly. The car goes through an ancient Roman gate.*
8. *High angle* LS: *a sunlit square in Rome. It is empty except for a white sportscar and three nuns who are crossing the square sedately, right to left, as Anna's car enters from the left and pulls up near the sportscar. The chauffeur opens the car door for the two women.*
9. MS: *Anna gets out of the car. Her expression is truculent as she looks up at the building behind her. Claudia leans against the car door and also looks up at the building.*

CLAUDIA: I'll wait for you here, Anna.

Instead of going in, Anna turns and moves away from the building toward the other side of the square, passing Claudia, who stands in the middle of the frame.

CLAUDIA (*turning toward Anna*): But where are you going?

ANNA (*sullenly*): To the bar. I'm thirsty.

Camera moves in slightly.

CLAUDIA (*surprised*): With a man you've kept waiting for half an hour and haven't seen for a month . . . ?

Anna stops. She looks back at the building sullenly and then turns back toward Claudia.

ANNA: Today I could gladly do without seeing him.

CLAUDIA: But we rushed . . . (*She pauses. The camera follows her as she moves back to the car, leaving Anna offscreen.*) Oh, all right. Goodbye cruise! (*She takes her purse out of the back seat.*)

ANNA (*off*): It's awful to be apart, you know.

Claudia turns to her abruptly.

10. *Anna alone in* MS, *facing the camera. Behind her there is a building with arcades.*

ANNA (*absorbed*): It really is, believe me. (*She walks to the left and leans on the car.*) And it's hard to make it work when one person's here, . . . (*Gestures in exasperation.*) . . . the other far off somewhere. But . . . it's also convenient. Because then at least you can think whatever you want, however you please—if you know what I mean. But instead when . . . when someone's right there, right there in front of you, everything's right there, do you understand? (*The camera moves right with her, discovering Claudia's back at the right of the frame.*) Let's go back. Come.

They start walking away from the car. Suddenly a man's voice shouts Anna! *and they look up at the building.*

11. *Low angle* LS: *Sandro, a man of thirty-five, his shirt unbuttoned, leaning out of the second-story window, waving and smiling. In the foreground, we see the two women from behind, in* MCS, *looking up at him.*

SANDRO: I'll be right down. (*He goes inside.*)

12. *As in 10. Claudia turns to look at Anna. Anna touches her arm and walks rapidly out of the frame left, toward the house.*

13. *Anna in* LS, *shot from inside the entrance hall of the building through the open door. She enters the hallway, approaches camera, and disappears offscreen left, so that all we see of her before she exits is her torso. Claudia can be seen outside, settling down to wait.*
14. *Low angle* MLS *of Sandro's apartment:*[1] *a small room with white stucco walls and vaulted ceiling, crowded with books and drafting materials. Sandro enters right, moves left across the room quickly, picks up a suitcase with his left hand and a towel with his right, and exits left.*
15. MS: *Sandro's torso to the right of a stairway leading downstairs. He moves to the right, into the bathroom, drops his towel inside, and then returns to the head of the stairway, where he meets Anna arriving at the top.*
    SANDRO: (*surprised*): Eh? Hi!
    He grabs her chin and kisses her on the lips. She does not smile. They part, and she stares at him. He walks back and looks at her quizzically. The camera follows her as she walks to the center of the room. Then she swings around and stares at him even more intently. As she backs away from him, she drops her purse on the coffee table with a loud bang, turns and goes to the french doors leading to a balcony behind her, then opens them. Sandro enters left foreground. We see his back as he advances uncertainly to the center of the room toward Anna, who has turned around and is framed full-length, facing him, against the balcony rail. (Camera line is established as right of the couple, with Sandro's back in left foreground and Anna to his right in the background.)
16. *Reverse* MS *of Sandro looking at Anna. He puts down his suitcase.*
    SANDRO: Would you like me in profile?
    He strikes a grandiose pose as in a Renaissance painting, turning sideways and laughing.
17. MCU: *Anna looks in his direction without amusement.*
18. *As in 16. Sandro drops the pose and moves toward her.*
    SANDRO: Is something wrong with me?
19. *Anna looks to the right of the space which—from the previous shots—we assume is occupied by Sandro. Then she moves to the right of the window, where she approaches Sandro, who is on the right.*[2] *She passes behind him slowly and silently, smiles enigmatically, grabs an iron bar (the kind used to reinforce old buildings) and ducks under it. It crosses*

*her forehead diagonally. With her back to Sandro, she begins to unbutton
her dress. Sandro enters frame left and leans on the bar with both hands,
resting his chin on his wrist. Anna turns and gives him a significant look.*

SANDRO (*leaning toward Anna*): But your friend is waiting for you
    downstairs.

ANNA (*still unbuttoning*): She'll wait. (*She turns and exits right.*)
*Sandro ducks under the iron bar, crosses behind, and follows her out of
the frame.*

20. *Sandro's bedroom. Low angle* MS *behind the elaborate grillwork of the
    bedframe, through which we see Anna removing her dress and turning
    toward the door as Sandro enters. He takes her in his arms and kisses
    her. She embraces him warmly.*

21. *Reverse* MCU *of the embracing couple; now we see Sandro's back,
    Anna's arms around his neck, her fingers stroking his hair. They kiss.
    Behind them, through the window, we can see the out-of-focus image of*

Claudia swinging her purse as she waits in the courtyard. Sandro moves off to the right and peers out the window at Claudia.

22. *As in 20. Sandro's torso exits right as Anna lies back on the bed; her head goes offscreen. She waits for Sandro to return. Her figure is partially obscured by the elaborate grillwork of the bedframe.*

23. LS: *Claudia, from the back, in the courtyard, as she looks up at the bedroom window and watches Sandro closing the draperies.*

24. MCU *of Sandro, inside, standing by the window and closing the draperies with his right hand. He exits left. A temps mort: all we see are the curtains, almost but not quite closed. Through an opening Claudia can still be seen downstairs in* LS. *The draperies flutter in the breeze.*

25. MCU: *Sandro and Anna in bed. Sandro, in profile on the right, leans over Anna and is about to kiss her gently; Anna seems very willing. He caresses her hair.*

    SANDRO: How are you?

    ANNA: (*sullenly*): Awful.

    SANDRO: Why?

    ANNA (*she flails at him half-seriously, half-jokingly, gritting her teeth and trying to punch him*): Oh . . . why . . . why . . . why, why why?
    He laughs, playfully, freeing himself, rolling on his back and holding Anna's head, smiling. Anna has twisted over and is lying on top of him, her back to the camera. She pounds his chest with her fists. Amused, he defends himself.

    ANNA (*furiously*): Why, eh? Why, why . . . ?
    They embrace passionately. Sandro clasps her hair tightly and closes his eyes. Anna, her back to the camera, gives up the struggle, strokes his forehead, and cuddles up against him.

26. LS: *Claudia enters an art gallery off the square. The camera follows her as she walks from left to right; she pauses for a moment, looking to the left.*

    WOMAN (*off, in Italian*): No, I would also like that small painting.

    MAN: (*off, in English*): What do you think?

    WOMAN (*off, in Italian*): I don't mind.

    WOMAN (*off, in English*): Very original concept. And he really knows how to use paint.
    The camera follows Claudia as she continues moving right and disap-

pears behind a partition hung with paintings. MCU *of an American couple discussing a painting.*

MAN (*in English, positively, taking his pipe out of his mouth and cross-ing his arms on his chest*): I agree. Lots of power and vitality.

The camera pans past an abstract painting to the right, following Claudia as she emerges on the other side of the partition, passing a worker in MCU, *who is facing screen right, studying a painting on the side of the partition opposite to the American couple. He turns to speak to his com-panion, who is offscreen right.*

WORKER (*in Roman dialect, turning around toward other worker*): He's got a long way to go.

Claudia walks toward the men from the background, looks at the dis-paraged painting, which the worker scrutinizes anew, and smiles sympa-thetically. She passes behind the second worker, who is looking toward a painting offscreen right with an empty stare. Claudia turns her back away from the camera and pauses to look at another painting.

27. *Low angle* LS: *the back window of Sandro's apartment. The draperies flap in the breeze. In the foreground, in* MS, *we see the iron rail of the balcony of the art gallery below; Claudia comes out on the gallery bal-cony, leans against the rail, looks right and then up at Sandro's window.*

28. *Claudia, at the right of the frame, leans back against the balcony rail in* MCU, *looking up. A bridge across the Tiber extends behind her. The rushing noise of water is audible.*

29. *Sandro's apartment.* CU: *Anna raises her head into the frame, her eyes almost closed and her hair ruffled. Then the back of Sandro's head also rises from behind. He kisses her chin and cheek as she lies back. He turns and puts his head down while Anna lifts hers slightly, without responding, her eyes open and aloof. She stares at the ceiling, then turns her eyes very slowly in his direction. The bedsprings creak as they move about.*

30. *As in 27. Claudia, her back to the camera, leans on the rail of the balcony below in a low angle* MS. *She goes back inside the gallery.*

31. *Claudia enters frame right into a very low angle* MCU *and looks up at the beamed ceiling behind and above her, back at the door, then up-wards, and evidently concludes that her friend is making love right above her head. She nods to herself, smiling and sighing, then readjusts her purse on her shoulder.*

32. CU *of Anna and Sandro as in 29. Anna, aloof and almost annoyed, faces the camera; the back of Sandro's head obscures most of her face. They kiss again. She looks up for a moment, then kisses him angrily back.*
33. MS: *inside the entrance hall of Sandro's building, as in 13, but now Claudia, in profile, is framed in the doorway. She turns, looks inside, then closes the door gently.*
    Dissolve.
34. LS: *a country road, trees in the background. A white sportscar roars in at high speed from left foreground, skids around a curve, and races away, disappearing in the distance.*
35. MCU *of Claudia, Anna, and Sandro in the car, framed by the windshield. Anna's head is higher than the others'. Presumably she is sitting in the tiny seat in back. The roar of the car's motor is very loud.*
    Fade out.
36. *Fade in.* LS: *a calm sea. On the left background, we see the shadowy silhouette of a pyramid-shaped island. On the right, a motor-yacht sails toward it.*
37. *Camera shoots over boat's stern, the noise of the yacht over. A sailor leans over the stern in* MS, *squeezing out a sponge. In the foreground is a tray with cups on it. The sailor turns around, puts the sponge in a bucket, and exits left.*
38. MCU: *Claudia, in profile, sits on one side of the boat, her knees drawn up to her chest, her forehead resting on her knees. Claudia slowly raises her head and turns toward the camera.*
39. LS: *the calm sea. A dolphin surfaces twice.*
40. MS: *Raimondo, a man in his thirties, lies asleep in the sun on top of the boat's cabin; a whippet lies on his stomach. He wakens and pushes the dog off with a grunt.*
    RAIMONDO: Get away, mutt.
    He resettles himself and closes his eyes. Behind him Corrado, a middle-aged, bald man, enters left. He comes up the ladder and stands near the stern, looking out over the sea. He grabs the awning-support with his right hand and, smiling, turns back to look at Raimondo. A young woman, Giulia, enters behind him, comes up the ladder, passes Corrado, and also smiles at the spectacle of Raimondo's repose.
41. MS: *Corrado gazes toward the right; he is smiling, holding onto the*

awning post. Giulia is on the left; the couple are separated by the horizon of the sea, crossed diagonally by the forward awning-support. Giulia turns toward him.

GIULIA (*addressing Corrado's back*): It's as smooth as oil.

CORRADO (*turning around, but not quite far enough to face her, holding onto the rail*): I don't know why, but I detest comparisons with oil. (*He returns his gaze to the sea, on the right, while Giulia, snubbed, turns her head left.*)

ANNA (*off*): Good morning. (*She emerges from the cabin, below deck, behind Giulia. Giulia turns in her direction.*)

GIULIA: Did you sleep well?

The camera follows Anna as she moves left, away from Giulia and Corrado, who are left offscreen. Anna stands in MCU *with her back to the camera, holding onto a pole with her right hand and looking toward the bow. She leans against the pole, trying to see better. The yacht is heading toward a rocky island.*

ANNA: Claudia!

CLAUDIA (*standing on the bow, points the island out to Anna*): Look! (*She gets up and walks along the edge of the deck toward Anna, almost slipping.*) Oh dear . . . (*She regains her balance, sits on the edge of the boat's railing, facing camera, and puts her right arm around Anna's neck. They kiss.*)

42. *Reverse angle of 41. In the right foreground, Raimondo, in* MCU, *still lies with his eyes closed. Behind him,* MCU *of the two young women: we see Claudia's back, her hair in the wind, Anna in profile at the left of the screen, looking at Claudia.*

CLAUDIA: Did you sleep well?

ANNA: So-so. Last night I went to bed planning to think over a whole lot of things. . . . But I fell sound asleep.

CLAUDIA (*smoothing her hair in back*): I didn't know one could sleep so well in these things. They rock you like a cradle.

RAIMONDO (*turning his head slightly toward the two women*): I didn't sleep well at all.

SANDRO (*off*): Greetings. Hi.

They all raise their heads and turn to look at him.

43. *Reverse, as in 41. In the right background, Sandro emerges in* MS *from below, just behind the yacht's windshield. Claudia continues turning so that she ends up facing the camera.*

CLAUDIA: Good morning!
Claudia continues to move forward along the edge of the yacht, toward camera, swings around an awning pole, and steps down onto the deck into CU, *her face and hair temporarily obliterating the images of Anna and Sandro. Then she exits right. Anna remains leaning against the rail, looking at Sandro, but then she turns her head, looks down and then out to sea, and exits left.*

44. *Reverse angle of 43.* CU *of Anna looking out to sea on right, then turning left to look in Sandro's direction.*

45. MCU: *Sandro, a magazine in his hand, climbs out on the wheelhouse. He sits for a moment on top of the cabin, then, coming into a low angle* MCU, *he crawls on his knees to the right. Anna enters right. He puts his head on her shoulder and opens the magazine as she turns to look at him, then at the water.*

ANNA: Get some sun instead.
Behind her shoulder, Sandro looks up at her, then, raising his eyebrows, smiles and throws the magazine overboard behind him. Anna looks at him, then turns her face to the right, directly away from him (facing in a totally opposite direction).

46. LS: *the pages of the magazine fly along the side of the boat and get caught in the wake. The camera pans to the right, revealing Claudia sitting in the stern. We see her from the back in* MCU. *As the pages fly past, she gestures as if in protest, then watches them float away.*

47. MCU-CU: *Anna stands on the edge of the boat, looking down. She kneels down, and we see Sandro's torso and head as he lies on his back. He reaches behind his head for Anna with his right arm; they kiss, and she rests her cheek on his forehead for a moment. Sandro raises his head, looks at the sea, then sits up and turns around.*

SANDRO: Shall we go for a swim?
He gets up, takes off his shirt, and, crossing to the right, his back to the camera, joins the others standing in the stern.

CLAUDIA: Not here. It's scary.
MCU *of Claudia, Corrado, and Sandro standing in profile, looking at the rocky cliffs of the island.*

48. LS, *from the moving boat. On the right, the steep, forbidding cliffs of another island rise abruptly from the sea. The boat moves alongside them. They are first in shadow and then turn brighter in the sunlight.*

GIULIA (*off*): Once, the Aeolian islands . . .

49. MCU: *Corrado, Anna, and Giulia (in the foreground) are standing in the stern, looking to the right, out to sea.*

   GIULIA: . . . were volcanoes.

   CORRADO: Just think, twelve years ago, when you and I came here, you said the same thing.

   Giulia turns around, looking at him, and breaks into confused laughter, then gets up, leaning against the edge of the boat, remaining on the extreme right.

   CLAUDIA (*off*): What's this one called?

   CORRADO (*over his shoulder*): It must be Basiluzzo.

50. *Claudia, her back to the camera, in foreground in* MCU, *contemplates the island.*

   CLAUDIA: "Basiluzzo"—it sounds like the name of a fish.

51. *As in 49. Corrado gets up and points to an island on the right.*

   CORRADO: And that one is Lisca Bianca.

52. MCU: *Anna, holding on to an awning pole with her left hand, looks annoyed. She lets go and moves toward the left.*

   ANNA: (*angrily*): Oh God, what a bore!

53. MS: *Anna takes off her robe and stands in her bikini.*

   ANNA: What a fuss you all make over a swim!

   In the left foreground, Claudia, her back to camera, turns toward Anna. The camera pans to the left, revealing Sandro, who is standing at the edge of the boat looking at Anna. Anna picks up her bathing cap and exits right, leaving only Claudia (center frame MCU *from behind) and Sandro (left foreground, facing the camera and looking to the right) onscreen.*

   SANDRO (*protesting*): Anna!

54. MS, *camera in the stern. On the right Anna, her back to the camera, puts on her cap and dives, riskily, from the speeding boat. On the left, Corrado, his back to camera, gestures as if to stop her.*

   CORRADO: But . . . wait . . .

   Anna seems to disappear in the boat's wake. The camera moves to the right, so that we also see Giulia and Claudia, from behind, as they look at Anna, hardly visible in the water. The camera remains on Claudia's back; she gestures helplessly with her right hand. The wake in the background occupies most of the screen. The sea looks rough. Anna swims away from the boat toward the island.

55. MCU: *Sandro looks out over the water, concerned. He throws his shirt down.*

56. *Reverse of 55: camera in the bow. Sandro crosses the deck diagonally from right foreground to left background. Giulia, Claudia, and Corrado are standing with their backs to the camera, looking out over the water. Sandro dives into the water, the camera following him as he swims left. The boat goes offscreen right.*

57. MS: *Raimondo in his bathing suit, with fishing gear in his left hand and a pair of fins in his right hand. He throws the fins on top of the cabin behind him and rings a bell on the wall of the cabin.*

58. *Reverse of 57: camera in the bow.*

   RAIMONDO (*slightly ironically*): Mario! Woman overboard!
   A sailor enters in MS *from left foreground, walking on the edge of the boat toward the bow, where we see Raimondo turning toward him; in the background are Corrado, Giulia, and Claudia, who is pulling on her bathing cap. Giulia giggles while Mario, the sailor, moves the table, opens a cabinet, takes out a ladder, and lowers it over the side of the boat. Behind the ladder in the left background, standing on the edge, Claudia turns toward the camera. Claudia prepares to dive, but she wants the yacht to stop moving first.*
   CLAUDIA: Stop! Stop!

59. LS *from the island of the yacht's approach. Jagged rocks are on the left and in the foreground. Noise of the motor is very distant.*

60. *Motor's noise at half-throttle. High angle* MS *of Giulia swimming on her back away from the boat. She is enjoying herself in the water. In right background, Claudia enters frame swimming on her back. The sea is tranquil.*

61. MS, *camera in the stern. In the foreground, we see two lounge chairs and the ladder coming up from the cabin. In the background are the rocky cliffs of the island. Patrizia, the owner of the boat, comes up the ladder. She is wearing a peignoir.*

   PATRIZIA: Raimondo!
   RAIMONDO (*in a resigned tone*): I'm here, Patrizia!
   PATRIZIA (*surprised, standing between the two chairs, turning to the left where Corrado approaches her along the edge of the boat*): Why did we stop?
   RAIMONDO (*off, then as he enters right foreground, his back to the camera, in elaborate diving gear*): Aren't you going for a swim, Patrizia?
   PATRIZIA (*looking at Corrado behind her, then turning to the camera,*

looking at Raimondo): Imagine. I was swimming even in a dream I had. You go ahead, Raimondo. (*Surprised at seeing him in diving gear.*) Raimondo?

Raimondo flops toward her and kisses her hand. From the way he walks, we can tell that he's wearing fins.

RAIMONDO: Lady Patrizia . . .

PATRIZIA: Do you like underwater fishing?

RAIMONDO (*turns around facing camera, then moves to the right foreground, putting on his mask and walking offscreen*): I hate it. But what can I do? I have to conform.

Patrizia walks to the right railing and looks out to sea; the camera follows her and then keeps panning to the right, showing Raimondo as he lowers himself into the water, leaving Patrizia offscreen. Raimondo drops into the water and sighs.

RAIMONDO: Who said that man originally lived in the sea?

He swims away, then dives. All we see is the edge of the boat.

CORRADO (*off*): Patrizia! If you give me your yacht's flag . . .

62. MS: *Patrizia, looking out to sea.*

CORRADO (*off*): . . . I'll plant it on the island.

PATRIZIA (*perplexed*): Mah!

Patrizia turns toward the camera, moving into CU, *center frame.*

PATRIZIA: Islands. . . . I could never understand them. . . . With all this water around them, poor things. . . . (*She turns to the left and smiles at her whippet, who comes onscreen.*) Cosimo! Come!

She picks up the whippet and disappears below deck. The frame is left empty in the background except for the sea and, in left foreground, the roof of the cabin, as we hear Corrado's voice.

CORRADO (*off*): Mario! Launch the raft!

MARIO (*off*): Right away, Mr. Corrado!

63. MS: *the sea. In left foreground, Giulia floats on her back, moving slowly toward the center of the screen. Sandro and Anna are swimming toward her from left. In the background is the rocky island.*

GIULIA: Sandro! Where are you guys going?

SANDRO: Ask her.

64. MS, *high angle from the edge of the boat to the water below. A tiny rubber dinghy enters from the left foreground: sitting in it are Corrado, facing the camera in* MCU, *then Mario, rowing, his back to the camera.*

MARIO: I've never worked on anything but cruises like this. Luxury boats. Even though the work's harder.

CORRADO: It is? Why?

MARIO: Because the owners never have set schedules. For instance, we had to stay up all night navigating. (*The raft moves toward the background, where we can see the rocky shore. The men's voices fade away in the distance.*) No time for sleep. But I'd rather have it that way.

65. MS: *the open sea. In left background, we see Anna as she swims alone.*

ANNA (*screaming*): A shark! A shark!

66. MS: *Sandro, who has been floating lazily on his back, right, turns around and begins to swim vigorously toward the left.*

MARIO (*off*): Don't move, miss. Stay right where you are. Don't move, anybody.

SANDRO (*gesturing with his hand*): Anna! (*Ignoring the sailor's command, Sandro continues to swim toward Anna.*)

GIULIA (*off*): Claudia! Wait for me!

67. MCU: *Anna, flailing about in the water, calling out.*

ANNA: Everybody! Stay away! Stay away!

Sandro, entering from the right, reaches her. Anna lets him tow her.

SANDRO: Lean on me! (*He tows her toward the camera.*)

68. *On the boat. Patrizia, in* MS, *left, watches a sailor (center) helping Giulia and Claudia climb aboard. We don't see their faces as they quickly turn their backs to the camera.*

69. LS: *Corrado standing on the rocky shore.*

CORRADO (*calling out*): What's happening?

70. MCU: *Giulia on the boat, her bathing cap still on, shouting back.*

GIULIA: There's a shark circling around here. (*Gesturing with her arms.*) Don't move!

71. *As in 69.*

CORRADO (*calling*): Who's moving?

72. MS: *on the boat. Patrizia and Giulia, their backs to the camera, and Claudia, facing the camera but looking right, all watch as a sailor in the center background helps Anna out of the water onto the deck.*

CLAUDIA (*eagerly, helping Anna, who holds onto her arm*): But how did you realize it was there? Did it touch you?

Sandro's face also emerges right as he climbs on board, while Anna, avoiding Claudia's, Patrizia's, and Giulia's eyes, brushes past them,

*walking toward the camera and exiting left foreground. Claudia follows
her, exiting center foreground, as Giulia, in high angle* MCU, *turns to
Patrizia, left.*

GIULIA: I would have died.

*Sandro, following Anna and Claudia, walks toward the camera and comes
between Patrizia and Giulia.*

PATRIZIA: And the horrible faces they have . . . with all those teeth . . .

73. MS: *camera inside the cabin. Anna comes down the ladder into* MCU,
*followed by Claudia. Anna dries herself, looking to the left, as Claudia,
on the right, watches with concern. Anna turns toward her and gently
touches her on the shoulder with her right hand.*

SANDRO (*coming down the ladder, his figure blocked by Claudia's
torso in the foreground; we see only his arm reaching out to touch
Anna*): Drink some cognac, Anna!

*As Sandro moves behind Anna and to the left, she takes off her cap, passing
her hand through her hair and turning toward Claudia, who is putting a
towel on her shoulders.*

ANNA (*looking annoyed*): No, it's nothing. Let's go. (*Sandro puts a
towel on her back.*) It's all over now. I'd just like to change, that's all.
(*She shakes her hair and sighs.*) I'm cold.

SANDRO (*moving away from her toward the ladder, then stopping to
look at Anna*): Yes.

ANNA (*addressing Claudia, whose back is now to the camera, then
glancing at Sandro's back*): The summer's really over.

PATRIZIA (*partially visible behind, in the corridor*): But where could
the shark have gone, I wonder?

*Claudia, her back to the camera, takes off her cap and shakes her head;
Anna's head is turned toward the door as Sandro leaves the cabin, closing the door behind him. The two women stare at the door for an instant,
then Anna moves to the background to shut the door tightly; she is obscured by Claudia's back as Claudia moves slightly to the left to get a
towel. She reappears, opens a closet, and disappears into it for a moment, then closes it, having taken out a black blouse. She turns to face
Claudia and the camera. Claudia's back is still toward the camera. Anna
sits on one of the berths, left. Her entire mood is changed. She smiles at
Claudia enigmatically.*

74. CU: *Claudia on left side of screen.*
   CLAUDIA (*blinking, perplexed*): Well? What's the matter?
   The camera follows Claudia as she moves one step to the right, looking down at Anna, whose head emerges into lower right foreground. Anna starts laughing as Claudia, perplexed but half-smiling, takes off one strap of her bathing suit, then the other. Leaving Claudia off, the camera pans right to Anna alone in MCU, *who continues laughing, looking away from Claudia to the right. She lowers her face, still laughing, looks up at Claudia again, then turns around so that her back is to the camera. She reaches for two blouses on the berth.*
   ANNA (*still laughing*): Which one should I wear? This? Or this? (*She looks toward Claudia again, in* CU. *She lifts up first a white and then the black blouse, holding them up in front of her.*)
   The camera pans left and reveals Claudia, still standing. The top of Anna's head is level with Claudia's eyes.
   CLAUDIA: This one. It's so cute.
   ANNA: (*looking up at Claudia, still smiling as if amused*): So why don't you try it on?
   Claudia turns with pleasure toward her, then slips on the blouse and starts walking away from Anna, followed by the camera, which leaves Anna off. The camera follows Claudia to the bathroom, where we see her from the back, left screen, looking at herself in the mirror. She turns around and stands facing Anna, who is smiling.
   ANNA (*reentering right, standing with her back to the camera in close foreground, undoing the strap of her bikini top at the back of her neck. Framed by the bathroom door, Claudia could be Anna's reflection, if it were not for her blond hair.*): It looks better on you than on me. Keep it.
   CLAUDIA (*smiling, looking pleased with herself, smoothing the blouse's collar, then shaking her head*): No . . . .
75. CU: *Anna, at extreme left (the left half of her face offscreen), smiles at Claudia, then turns away, moving back to* MCU, *taking off her bikini top. We see her from the back as she silently slips a dress over her head. Claudia enters left foreground, her back to the camera, and stands next to her.*
   ANNA: You know, that story about the shark was all bull.
   CLAUDIA (*turning to her in amazement*): Bull?

ANNA: Yes.

CLAUDIA: Why?

ANNA (*reaching for a cigarette, slightly annoyed*): It just was, that's all. (*Decisively, as if to settle the matter.*) Don't worry about it. (*She lights the cigarette.*) It's all over now.

CLAUDIA (*serious, reproachfully*): I don't even want to know why you do things like that. It's Sandro, I guess. Did it do you any good, at least? C'mon, let's go.

Claudia exits right. Anna sits down, lowers her eyes, then turns left, first putting the cigarette in her mouth, then reaching for the black blouse. She stuffs it into Claudia's bag and looks up again at the door through which Claudia has exited. Creaking noises of the yacht and the slapping of waves can be heard.

76. *High angle* MCU *of Patrizia, left, her back to the camera, sitting at a small table in the cabin and working on a very complicated jigsaw puzzle.*

77. *Low angle* MS: *camera in the cabin. Patrizia, in lower right foreground,*

sits at the table, facing the camera; Claudia appears from the deck above, entering center background, and leans against the cabin doorway.

CLAUDIA (*moving her right leg forward and leaning on her bent knee*): Aren't you going ashore?

PATRIZIA: You call those rocks shore?

Claudia backs away to permit Raimondo to enter from the left; he bends down to come into the cabin, crossing in front of Claudia.

PATRIZIA (*turning to Raimondo*) Were you still in the water? (*She returns to her puzzle.*) Don't you know there's a shark around here?

RAIMONDO (*after freezing for a moment, he walks into the cabin behind Patrizia, taking off his gloves*): A shark? (*Patrizia laughs without taking her eyes from the puzzle.*) I could have been killed, eh? Is that what you guys mean?

PATRIZIA: Uh huh.

RAIMONDO: I see, of course.

Raimondo sits down at the table in the left foreground, shaking his head once, slowly. Patrizia remains in extreme right foreground, studying her puzzle. In the center background, obscured by the bright sunlight, Claudia has sat down on the top step, watching the two below her as she leans against the wall, her arms crossed behind her head. Raimondo watches Patrizia avidly.

PATRIZIA (*without looking at him, coldly*): What do you want, Raimondo? Me? (*She looks up at him, more affectionately.*) At this hour? (*Raimondo nods wistfully, as if to suggest that his silent request is not unreasonable.*)

CLAUDIA (*getting up, her head disappearing outside the cabin*): Goodbye!

PATRIZIA (*looking down, continuing with the puzzle*): No, Claudia. Stay. There isn't any romance going on.

Claudia stops and sits down on the steps again, her legs crossed. The camera moves left and down, following Raimondo, who has bent his head to look under the table. Patrizia's foot, in an elegant summer shoe, appears in right foreground, as she stretches out her leg to Raimondo.

PATRIZIA (*off, except for her leg; she pulls up her gown*): All right like this? Have you seen it? Are you happy? (*She laughs.*)

Raimondo nods and then straightens up.

78. MCU: *Patrizia is sitting at the table, still studying her puzzle. Raimondo,*

in profile on the left, straightens up, stretching out his right arm to put on his shirt. He looks pleadingly at Patrizia, who sighs wearily at his attentions. He gets up and stands by her chair, timidly placing his right hand on the backrest and gazing at her adoringly. She leans back, looking down, annoyed, and holds a cigarette to her mouth; he kneels down, getting closer to her, and as she lights her cigarette, her face is obscured by the smoke. He slips his hand into her peignoir to feel her breast. She sits up, and he removes his hand.

PATRIZIA: You're a bit disappointed; tell me the truth.

RAIMONDO (*shaking his head, his arm around the back of the chair*): No, on the contrary . . .

PATRIZIA (*turning toward Claudia*): How would you describe Raimondo's face?

CLAUDIA (*off*): A bit corrupt, I'd say.

PATRIZIA (*looking at Raimondo, then lowering her gaze, amused*): Not at all! He's a child, that's what he is!

RAIMONDO (*not amused*): Don't start in on that, Patrizia. I prefer "corrupt." Unless you happen to love children. (*He adjusts his shirt at the shoulder.*)

PATRIZIA (*looking down, indifferently*): I love no one. You know that.

RAIMONDO: I know, I know, damn it.

The camera follows him as he gets up, turns around, and walks toward Claudia, who is still sitting on the steps. As the camera moves, Patrizia goes off right. Claudia, her arms crossed and resting on her lap, watches him, half-smiling.

RAIMONDO (*turning around to face the camera again, smoothing his shirt collar and gesturing theatrically as he talks, then putting his hands on his waist*): If anyone was ever cut out—custom-made—for dissipation, betrayal, depravity, debauchery . . . (*He turns to Claudia, now holding her bent knee with both hands, grinning.*) . . . she's the one. But . . . (*Rolling up his shirt-sleeves, half-turning toward Patrizia, right.*) . . . she's faithful. Faithful out of sheer inertia, apathy.

79. MCU: *Patrizia, on left, looks up toward both of them.*

PATRIZIA (*laughing*): It amuses me. It's the only thing I find amusing . . . (*Looks down again.*) . . . besides my dog.

80. *As in 78. Raimondo looks down.*

CLAUDIA (*getting up decisively, her head again going out of upper frame, grabs a straw hat hanging on the wall next to the stairs on her way out*): Shall we go ashore?

Claudia exits left background. Raimondo, looking down pensively, moves forward, toward the camera.

81. *The rocky shore of the island, Lisca Bianca. In right foreground, the back of Corrado, in* CU, *wearing a panama hat. In left background,* MLS, *Anna hangs onto the rocks as if afraid; Sandro is behind her with a towel in his left hand.*

CORRADO: There should be some very ancient ruins up there. Why don't we go see? Giulia . . .

The camera pans left, following Corrado as he climbs up the rocks, Anna and Sandro going off right.

CORRADO: Do you remember . . .

GIULIA (*off*): Yes. (*She moves to the left to meet him, moves past him in left background, and spreads a blanket.*)

CORRADO (*his back to the camera in center foreground*): No, no, you'd better go to sleep. For you, everything is beautiful . . . the sea, a child, a cat. . . . You have a little heart so sensitive . . . (*His speech overlaps the next shot.*)

82. MS: *Claudia, swinging her hat, walks across the gangway from the yacht to the shore, then sits down, her left leg stretched out and the other bent, her arm resting on her knee.*

CORRADO (*off*): . . . that everything makes it go pit-a-pat.

GIULIA (*off*): Well, if they are beautiful, why shouldn't I say so?

Claudia leans down, dipping her hand in the water as if caressing something under its surface.

CLAUDIA (*in a fond tone*): Nice boy!

GIULIA (*off*): Who are you talking about?

CLAUDIA (*stretching out on the gangway, looking up*): That shark!

83. MCU: *Sandro, in profile, stands on the rocks, holding a towel under his left arm and looking up.*

SANDRO: Again?

The camera follows him as he turns and climbs the rocks toward the left; he throws his towel aside. He turns his back to the camera and begins to climb up after Anna, now revealed climbing on rocks higher up. Anna continues into right background, and Sandro follows her, stopping for an instant as if puzzled.

84. MS, *high angle: a sailor runs down the gangway, coming into* MCU
    from left background and holding up a basket of fruit.
    CLAUDIA (*entering frame from lower right, with her back to camera*):
    How wonderful!
    *She takes an apple from the basket and gives the sailor her hat. Holding
    up the apple, she looks upward, smiling, then exits right foreground.*
    CLAUDIA: Corrado!

85. MS: *Corrado's back moves into frame from left as he walks across the
    rocks; waves splash against the island's dark silhouette.*
    CLAUDIA (*off*): Do you[3] want one?
    CORRADO (*continuing to walk to the right, then half-turning, smiling
        gently at Claudia, who enters left foreground with her back to the
        camera, showing him the apple*): This is Patrizia's own special way
        of being with us.
    *Claudia walks up to him and offers him the apple. They face each other
    in profile, but at a slight distance. Claudia bites into the apple.*
    CLAUDIA: You know, I really like you.[4]
    CORRADO: Even more than the shark?
    CLAUDIA: Oh, there's no comparison. (*She turns and looks to the left.*)
    CORRADO (*gallantly offering his hand*): Then why don't you come with
        me . . . (*Corrado's speech overlaps the next shot.*)

86. MS: *Giulia, lying on the blanket. Hearing Corrado, she looks up, facing
    the camera.*
    CORRADO (*off*): . . . and have a look at these ruins.
    CLAUDIA (*off*): Ah. It might be an idea.
    Giulia sits up, watching them anxiously.

87. MCU: *Sandro cautiously walks sideways from left to right along a ledge,
    his hands holding onto the sheer rocks.*
    CLAUDIA (*off*): No, we'd better stay here.
    *The camera continues to pan right with Sandro, finally revealing Anna in
    right frame; it follows Sandro as he steps easily down to her, holds her
    right arm briefly (as much to support himself as to caress her), and then
    passes in front of her, coming into right foreground. She stands slightly
    higher than he, on the ledge.*
    ANNA (*as Sandro turns around, looking at her*): Sandro . . . a month is
    much too long. I had gotten used to being without you.

SANDRO (*touching her left arm in a quick gesture of reassurance*): It's the usual discomfort. Then you get over it. (*He casually turns away. The camera follows him from behind as he walks away to the right, leaving Anna off-frame.*)

ANNA (*off*): A little more this time.

SANDRO (*unconcerned, still walking to the right. At the edge he looks out to sea, then turns and looks upward at Anna; as she reenters left frame he turns back to look at the sea*): Then it will take just that much longer for you to get over it.

ANNA (*moving right to stand next to him, in profile, again standing a little higher than he*): No, really. I think we should talk about it. (*Almost aggressively.*) Or are you convinced that we'll never understand each other, either?

SANDRO: We'll have time to talk about it. We're getting married. Plenty of time then.

Anna frowns and turns away, while Sandro stares at her. The camera follows Anna to the left, leaving Sandro offscreen right. Anna sits down on the rocks, then turns her head right, toward Sandro.

ANNA: In that case, what would our getting married mean? Nothing. Even now, we're living as if we were married, aren't we? (*Increasingly excited.*) Giulia and Corrado . . . aren't they just as good as married already?

Sandro's arm enters right, gently strokes her hair, but she shrugs it off.

SANDRO (*entering right, sitting down next to her, his back to the camera, as she rests her chin on her knee*): But why waste time discussing, talking . . .

88. MCU, *reverse: Anna is now on the right, hugging her knees, her back to Sandro. Sandro, on the left, toward the camera, looks down.*

SANDRO (*quietly positive*): . . . talking, talking. Words. Believe me, Anna, . . . (*Looking up at her.*) . . . they're no help. Words only confuse things. I love you. Isn't that enough?

Anna turns only her head toward him. But as he tries to kiss her, she turns away, staring blankly to the right, while Sandro, behind her, looks at her intently.

ANNA: No, it's not enough. (*Pause.*) I'd like to try to be by myself for a while.

SANDRO (*surprised, and as if only now understanding the seriousness of the discussion, he grasps her elbow*): But you just said that a month without me . . .

ANNA (*pulling away angrily*): I mean longer. Two months, a year! Three years! (*She shakes her head, annoyed, then gets up and exits right.*)

Sandro stares at her, baffled.

89. CU: *Anna, in profile, in center foreground. Behind the rocks, in far left background, Corrado is looking over the cliff. Giulia is behind him.*

CORRADO: Look, so many fish. (*He turns and disappears behind the rocks, Giulia trailing behind him.*)

ANNA (*leaning against the rocks, softly, as if speaking to herself*): I know, it's absurd. I feel awful. (*Louder, turning left and looking intently toward Sandro, who is offscreen.*) The thought of losing you makes me want to die. (*She turns slightly, her eyes now not focused on him but on something far away.*) And yet . . . I don't feel you anymore.

She looks toward him again, then lowers her gaze as he enters from the left and stands close to her, gently stroking her hair. She turns her face toward his, as if to kiss him, then looks down again.

SANDRO (*in a calm but challenging tone*): Not even yesterday, at my house? You didn't feel me then?

90. *Reverse angle,* MCU, *of 89. Sandro's back is now on the right; Anna faces the camera left, staring at him angrily.*

ANNA (*with a searching, accusing look*): You always have to drag things down.

Sandro turns left, lowering his eyes with a sarcastic nod, and plays with a pebble, marking the rocks in front of him with it three times, as if it were a crayon. Then he lets it go, confronts Anna, and finally turns his back to her, staring out to sea as if at a loss for words. Anna rests her chin on a ledge, facing the camera left, CU, *her fist in front of her mouth. She looks very troubled. Sandro idly throws a pebble into the sea, then crosses behind Anna to left background, sitting down on the rocks and looking out at the water. She turns around to watch him, the back of her head to the camera. He leans back and stretches out on the rocks, crossing his arms over his eyes, and falls asleep.*

Dissolve. Anna's head dissolves more rapidly than does Sandro's body.

91. LS: *a side view of cliffs very much like those in 90, descending from left to right into the sea. But these are steeper and more menacing. The lighting is much darker. Sounds over of a motor launch, off, and of the waves breaking against the shore.*

92. MCU: *Giulia, her head in left frame, lies asleep on the rocks; she turns her face, wakes up, looks at the sky, and sits up, leaning on her forearms as Corrado crosses behind her, left. He passes by without looking at her and stares out to sea.*

    GIULIA (*turning toward Corrado, now on right*): The weather's changing.

    CORRADO (*turning to look at her as she throws back her head, shaking her hair*): For God's sake, Giulia, don't talk in captions. I can see for myself that the weather's changing.

    Corrado smiles at her, then turns his head to stare back at the sea. Hurt, she abruptly turns her head away from him, toward the camera, her eyes cast down.

93. LS: *steep high angle from above a ledge hanging over the sea. Claudia's figure, much foreshortened, moves along the ledge. She puts her shoes on the rock and hangs tightly to it with her arms behind her back, above the powerful breaking waves that could sweep her away.*

94. MLS, *reverse angle of 93. Claudia, center, faces the camera with her back to the rocks, kicks idly at a wave, then turns around to pick up her shoes. She turns back toward the camera and exits right. The sound of a motor launch can be heard over the waves.*

95. MCU, *reverse angle of 92. Corrado in the foreground; behind him, Giulia sits on the towel in profile, facing left. The camera pans right, follows Corrado's back as he walks away from her down to the sea, leaving her off-frame left. He stands looking intently out to sea, his hand on a rock to the left.*

96. LS: *Sandro, facing the camera, lying on the rocks as in 90, but now alone. A big wave washes ashore on the left, spray filling the air.*

97. MS, *as in 95. Corrado from behind as he stands at the edge, his left hand still resting on the rocks and the other in his pocket, looking out to sea. A sailor enters from right background, moving first into center background, then approaching Corrado.*

    SAILOR: We should leave.

CORRADO: Why?

SAILOR (*pointing to the sea without looking at it*): The sea's getting too rough.

They start walking away from the sea.

98. MS: *Claudia walks along the rocks. The camera follows her as she moves right, toward the sailor and Corrado, who enter from the right.*

CLAUDIA: And Anna?

CORRADO (*without looking at her*): I don't know.

The camera follows Claudia, passing between the two men, who are looking with concern out to sea. Her eyes search inland for Anna. As the camera pans with Claudia to the right, Giulia is revealed, still sitting on the rocks above, her back to the camera, near Corrado but staring in the opposite direction. The camera keeps following Claudia to the right as everyone else goes off left frame.

CORRADO (*off*): I thought I heard a boat.

SAILOR (*off*): Yes.

CORRADO (*off*): D'you hear? (*There is the sound of a motor, though not as distinct as before.*)

Claudia keeps walking, but now perpendicularly to the camera plane.

CLAUDIA (*in MS, calling to Sandro lying on the rocks*): Sandro! Where's Anna?

SANDRO (*in LS, sitting up in left background and looking left and right, as if surprised*): She was just here.

CLAUDIA (*turning around and addressing Corrado and the sailor*): Isn't she on the yacht?

In the background, we see Sandro as he gets up.

SAILOR (*off*): I don't know, miss.

In the background, Sandro walks to the water's edge. In the foreground, Claudia takes a few steps toward the yacht, which is offscreen right.

CLAUDIA (*calling out toward the yacht*): Patrizia!

99. MS: *Patrizia, working on the puzzle, is on the right, with the whippet sitting on her lap, and Raimondo on the left.*

CLAUDIA (*off*): Patrizia! Is Anna there?

Raimondo nods to Patrizia and the ladder, as if to make her aware of Claudia's call. As she remains engrossed in the puzzle, he nods again, acknowledging that he should answer Claudia, then gets up and walks up the ladder, exiting frame in center background. The camera stays on

Patrizia, who continues to do her jigsaw puzzle.

RAIMONDO (*irritated, off*): Anna! Anna!

100. MS: *a deeply shadowed part of the cliffs, sloping down into the sea. Sandro enters from left and moves toward the camera, and looks up at the cliffs above him.*

RAIMONDO (*off*): No! She's not here.

SANDRO (*he comes into* MCU, *stepping into a sunny patch, looks up again, then down, concerned but also irritated*): This is just the kind of thing that Anna does that drives me crazy.

101. *In extreme right foreground, Claudia's head in* MCU *is seen from the back as she looks at Sandro, in* LS *left background, his back to the camera, climbing up steep rocks to higher ground. Then she turns suddenly around, looking out to sea, then back toward Sandro, whom she follows up the rocks to the left. Sandro exits. Corrado enters from the right foreground, and follows Claudia up to the rocks into left background. Giulia energetically joins them.*

102. LS: *an expanse of rocky plateau, the highest part of Lisca Bianca. Sandro enters from the left foreground, picking his way across the terrain, moving into the center, his back to the camera.*

SANDRO (*cupping his hands and shouting*): Anna! (*He continues up the hill, jumping from rock to rock.*)

103. LS: *high angle of a deep and menacing crevasse in the rocks. An angry sea boils below. Sandro enters from right, walking along the edge. He stands in half-profile, looking down into the crevasse, then looks around, turns his back to the sea, and moves away, exiting right. The camera tilts up slowly to a long view across the island to the horizon of the sea beyond. In* LS *Claudia is searching for Anna.*

104. MCU-MS: *Claudia's torso in foreground, blocking the camera. She walks away toward the background, putting her belt on and looking around. Corrado enters right foreground, walking slowly after her. Mysterious music by a double bass and clarinet begins, and continues through 117. Giulia enters from the same spot where Corrado entered, but less solemnly.*

GIULIA: This island is really beautiful, isn't it?

She stops and turns toward the camera for an instant, then, as Claudia and Corrado go offscreen solemnly in the left background, she hops along to catch up with them.

105. MCU: *Sandro, on a steep ledge, half-turned toward the left, is looking*

out to sea. In the background is an island emerging from the sea like a whale. He turns, scanning the island, then starts walking to the right, the camera panning with him. He squats down to look at the sea at the base of the cliffs near him.

106. CU: *high angle on Sandro's back, foreshortened, as he continues to look at the sea directly below. His white shirt contrasts with the completely dark sea in front of him. He gets up, slowly turning toward the camera, an expression of intense concern on his face.*

107. LS: *on the plateau, Claudia is making her way across the rocks, followed in the far distance by Giulia and Corrado. Sandro abruptly enters left foreground, hopping from rock to rock until he stops in right foreground.*
     SANDRO (*calling*): Did you find her?
     Claudia, in LS, *shrugs and, as Sandro exits right frame, turns back toward Corrado.*

108. MCU: *Giulia, who walks toward the camera, coming into* CU, *looking slightly toward the right.*

GIULIA: Anna! (*She slowly turns her head to the left.*)

109. MCU: *Claudia, on the left. The camera pans with her as she carefully walks to the right, looking around intently. She stops and looks out to sea. In the right background, obscured by fog and clouds, there is another volcanic island.*

110. CU *of Corrado, in left profile, as he holds a large shell in front of him, examining it. He looks up at the sea, turns his back to the camera, casually dropping the shell, and exits left.*

111. MS: *Giulia runs into right screen, looking for Corrado.*

112. MCU: *Corrado, seen from the back in right foreground, slowly walks down and to the left. The camera follows him. He turns his back on Giulia, toward the camera, smiling, obviously ignoring her. Giulia is in deep left background, watching him. Corrado exits right foreground.*

113. MCU: *Giulia, standing; she stares in Corrado's direction, holding her hands together; then her head falls, she twists a stem or leaf in her hands, and throws it down in a gesture of helplessness and disappointment.*

114. *Low angle* CU *of Claudia against the sky. She squats down, her hair blown over her face by the wind. She shakes her head sadly, as if on the verge of tears, then turns and sits down, brushing her hair back in the breeze. Deep in thought, she fiddles with a small plant growing in the rocks. Then, seeing something on the left, she lets it go, gets up, and exits left, her torso filling the screen. A brief* temps mort *of the plant on the rocks.*

115. LS: *Sandro is walking inland from the cliffs toward the foreground. Suddenly there is the sound of a boat siren. He turns around in* MS. *The boat can be seen in the far background, near the whalelike island. The camera pans with Sandro to the right as he resumes walking, approaching a hut built into the rocks; he hurries down to the door.*

116. MCU: *Sandro, seen from the back, tries the door of the hut. Finding it locked, he steps backwards, turns toward the camera, looking around, and then moves toward the left.*

117. MS, *as in 115, of Sandro walking away from the hut, climbing up the rocks he just descended. As he exits left foreground, Claudia and Corrado appear from below, behind the hut.*

CLAUDIA (*approaching the hut's door and stopping there, calls*): Sandro! Anything?

Music ends.

118. MCU: *Sandro looking out to sea. He turns and shakes his head despondently. Then he exits left. The camera lingers on the vista of sky and island.*
Dissolve.

119. *High angle* LS: *Claudia, her back to the camera, is walking cautiously on the rocks by the sea. We hear the water pounding violently below. The roar of the waves is deafening.*

120. MLS, *reverse angle of 119: Claudia walking on the rocks toward the camera. The camera leaves her and pans across the rocks, then tilts down into a dark crevasse in the cliffs.*
   CLAUDIA (*shouting off over the roar of the waves*): Anna!

121. *As in 119. Claudia starts climbing the rocks to higher ground, exiting right.*

122. LS: *the hut, seen from below. Next to it, a figure is silhouetted against the horizon. The roar of the waves is replaced by the sound of a strong, menacing wind.*

123. *Slightly high angle* CU *of Corrado, looking down. The wind tosses his thinning hair about. He slowly looks up. Sound of the wind continues.*

124. LS: *the very dark sea. A storm gathers in the distance. The camera slowly tilts upward to the stormy sky, which takes over the entire frame. An enormous waterspout is visible on the left.[5] Sound of the wind continues.*

125. MCU *of Corrado, as in 123, looking the waterspout up and down. Sound of the wind continues.*

126. LS: *the part of the waterspout touching the sea, forming a bright circle. Sound of the wind continues.*

127. LS: *the cliff sloping to the sea. In center foreground, Claudia's head is miniscule among the rocks. As she watches, a large boulder tumbles down the slope on the right and splashes into the sea. Her back is to the camera and her hands clutch a rock.*

128. CU, *reverse angle of 127: the top of Claudia's head. She is lying prone on the rocks; her face is hidden from the camera because she turns her head to the right, laboriously and carefully, in order to get up. As she lifts herself, her entire body goes offscreen at the top; only her hands are visible as she pushes herself up from the edge.*
   CLAUDIA (*off, in a wondering, hesitating, excited voice*): Anna!

129. LS, *as in 122. In the far distance, the figure of a woman in a white dress against the sea suddenly disappears behind the rocks.*

130. *Low angle* MCU: *Claudia against the sky. She tosses her hair out of*

her eyes and gazes intently toward the left. She begins to run excitedly,
running off left foreground.

131. *Against the rocks shown in 129,* LS *of Claudia running onscreen from the
right toward the spot where the woman has disappeared.*

132. *Reverse angle of 131. Claudia runs toward the camera. As she comes into*
CU, *she stops, her face falling in disappointment.*

133. MS: *Giulia's back as she walks toward the edge of the rocks, looking
down into the sea.*
CLAUDIA (*off, upset*): Giulia!
*Giulia turns toward the camera, which follows her as she runs from right
background to left foreground.*
GIULIA (*in high angle, stopping and looking up*): Did you see that?
*The camera follows Giulia as she climbs up the rocks toward the right,
coming into* MCU *toward the foreground, and picks up the back of
Claudia's head. It remains in high angle for the remainder of the shot.*
GIULIA: You see how he treats me?
CLAUDIA: Who?
GIULIA (*smoothing her hair away from her face*): Corrado. All he's
   done today is insult me.
CLAUDIA (*still from behind, moving away impatiently, then glancing at
   her reproachfully*): Giulia!
*As Giulia looks down toward the sea, Claudia turns to the right, turns her
back to Giulia and exits right. Giulia remains in left foreground, high
angle, staring down to the right, then up at Claudia, and finally back at
the sea.*

134. MCU *of Sandro on the yacht, in left profile, scanning the base of the cliffs
as the boat skirts the island.*
CORRADO (*off, calling out*): Sandro! Sandro! (*As the yacht moves to the
   right, it passes Corrado, standing on a rock at the water's edge, while
   Sandro, turning his back to the camera, turns toward him.*) We didn't
   find anything. Not even a sign!
*As the boat carries him offscreen right, Sandro makes a helpless gesture.
Corrado begins to climb to higher ground. The camera pans left, following Corrado, who disappears behind a rock. The camera continues to
pan left and picks up the awning in the stern of the yacht. Patrizia and
Raimondo, under the awning, their backs to the camera, are scanning the
coastline.*

135. MS: *Claudia on the high ground, right foreground, her right hand keeping*

her hair away from her face. Giulia is wandering in the far background.
CLAUDIA (*looking around, bewildered*): Anna!
Dissolve.

136. LS: *the sea, the other dark rocky island in the background. Sandro walks into right foreground, his hands behind his back, and stands in* MCU *in center foreground, crossing his arms on his chest and slowly turning, first toward the camera, looking down, then all the way to the right. The camera follows him as he walks away, picking up Patrizia, Raimondo, Giulia, and Corrado, who form a kind of statuary group in center-right foreground. Raimondo is smoking a cigarette; Patrizia, behind him in left profile, stares out to sea; Giulia looks downward restlessly; and Corrado, on the far right, standing behind Giulia, also contemplates the sea. Sandro, who had disappeared momentarily behind the group, reappears and stands on the left, pursing his lips; Raimondo throws his cigarette away and turns toward him, his arms folded on his chest. As Sandro starts talking, everybody turns to him.*
SANDRO (*looking at them and gesturing with his hands*): Listen, you guys. Let's try to be practical. The best thing would be for the rest of you to go to the nearest island. . . . There must be some kind of police station or customs office there—something, anyway! (*He puts his hands in his pockets, shifting his weight nervously from one leg to another.*) Report her disappearance. I'll stay here. I'll stay here because . . . I don't know. (*Shrugging, then taking his hands out of his pockets, gesturing as if to cut any discussion short.*) Something may happen, that's all I know. Anyway, I don't feel like leaving.

137. MCU, *reverse angle of 136. Corrado, on the left, his arms crossed on his chest, Patrizia, in the center, holding the whippet, and Giulia, on the right, her face half-off the frame, are all gazing left toward Sandro, who is offscreen.*
CORRADO (*resolutely, putting his hands on Patrizia's shoulders as she turns away from the camera, to help her down the rocks*): Let's get a move on, then. No point in losing any more time.
The camera follows Patrizia to the right as she moves down to the water, where she meets Raimondo. Corrado is left offscreen. Giulia follows Patrizia, coming into center foreground.
PATRIZIA (*in profile, partially covered by Giulia, also in profile, standing in front of her. She addresses a sailor, who is offscreen right*): How long will it take to get there and back?

The sailor enters from right foreground.

SAILOR: A couple of hours if we can find the customs officers at Panarea. Longer if we have to go to Lipari. Depends on the sea, too.

RAIMONDO (*glancing at the sea behind him, nodding, while Giulia clutches her collar with her hand*): Ah, yes, the sea.

CORRADO (*off*): In any case, I'll stay here with Sandro.

Patrizia turns around and walks off.

GIULIA (*moving left into center foreground and looking left toward Corrado, who is still off-frame*): But why? And if it starts to rain?

138. MCU: *Corrado, in reverse shot, looking back at Giulia.*

CORRADO (*smiling condescendingly*): Well, if it rains, I'll buy myself an umbrella.

He turns his face to the left, where Sandro enters and approaches him. Sandro then quickly starts walking away to the right.

139. MCU *of Claudia, on the left, her back to the rocks, her arms folded on her chest. Patrizia, her back to the camera, enters right foreground, still holding the whippet.*

CLAUDIA (*moving away from Patrizia, crossing behind her, climbs a rock, her back to the camera, and says decisively*): I'm not going.

140. MCU, *reverse angle of 139. Claudia, in right foreground, a defiant look on her face; behind her, in left background, Patrizia, Corrado, and Giulia stand on a rock below her, Sandro on a rock above her.*

CORRADO (*coming toward her*): Claudia . . . I understand why you might want to stay, but there are two of us already staying behind.

SANDRO (*tilts his head to the left so that his whole face, in MS, is visible as he faces her*): Also, your[6] being here . . . I don't mean to offend you . . . but you might be in the way.

In the middle of his speech, Claudia turns toward him, then without a word, she rushes off left between Corrado and Patrizia. Before she reaches Sandro, she turns abruptly right and climbs the rocks, crossing in front of him and exiting right. The others follow her with their eyes as she climbs higher.

141. MS: *Claudia, with her back to the camera, climbs diagonally on the rocks from right foreground to left background (across the 180° line).*

142. MS: *starting from positions as in 140, Sandro and then Corrado follow Claudia, exiting right. Patrizia turns and gives her left hand to Raimondo, who helps her down the rocks. The two exit left. The camera holds on the empty scene.*

Dissolve.

143. LS: *the sea and the two islands from high up on the edge of the island. Claudia enters right, walking in* MS *to the center; she turns away from the camera and looks out to sea. Thunder can be heard. Claudia turns and starts walking toward the camera.*

144. MS: *the dark interior of the hut. Sandro enters the door on the left.*
SANDRO: Damn, we forgot to ask them to leave a lantern . . .
As he looks in his pockets for a match and lights it, first Claudia and then Corrado come through the door.
SANDRO (*holding up the match*): Ah, there's one. (*He lights the lantern.*) There!
They glance around, then Claudia exits right; Corrado moves toward the camera, putting a finger on his lips, pensively; Sandro turns toward the wall, his back to the camera, with his hands on his hips. He bends down to pick something up, then looks at a cloak hanging on the wall.

145. CU *of Corrado, in profile, facing right. He shuts the door, looks up, and turns around, removing his hat. The camera follows him as he walks in* MCU *to the back of the room, revealing Claudia, who is facing the wall, her back to the camera. She turns, looks up, and walks into* CU. *Corrado, in left background, faces the wall.*
CLAUDIA (*soberly*): As far as I'm concerned, she's still alive. Even this morning . . . (*She glances at Corrado from the corner of her eye; he quickly turns toward her.*) . . . that whole story about the shark . . . it wasn't true.
Sandro steps onscreen left, quickly moving closer to her; Corrado, behind her on the right, looks at her intently.
SANDRO: But why didn't you say so before?
CLAUDIA (*looking down*): But . . . I don't know . . . (*She quickly turns right to face him.*) It just didn't seem worth mentioning. . . . She was laughing. . . .
CORRADO (*looking intently at her, in an objective, inquisitive tone*): Sure, but what remains to be seen is why she invented that shark. What was she driving at?
She turns to the left and starts to move away from them. The light on her remains bright.

146. MCU *of Claudia, continuing to walk away from the two men into a totally dark area in the hut.*
CLAUDIA): Perhaps we should ask *him* that.

She turns around, coming into the light again, and sits down in a corner, with her arms crossed on her chest and her head resting against the wall.
SANDRO (*off*): Me? Why?
The look on Claudia's face is challenging, though her eyes are averted from the two men.

147. MCU *of Corrado, on the right, and Sandro, in profile on the left.*
     CORRADO: Why? Did you two quarrel? I'm sorry. . . . I don't mean to pry, but this is very important.
     SANDRO (*shaking his head, in a tone of dismissal*): The usual discussions . . .
     The camera stays on him as he walks restlessly away toward the right, crossing in front of Corrado. Corrado is left offscreen by the camera movement. Reaching the wall, Sandro turns around, sitting on a ledge.
     SANDRO: The only thing, if I remember correctly, was that she said she wanted to be alone.

148. *As in 146, but Claudia now looks pointedly at Sandro.*
     CLAUDIA (*contemptuously*): And how do you[7] explain that?

149. *As in 147. Sandro puts a cigarette in his mouth and looks up, surprised and a bit resentful, then takes the cigarette out of his mouth, as if about to say something. Noise of dripping rain and thunder.*

150. MCU *of Corrado, in profile in the center, taking off his jacket. The lantern flickers. He turns and walks toward the camera, coming into* MCU, *then sits down with his back to the camera in foreground. Claudia enters right and sits beside him. Footsteps can be heard approaching the door. They look up, hoping to see Anna enter.*

151. MCU: *Sandro, leaning against the wall. He slowly gets up, also looking toward the door expectantly.*

152. MCU, *as in 150. Corrado and Claudia, their backs to the camera, stare at the door in front of them. The upper portion of the door opens, framing an old man with a cape over his head to protect himself from the rain.*
     OLD MAN (*opening the lower portion of the door and looking around*): Excuse me! What are you all doing . . . ? (*He opens the lower part.*)
     Corrado gets up, partially obscuring the old man, then steps to the right.
     SANDRO (*off*): Are you[8] the owner?
     As the old man shuts the door and turns to the left, Sandro enters left, standing in profile in front of him.
     OLD MAN (*taking off his cape and putting his things down*): No, the owners are in Australia. (*Looking at Sandro and Corrado.*) I've been to

Australia too. . . . Thirty years! (*Gesturing to the wall on the right, in broken English.*) These are my photo.

As he says this, Claudia emerges from right foreground, getting up from her seat, her back to the camera, partially obscuring Corrado and the old man, who quickly moves to the right.

153. MCU: *the old man, on left, stands at the wall, his back to the camera, pointing at each of the pictures.*

OLD MAN (*in English*): This is my brother. My sister-in-law. My friends. (*He points to the ones in front of him, looking toward the left.*) My uncle. My mother. (*In Italian.*) My grandson. (*Patting the wall.*) Those were the days.

The camera pans with him to the left as he turns away from the wall, revealing Sandro, who stands behind him on the left.

SANDRO: But where did you come from? We've been all over the island.

OLD MAN (*stopping in center foreground, in profile, looking at Sandro*): From Panarea.

The old man moves away, exiting left, while Sandro follows him with puzzled eyes. Corrado enters right, and the camera follows him as he crosses in front of Sandro and then leaves Sandro offscreen. He reaches the old man on the left, by the table, his back to the camera.

CORRADO (*in profile, looking at the old man, who is leaning on the table*): From Panarea. . . . So it was you, around two o'clock. I saw a rowboat go by.

OLD MAN (*taking some bottles out of a bag and putting them on the table in front of him*): Must have been four or five.

CORRADO (*looking at him intently*): In the afternoon?

OLD MAN (*continuing what he is doing*): No, in the morning. (*Stopping, looking at Corrado.*) But why? (*Looking toward Sandro, in English.*) What happened? (*In Italian.*) What was it? What was it?

154. MCU *of Sandro.*

SANDRO (*shaking his head, cutting the discussion short*): Nothing, nothing.

The camera follows Sandro as he puts a cigarette in his mouth and moves right. Sandro passes in front of Claudia without looking at her.

CLAUDIA (*staring at Sandro, who stops, already half out of the frame*): Why don't you tell him?

She glances down, then looks up, first at him, then at the others, off to the left. Sandro looks at her, his back to the camera. She addresses the old man.

CLAUDIA: One of the girls who was with us has disappeared.

155. MCU, *reverse angle of 154. Claudia, in center foreground, with her back to the camera, looking at the old man in right background; Sandro, his face now visible, in left foreground, looking intently at Claudia. Corrado stands to the right of the old man, staring at him.*

OLD MAN (*looking at Claudia*): Disappeared? You mean, she drowned? *Sandro turns his head toward the old man, and Corrado continues to stare fixedly at him.*

CLAUDIA (*positively*): No, she didn't drown. Disappeared. We don't know where.

SANDRO (*looking at Claudia*): And it's my fault. Go ahead, say that, too. It's what you're thinking.

CLAUDIA (*taking her jacket off, she moves toward the left, leaving Corrado and the old man offscreen and passing behind Sandro, who turns around to watch her as she moves to the left*): You concern yourself too much with what I think. (*She stops and confronts him.*) It would have been better if you had tried to understand what Anna was thinking!

156. MCU: *the old man, on left, and Corrado, on right in profile.*

OLD MAN (*gesturing with his right hand*): Did you look behind the house? She might have fallen from those rocks. Because a month ago . . .

157. MCU: *Claudia, on left, facing camera, looking down with her arms crossed on her chest, and Sandro, on right, with his back to the camera.*

OLD MAN (*off*): . . . the same thing happened to me with one of my lambs.

As she listens to the old man, Claudia steps apprehensively toward the camera, looking up, then glances over her shoulder at Sandro, who has turned toward the camera, looking at her inquisitively.

OLD MAN (*off, continuing*): All day I looked for him. It wasn't until night that I found him.

Claudia, distressed, looks up distractedly and rushes past Sandro, exiting right, slamming the door behind her; Sandro, center, is left alone, turned to the right, staring after her.

OLD MAN (*off, concluding*): I guess it strayed there. . . .

158. LS: *Claudia runs out of the hut into the rain, climbing the rocks toward the camera. Sound of the rain pouring down.*

159. MS, *low angle. Emerging from left foreground, Claudia, already soaked, climbs up a small mound and stands with her back to the camera, in front of the sea.*
    CLAUDIA (*wailing desperately*): Anna! Anna!
    The rumbling of thunder. She bows and hugs herself in despair. Corrado rushes onscreen from the left foreground; he puts his arms around her shoulders, turns her gently, toward the camera, and then leads her away from the sea.
    CORRADO (*whispering*): Come back. Come.
    She turns, and they walk back toward the camera.
    Dissolve.

160. CU: *Claudia lies asleep with her left hand next to her face, which is turned toward the camera with a peaceful expression. The wind howls outside the hut (and continues for several shots). As if her sleep were disturbed, she hides her face in her arm. She tosses and turns, then opens her eyes, looking around slowly as if wondering where she is. As she props herself on her elbow, the camera follows the direction of her gaze to the right, revealing Corrado, who is sitting at the table, his eyes closed, resting his face on his hand, his finger laid thoughtfully on his cheek. Claudia, in center foreground with her back to the camera, smooths her hair back, sits up slowly, covering herself with the blanket, and exits right. Corrado remains immobile in the same position.*

161. MCU: *Claudia enters left, her back to the camera, and opens the door. She stands shivering in the doorway, looking out to sea; the wind whistles noisily. She turns and walks back inside, offscreen left. A temps mort— the doorway framing the grey sea and a cold sun rising on the horizon.*

162. MCU: *inside the hut. Claudia, shown only from shoulder to knee, picks up some clothes lying on a chair. The camera tilts up, fully revealing her in low angle. She puts her dress against her chest. She sighs, quickly turns to the right, and drops the dress. The camera follows her as she moves to the right and picks up her bag, takes a garment out and tosses it away, then finds the dark blouse that Anna had given her. She holds it up in front of her and looks at it intently.*

163. CU *of the blouse clutched against Claudia's breast. The camera tilts up, showing her face as she looks down at the blouse, feeling it with her hands, then looking reflectively in the direction of the camera, pondering.*

164. LS: *the sea, breaking on the rocks. Noise of the waves and whistle of the wind continue through the shot. The camera pans slowly across the rocks to the left, revealing Sandro, who stands on the edge, facing the sea, his arms crossed on his chest. The camera follows him as he turns his back to the sea, puts his hands in his pockets, starts climbing, and then stops to sit down on a rock, facing the sea again. He glances over his shoulder and gets up, turning his back to the camera and moving away from it. Claudia, also in* LS, *enters left and walks toward Sandro. They are framed against the turbulent sky.*

SANDRO (*as Claudia is coming closer*): How are you? Do you feel better?

CLAUDIA (*standing in front of him, a little higher up, in a soft tone*): Forgive me for last night.

165. *Reverse of 164.* MCU *of Sandro in profile, looking toward the right, facing the wind, smoothing back his hair.*

SANDRO: You're very fond of Anna, aren't you?

CLAUDIA (*off*): Yes, very.

SANDRO (*looking intently at Claudia, who is facing camera, evidently on a rock, for she stands a head above him*): Did she ever talk to you about me?

CLAUDIA (*looking down, shaking her head sadly*): Just a few times. But always with tenderness.

Sandro looks down, shakes his head as if puzzled, and, turning his back to the camera, paces behind her toward the sea, clutching his forearms with his hands.

SANDRO (*turning around, hesitantly*): And still . . . still she behaved as though . . . our love . . . (*Walking toward the camera, more decisively.*) . . . yours, mine, her father's too, in a certain sense, wasn't . . . just wasn't enough for her . . . (*He steps into the foreground, turning his back to Claudia, who looks down, deeply saddened.*) . . . wasn't of any use to her.

CLAUDIA (*fighting back tears, she does not try to keep her hair out of her eyes*): Sometimes I wonder what I could have done . . . (*Sandro smooths back his hair, turning toward her.*) . . . so that all this wouldn't have happened.

While Sandro looks away, Claudia observes him for a moment from the corner of her eye, then, as if hearing something, she turns to look at the sea behind them. The sound of a motorboat is audible through 168.

166. LS: *the sea, the islands, in the glow of the morning sunshine. The camera pans slowly to the left, but nothing can be seen except rock, sea, and sky.*

167. MCU, *as in 165, of Sandro, looking toward the sea behind him, and Claudia, looking toward the right. They both suddenly turn and look at each other at the same time for a moment; Claudia gestures to the right, and Sandro looks toward where she's pointing.*

168. LS: *a cliff descending into the sea. The camera moves slowly up and to the right, across the rocks; Claudia emerges from left foreground, her back to the camera. The camera follows her as she walks slowly, hugging herself against the wind. Then she runs to the background, Sandro emerges in* MCU *from left foreground; he is shown in profile, a bewildered expression on his face. He turns his back to the camera, looks at Claudia, then looks back toward the right.*

169. LS: *low angle from the top of the plateau down to the sea. A figure emerges from the rocks, walking slowly toward the camera.*

170. *As in 168. Sandro rushes off, exiting right; Claudia remains in* LS, *turned toward the camera and framed against the sea.*

171. MS: *the camera follows the old man as he makes his way across the rocks, walking from left to right until Sandro jumps onscreen from the right.*[9] *Sandro grabs the old man roughly by the shirt.*

SANDRO: Whose boat is that?

OLD MAN: What boat?

SANDRO: Didn't you hear the noise? (*Gesturing to the sea with his right hand, while he vehemently holds onto the old man's shirt with the other.*) A minute ago. Didn't you hear the noise?

OLD MAN (*calmly, gesticulating*): There are a lot of boats around here in the summer.

Sandro pushes him away impatiently, moving right and toward the camera, his hands in his pockets. Then he turns toward the old man.

SANDRO (*aggressively*): How come you got up so early?

OLD MAN (*sarcastically*): Five o'clock in the morning is early?

Sandro looks away toward the right and exits right; the old man follows him.

172. *Claudia stands in* MCU *in left foreground, her back to the camera. Sandro, in* MS, *is walking up toward her with his hands in his pockets. The old man disappears behind a rock below. Before Sandro can reach the top, Claudia turns around and exits left. Sandro walks slowly into* MCU; *the camera follows him as he walks toward the left. He stares*

intently at Claudia. *Enigmatic clarinet music begins again, and continues through 178.*

173. MS: *a pool of rainwater in a hollow in the rocks. Claudia's arms and hands come into frame from the left, dipping into the water. She lifts the water to her face, which enters the screen at the top. Then the camera tilts up, fully revealing Claudia and remaining focused on her as she brings some water to her forehead. She looks down, holding her hands open in front of her, as if assessing the cleanliness of her palms. Then she looks up toward the sky. Sandro crawls over the rocks behind her, quietly. His figure is partially obscured by Claudia's in the foreground. She does not know he is behind her. He sits on a rock on the right, contemplating her with his hands in his pockets. She dries her face with a handkerchief and suddenly senses his presence. She turns around to look at him, her back now to the camera. He looks away and stares blankly in front of him. Claudia lowers her gaze, still rubbing her hands in the handkerchief. Then he looks at her again. When she turns toward him, he looks away again and raises his shirt collar and folds his arms. Then, as their glances cross again, she begins to climb toward the right, past him.*

174. MCU: *Sandro, standing on the right, watches Claudia walking up from the left; as she comes into center foreground, crossing in front of Sandro, she slips. He catches her, smiling sympathetically.*

175. MCU, *high angle, reverse of 174: Sandro is now on the right, his back to the camera, Claudia on the left, looking at him with puzzlement, as if trying to guess what is in his mind. Then she starts to get up, moving to the right, in front of him, and still looking at him.*

176. *Another reverse;* MCU, *as in 174:*[10] *Sandro continues to hold Claudia's wrist, even though she has regained her balance, gazing at her with a tender half-smile. She slowly extracts her wrist, but he holds on as her fingers pull away from his.*

177. MCU, *as in 175: Sandro is in the foreground with his back to the camera, his sweater and dark hair covering most of the screen. Only Claudia's head is visible, over his right shoulder in low angle. She is looking at him with puzzlement and even resentment at the intimate exchange of touches. Then she looks down, clutching her coat collar, and exits left behind him. Alone on the screen, he slowly gets up, then exits left after her.*

178. LS: *the open sea. A boat approaches the island, blowing its horn loudly.*

(The clarinet music ceases.) Claudia enters from right foreground and stands, watching the boat, her back to the camera. Sandro enters from the same spot, crosses in front of her, and stands to her left, his back also to the camera. They exchange glances, and then watch the boat again. The camera pans slowly to the right, following the boat coming to the shore.
Dissolve.

179. LS, *high angle from the top of the cliff. A dinghy approaches. The camera continues panning to the right, revealing the backs of two policemen and of Corrado and Giulia watching a man, secured by heavy lines, examining the shoreline at the base of the cliff.*
     MARSHAL (*leaning down, shouting*): Bartolo!

180. LS, *low angle, reverse of 179: the four people standing on the cliff. Sandro comes up from behind to join them. The policeman on the right is holding the ropes that secure the man.*
     POLICEMAN (*shouting*): Well?
     BARTOLO (*off, shouting*): Nothing! Nothing!

181. *As in 179.* LS, *high angle, from the cliff, where the policemen and Corrado stand.*
     MARSHAL (*shrugging his shoulders as he addresses Corrado*): Nothing!

182. MCU: *Giulia, on the left, blinking in the sun, looking out to sea; Corrado, in the middle, staring at the policeman in front of him.*
     CORRADO: Don't look at me like that, Marshal. It is quite uncalled for, you know.
     All three turn to look down at the shore again. The marshal shrugs, as if he doesn't know what more to say.

183. MS, *high angle: Claudia is standing alone, her back to the camera and her arms crossed on her chest, looking down into a deep crevasse in the rocks.*

184. MS: *Sandro walking down the rocks. He stops, hearing some voices off to the right. He moves down a few steps farther toward the camera, glancing toward the left, perhaps at Claudia. He looks indecisive, perhaps unsure whether he should approach her or not.*

185. MS, *as in 183, of Claudia as she turns around and starts walking up, left and toward the camera. Enigmatic clarinet and flute music begins again (through 193). As Claudia looks up, however, she quickly changes her mind, because of something or someone she has seen (perhaps Sandro).*

> *She immediately sets off in the opposite direction, to the right, behind some rocks. The camera follows her. A policeman's voice, off, says "Yes. There!" As it pans right, the camera picks up some policemen in the background.*

186. LS: *Claudia, making her way from the left across the rocky cliff to the edge, looking out to sea. In the far background, scarcely visible, Sandro turns away.*

187. LS, *high angle, from the cliff. Divers search in the sea down below. They converse among themselves, their words are not quite audible.*

POLICEMAN: Wait . . .

> *The camera tilts downwards slowly, revealing Patrizia's head in the foreground, very foreshortened. Her whippet is at her side. She is watching the divers. Another diver jumps into the water.*

PATRIZIA (*turning right, addressing Claudia unemotionally*): Let's hope these people don't find her. They would find her dead.

188. MCU: *Claudia, kneeling on the rocks, breaks down, sobbing uncontrollably and holding her head in her right hand. Patrizia enters left, and stands silently in front of her. She takes off her glasses and turns toward the camera, apparently at a loss for words. Claudia continues weeping. They are both startled by Sandro's voice.*

SANDRO (*off*): Listen, Patrizia . . .

> *They quickly look around toward the background. Claudia stands up and takes a step to the right, the camera following her and leaving Patrizia off. She smooths her hair and dries her eyes with her handkerchief. Sandro and the marshal emerge from the right and pass behind her as they walk quickly toward Patrizia.*

SANDRO (*to Patrizia*): . . . he says there's a current that runs past this island across to another . . .

> *He quickly moves off left, followed by the marshal; the camera stays on Claudia, in MCU in the foreground. She wipes her nose and dries her tears, but her face remains grave.*

SANDRO (*off*): . . . I'm not sure which. But at least it's a clue to go on, isn't it? The marshal says . . .

189. MCU: *Sandro descending the rocks.*

SANDRO: . . . that he'd like to send one of his men over to see. You never know . . . (*He sits down on a rock. A policeman crosses the screen walking from right to left behind him. Sandro turns slightly to the right, still addressing Patrizia.*) Do you[11] mind if . . . ? (*As he looks up, he suddenly stops, startled.*)

190. MCU: *Patrizia, right foreground, staring soberly toward the left; Claudia, behind her, with her back to the camera, looking in the opposite direction.*

191. MS, *reverse angle of 190: Claudia, standing in right foreground, her face toward the camera; the back of Patrizia's head on the left; Sandro, sitting behind and between the two women, looking at Patrizia.*

SANDRO (*to Patrizia*): Do you mind if I ask Raimondo to go along with him?

Patrizia turns meaningfully toward Claudia.

192. As in 190.

PATRIZIA (*glancing at Claudia, then looking up and responding with her usual coolness*): I don't see why I should mind.

She turns toward Claudia, who has turned around to confront Sandro.

CLAUDIA (*scornfully*): I think that you should go.

193. *Reverse angle, as in 191.* MS *of Claudia, standing in right foreground with her back to the camera, looking at Sandro in front of her; Patrizia, in left foreground, also with her back to the camera, looking at Claudia; Sandro sits between them, but looks at Claudia.*

SANDRO: Yes. Yes, perhaps that would be more useful. (*He looks downward.*) More useful.

Claudia turns around, looking downward, biting her lip, and exits right foreground, while Sandro follows her with his gaze. Then he gets up, turns around and exits left. Patrizia turns to the right, camera following her as she sits down on the rocks next to Claudia. Both face the camera, looking downward.

PATRIZIA (*staring into the camera*): The one who amazes me is Sandro. He seems almost calm.

CLAUDIA (*looking at her*): Calm? He doesn't seem calm to me. (*Patrizia turns toward her; Claudia softens her voice while making her point.*) He was awake all night . . . (*She continues to look down, hugging her knees and moving her finger nervously.*)

194. MLS: *Raimondo makes his way across the rocks from left to center, carrying a thermos-bottle. The camera tracks right with him, revealing Corrado and Giulia in background, then Giulia in left foreground. Patrizia is in right foreground, her back to the camera.*

RAIMONDO (*kneeling down, addressing one of the divers*): What is it?
DIVER (*coming up the rocks carrying a vase*): An ancient vase. There's
  a whole city down there. It's full of these things.
*He hands it to Patrizia, who has moved down to meet him. She looks at
it and turns left, climbing the rocks toward Raimondo.*
PATRIZIA (*ignoring Raimondo and continuing past him toward the
  left*): Of course *he* would show up just now.
*The camera stays on her as she keeps walking to the left, carrying the
vase, thus revealing Corrado in center, and Sandro and Claudia standing
side by side in left foreground. Claudia is looking at Sandro coolly; his
eyes are lowered.*
CORRADO (*to Patrizia*): Let me see.
PATRIZIA: Okay, so tell us, what century does it belong to?
*Giulia emerges on center, running up from the rocks below; everybody
turns toward her.*
GIULIA (*brightly, excited*): Corrado! Why don't we ask them to let us
  have it?

CORRADO (*sarcastically*): Sure. So you can put your geraniums in it. (*He hands the vase to her, and she hands it to Raimondo, who is standing to her right.*)

PATRIZIA (*in right foreground, turning to Sandro on left*): And you? Weren't you supposed to go?

SANDRO: Well, no, it's pointless.

195. MCU: *Sandro and Claudia. She rushes offscreen right. He stares down intently, as if deep in thought. Then he turns and stares in Claudia's direction.*

196. MS: *Claudia, with her back to the camera, moves silently behind Corrado and Giulia, who are standing in center, turned toward the right. As the camera follows her off toward the right background, Raimondo is revealed standing in right foreground, holding the vase. Everybody turns to stare after Claudia. Raimondo drops the vase.*

197. CU *of the vase smashed on the rocks in front of Giulia's feet, as she exclaims "Oh!"*

198. CU *of Raimondo, looking down at the pieces.*

PATRIZIA (*off*): What a shame!

Raimondo nods in mock sorrow, shrugging and looking left, then right.

RAIMONDO (*looking into the camera, resignedly to himself*): As usual. (*He turns and appeals to someone for understanding.*)

GIULIA (*off, excitedly*): Here's Anna's father!

199. MLS: *a hydrofoil speeds across the sea to Lisca Bianca. A horn sounds. Dissolve.*

200. MLS: *Giulia, on right, moves down to join Corrado. Claudia climbs in the opposite direction, toward the camera. As she comes into* MS, *a policeman quickly enters from right foreground, his back to the camera, and salutes her. Claudia ignores him and proceeds forward, holding out two books. She stops in front of Anna's father, who is just offscreen left.*

CLAUDIA (*holding out the two books*): I looked through Anna's suitcase . . . (*She stops, suddenly aware of the dark blouse that she is wearing, the one Anna had given her. She looks down, embarrassed, clutching the collar and smoothing it down in front.*)

201. MS, *reverse angle: Anna's father, standing center, slightly above her; Claudia in front of him, with her back to the camera.*

CLAUDIA (*apologetically, softly*): Yes, it's Anna's. She gave it to me yesterday. I found it in my bag. I didn't really want it, but I didn't have anything else to put on this morning. I'm sorry.

He reaches out and pats her shoulder reassuringly. Claudia hands him the books.

CLAUDIA: I found them in her suitcase.

202. CU: *the books in his hands (only the lapels of his jacket are also in the frame). He hands one of them back to her; it is F. Scott Fitzgerald's* Tender is the Night. *He looks at the other—the Bible—and moves toward the background with it, so that his head comes into view. He moves behind Claudia, who sits in the foreground with her back to the camera, and turns toward her so that we now see him full face.*

    FATHER (*pensively*): I think this is a good sign. (*He moves to the right, the camera following him, leaving Claudia offscreen left, looking at her.*) Don't you[12] agree? (*He raises his voice, and speaks more excitedly.*) I believe that anyone who reads the Bible could never do anything rash . . .

203. *Reverse angle,* CU *of Claudia, looking at him.*

    FATHER (*off*): . . . because it means she believes in God. Therefore . . . *Claudia looks down as he continues what begins to sound like an argumentative speech to a public assembly.*

204. *Reverse angle,* MS: *Claudia, standing with her back to the camera in front of Anna's father. In the right background, Corrado and Giulia are watching them.*

    FATHER: . . . I would rule out the possibility of suicide, wouldn't you? *Claudia steps back, then to the right, as if to get away from his intensity. She brings her hand to her mouth and moves down the hill to the right. Anna's father turns to watch her.*

205. LS: *a helicopter approaches the island and passes overhead. The camera tilts up and follows it as it circles from right to left, then down, disappearing behind the rocks. A policeman stares after it.*

206. MS: *Anna's father stands watching the helicopter, holding the book in his hands. He puts it down on a rock and rushes off right foreground.*

207. LS: *the high plateau. The helicopter reemerges in left background and, as it circles, approaching the ground, people run toward it. The helicopter lands, kicking up clouds of dust. Anna's father runs toward it from left foreground. Two men get out, one from each side; the one on the left approaches a policeman, the other, on the right, Anna's father.*

208. MS: *Anna's father, in center, standing in front of the pilot, who has his back to the camera, and talking to him.*

FATHER: Thank you, anyway.
He turns abruptly and walks away. The policeman turns around and tosses a report into the helicopter.

209. MCU: *in foreground, Sandro (center), Corrado (right), and a policeman watch a police launch which is passing below them.*

VOICE FROM LAUNCH: Captain! From headquarters! Some important news, sir!
Sandro rushes offscreen right.

OFFICER (*from shore*): Yes? What is it?

SAILOR (*yelling out*): They've stopped a suspicious boat a few miles from here. The crew is being held for questioning in Milazzo!
The marshal enters from left and stands in center foreground with his back to the camera. Then he turns to his subordinate.

MARSHAL: We'll have to go and take a look.

OFFICER: Yes, of course.
They both turn toward the camera; the marshal exits center foreground.

210. MS: *the old man is sitting alone in right background, in deep focus, on the rocks above; the marshal enters in MCU from left foreground, looking up at him; he turns toward the camera and rubs his chin thoughtfully.*

211. MS: *Corrado is helping Anna's father down the rocks toward the water.*

CORRADO (*lending his shoulder*): Did you hear that?

FATHER (*getting down the rocks and starting to walk past Corrado toward the right, along the edge*): We are in God's hands.

SANDRO (*off*): Sure. Still, in my opinion we should definitely go to Milazzo.
The camera follows Anna's father as he moves down to the right, toward the police launch and the yacht. Corrado and Sandro follow him.

212. CU *of Sandro. Behind him, Claudia listens without looking at him.*

SANDRO (*softly, but firmly*): Forgive my frankness, but do try to understand.

213. *Reverse angle,* MS: *Sandro standing on right with his back to the camera; Anna's father in center; Corrado on left.*

SANDRO (*looking at Anna's father*): I am the one who's closest to your daughter.
Anna's father starts abruptly to walk upwards, pushing past him.

FATHER: Wherever she may be now . . .
He exits right foreground.

FATHER (*off*): . . . my daughter needs her father now more than she
needs you.
*Corrado and Sandro look downwards; then Sandro exits after Anna's
father.*

214. MS, *high angle: Anna's father is standing with his back to the camera at
the water's edge, beckoning the captain to pick him up. Then he stands
clutching his hands behind his back. Sandro enters from left foreground
and turns toward the camera in* MCU, *looking up.*
SANDRO: What are the rest of you going to do?

215. MS: *on the rocks above. Raimondo, on the right, leans against the rocks,
holding a woman's parasol. Next to him is Patrizia, holding her whippet,
and on the left, Giulia.*
PATRIZIA (*piqued*): What do you want us to do? I don't know! (*Turning
toward Raimondo.*) We'll go to the Montaltos.
RAIMONDO (*looking down, sighing in agreement*): Eh!

216. *As in 214.* CU: *Sandro looks away, turns around and starts moving down
toward the yacht below; he stops pensively as Corrado enters from the
left and pats him on the shoulder, then walks behind him, exiting right.
Sandro turns back toward the camera and speaks to Patrizia.*
SANDRO: I'll get my suitcase. (*Ambivalently.*) I'm sorry. . . .
*He glances back at the yacht. Behind him, Corrado reenters from the
right and crosses to the left.*

217. *As in 215.* MS: *Giulia, Patrizia, and Raimondo, who idly twirls the
opened parasol.*
PATRIZIA (*upset*): Imagine that.

218. MS: *inside one of the yacht's cabins. Claudia, with her back to the
camera, looks into a small mirror and tries to smooth her hair in the
back. She turns around. She can't find her brush, so she enters another
cabin and picks up a brush that was hanging on the back of the door. [Is
it Anna's?] In* CU, *she stares at herself in a mirror off-frame left. She
brushes her hair vigorously, but suddenly stops and turns toward the
cabin door behind her. Sandro has silently appeared. While Sandro hesitates at the door, she turns her back to him, opens another door, and exits
left into another room.*

219. MCU: *Sandro comes through the door of the room Claudia has just
entered. Claudia, with her back to the camera, emerges from right foreground and tries to leave, but he blocks the door with his left arm, look-*

ing intently at her with a half-smile. The camera moves in close as Sandro steps forward, his eyes fixed on her lips, embraces her cheek and hair and kisses her passionately. She reaches for his hand, which is around her neck, loosens his grip (though not aggressively), and pulls free, turning around to face him. Bemused, she stares at him, breathing heavily, then abruptly turns away, running up the ladder on left and exiting. Sandro, with his back to the camera, leans his head against the door.

220. MS: *the lower half of Claudia's back as she moves away from the camera, out of the boat, runs down the gangway, and onto the rocks. The camera follows her as she passes Raimondo, sitting below, then climbs up and stands next to Patrizia. Sandro emerges with his back to the camera from right foreground. He begins to walk slowly down the gangway, carrying his suitcase. He stops at the edge, calling up to the others.*

SANDRO: I'll meet you at the Montaltos', then.

PATRIZIA: Very well.

He starts to move away.

221. CU *of Patrizia (on left) and Claudia (on right, a few steps ahead), their backs to the camera.*

PATRIZIA: Yes, I think this is the best thing. (*Claudia turns quickly toward her.*) In fact, I'm sure Ettore has already gotten there by now.

CLAUDIA (*turning toward Patrizia, her arms crossed on her chest, her hands clasping her forearms*): I'm going to look around the islands.

PATRIZIA (*amazed*): You're[13] going to do what?!

CLAUDIA (*firmly and solemnly*): I can't leave until I've seen all those islands, . . . (*Gesturing with her head.*) . . . one by one.

222. MCU, *reverse angle.*

PATRIZIA (*pleading*): But aren't you exhausted? I certainly am; it's a miracle I can still stand up. (*She turns toward the left, calling out.*) Raimondo!

As Claudia leaves frame right, Raimondo emerges from behind her and stands center, beside Patrizia.

RAIMONDO: Here I am, Patrizia, as always.

PATRIZIA (*turning toward him and starting to walk away, her back to the camera*): Claudia is not coming with us. Will you take care of her baggage?

RAIMONDO (*holding her hand, helping her down the rocks in the usual, resigned tone*): Yes, of course. (*He leads her away toward the right.*)

223. *As in 220.* LS: *Raimondo and Patrizia make their way down the rocks.
Corrado starts to climb up to meet Giulia, who has appeared in left back-
ground, but Claudia ignores their departure, gazing right, at the sea. As
Raimondo and Patrizia reach the gangway, the camera pans to the right.
Sandro, the officer, and Anna's father, in a boat being rowed from the
island, exit right.*

224. LS, *from above: all the boats lie anchored side by side offshore.
Fade out.*

225. *Fade in to* MS *of the spacious lobby of the customs station of Milazzo,
Sicily, housed in an old palazzo.*[14] *The walls are covered with faded
frescoes, a crucifix, and several frames containing pictures and docu-
ments, busts in niches, and so on. A policeman, center right with his back
to the camera, sits behind a typewriter. A large table is on the left; behind
it, two customs officers, one sitting and one standing, interrogate a man
in a plaid jacket who is standing before them.*

LIEUTENANT (*speaking in standard Italian*): I hear things aren't going
too well at home. Is that right?

*Another policeman enters from extreme right, closing the door behind
him and standing, his arms crossed on his chest, looking toward the
table.*

FISHERMAN (*humbly, in Sicilian dialect*): Yes. My sister's been sick all
year. My father, too. . . .

LIEUTENANT: Ah, so you've turned to smuggling . . . you need the
money. . . . (*Leaning forward on his chair.*) But I can help you.[15] I can
arrange for relief if that's what you want. But let's take care of this
formality first, shall we? (*Accommodating.*) Just a few questions, and
then we can all go have lunch, okay? (*He gets up and walks around the
table, passing the policeman at the typewriter, and stands in front of
the fisherman, his thumb in his belt.*) Your friend told me that you
dropped the net three times.

FISHERMAN (*turning toward him and looking him in the face, responding
in Sicilian*): That's right, sir. Three times.

LIEUTENANT (*changing tone, gesturing to the policeman standing at the
door*): Bring in the rest of them.

*As he exits frame left, three men enter from right, in single file, and take
their place by the table, as the guard indicates where they are to stand.*

226. CU: *the lieutenant, from behind, as he opens a door and nods; Sandro*

appears on the left, but does not enter the room.

LIEUTENANT (*quietly, to Sandro*): That's it. They're starting to contra-
   dict one another. (*Sandro lowers his eyes.*) Excuse me.

*He turns around, closes the door behind him (leaving Sandro outside),
and walks off right. The camera rests for a moment on the shut door; then
Sandro opens it a crack and peers in.*

227. MS: *the four fishermen are standing in a row, facing the camera in the
   foreground. Behind them, in center background, Sandro is watching from
   behind the door. The lieutenant comes up behind the men and taps the one
   on the right on the shoulder. The man turns around.*

LIEUTENANT: Look, your friend over there . . . (*Nobody turns.*) . . .
   has confessed to me that the sea was too rough for fishing.

228. MS, *reverse angle: the lieutenant's back is now to the camera, on left,
   and the accused man faces the camera; on right, the two other fishermen
   standing in front of the table with their backs to the lieutenant and their
   friend. Behind them, the policeman is typing.*

LIEUTENANT: Well then? And the other boat?

FISHERMAN (*surprised*): What boat?

LIEUTENANT (*moving away with impatience*): The one my men saw.
   (*Turns around and faces the camera, with his thumbs in his belt.*) And
   they clearly saw you tossing crates overboard. (*He walks to the right
   and, as he goes off, all the men turn, staring after him.*)

LIEUTENANT (*off, decisively*): Now then, how is it going to be?

FISHERMAN (*shaking his head, playing with his ear*): I didn't feel
   well. . . . I'm all mixed up. . . . I don't know anything. . . .

*Sandro rushes onscreen left, his back to the camera, and grabs the fisher-
man by the collar, shaking him angrily. The lieutenant reenters quickly
from the right, rushing toward him.*

SANDRO (*furiously*): What? What are you[16] saying?!

*The lieutenant grabs Sandro by the arm and pulls him away, while Sandro
angrily frees himself from his hold. The camera follows them as they
move away toward the left, leaving the others offscreen.*

SANDRO (*impatiently gesturing with his hands*): What does all this have
   to do with Anna?

LIEUTENANT: Come.

The lieutenant firmly leads him away; they both exit left.

229. MCU: *the lieutenant and Sandro, with their backs to the camera, as the*

officer leads him back to the door. Sandro turns toward camera.

LIEUTENANT: At least stay here.[17]

SANDRO: Okay.

The lieutenant turns back, exiting from right foreground; Sandro stands by the door, watching, with an impatient look on his face.

LIEUTENANT (*off*): Now I'm willing to forget all about everything else—cigarettes, smuggling, everything. All I want to know is, did you take the girl anywhere?

None of the fishermen respond. Sandro shrugs, turns around, and slowly leaves.

230. LS: *Sandro emerges from behind a crudely built screen into the lobby. On right, against the wall, a bench; a man is sitting there, with his back turned to the door from which Sandro has just emerged. Sandro walks toward the right, looking back once at the door; then he turns and exits right. The fishermen also emerge and walk toward the camera, pushed along by a policeman. As they come into* MCU, *they disappear into right foreground.*

FIRST FISHERMAN: What did you say?

SECOND FISHERMAN: Me? Nothing.

POLICEMAN: Shh!

231. MCU: *Sandro, his back to the camera, is looking up at the wall. The camera moves slightly left to reveal a policeman sitting against the wall, facing Sandro. He points to one of the busts high up behind him, offscreen.*

POLICEMAN: This is the one who built the villa.

SANDRO: If someone had told him it was going to end up like this . . .

As he steps to the left, looking up, the camera tilts up, leaving Sandro and the policeman off, slowly revealing the extremely ornate wall and continuing up to the baroque ceiling.

232. MS: *Sandro, his back to the camera, walking away slowly. As the lieutenant enters right foreground, Sandro quickly turns around and walks back toward him, opening a newspaper he has folded in his hands.*

SANDRO: Ah, Lieutenant! (*Coming up to him and showing him the paper.*) Do you know this "F.Z." who wrote this article in the paper?

LIEUTENANT (*looking up at Sandro*): Francesco Zuria, the reporter.

SANDRO (*looking at the officer, then down, considering*): Where can I get hold of him? Do you think if I offered a reward for anyone who could provide information . . . ?

LIEUTENANT (*encouragingly*): Zuria's in Messina. We could try. (*Gesturing to the right.*) Would you like to call?

SANDRO (*decisively*): No, no, thanks. Don't bother.

Sandro turns around and starts to walk briskly away, while the lieutenant follows him; they both stop as a sailor comes through a passageway in front of them.

BRIGADIERE [18] (*stepping in front of the lieutenant*): Any further orders, Lieutenant? May I return to Lipari?

LIEUTENANT: Yes. By the way, where did you [19] put that box with the cigarettes?

BRIGADIERE: In the storeroom.

LIEUTENANT: Very well.

BRIGADIERE: Yes, sir.

The brigadiere quickly leaves the passageway. Sandro, who had been standing by the lieutenant looking back and forth at him and the brigadiere, pauses for a moment, then calls him back, starting to follow him.

SANDRO: Brigadiere!

He runs after him, disappearing behind the columns in the background, while the lieutenant starts off in the opposite direction.

233. MS: *the ornate balcony of the customs station. The brigadiere emerges from the door and starts quickly down the steps to the street. Sandro rushes down the stairs and catches up with him, the camera following them to the right, from below.*

SANDRO: Excuse me, brigadiere. But when did you [20] get here?

BRIGADIERE: (*stopping and turning, so that they face each other in profile*): Two hours ago.

SANDRO: And the young lady who was with you—where is she now?

BRIGADIERE: I don't know. She said she had to catch a train. . . .

Sandro looks away pensively, then turns around and hurries down the stairs off left foreground. The brigadiere makes a move as if to follow him, but pauses behind a large, ornate stone vase on the stairway.

234. MS: *Claudia is sitting in the corner of the dingy waiting-room of the train station, leaning back with her legs crossed, idly shaking her foot. Enigmatic music similar to that played during the search for Anna on the island is mixed with the sound of a train arriving (continuing through 237). She picks up a newspaper, opens it up, and leafs through without interest. Suddenly an item catches her eye, and she sits up.*

235. CU *of the newspaper's page from over Claudia's shoulder. The headline reads: "Rich Roman Girl Vanishes on Lisca Bianca." The sound of foot-steps. Claudia turns her head to the right.*

236. MS: *Sandro appears in the doorway, stops, then slowly enters the waiting-room. The camera follows him to the right, where Claudia is sitting, her back to the camera, looking up at him silently. As he gets closer to her, she moves as if to get up, but remains seated. Sandro stops in front of her.*

SANDRO (*quietly*): Where are you[21] going? To the Montaltos'? (*She nods.*) Can I come along?

CLAUDIA (*looking down and handing him the newspaper, sadly*): Have you[22] read it?

He takes it, steps toward the foreground, circles in front of her and then sits next to her, so that they both come into MCU, *facing left. Claudia looks down; Sandro leans back, looking up as if exhausted.*

CLAUDIA: They ask anyone who has any information to notify them in writing. . . .

SANDRO (*sitting up, looking down*): Yes, I thought of going, of speaking to . . .

CLAUDIA (*urgently, looking him in the eyes, as he turns toward her*): Yes. You must go.

SANDRO (*sitting closer, turning toward her, his back to the camera*): But then when are we going to see each other?

Claudia stares at him for a moment, looks down, then examines his face intently, shaking her head slowly.

237. *Reverse angle,* MCU: *Sandro stares at her with an imploring look, then nods sadly. He gets up, moving to the right, the camera following. Claudia is left off-frame. He passes a bright poster with a cartoon drawing of a boy in a bathing suit, sunglasses, and a sailor-cap that reads "Summer in Sicily." On Sandro's face is a fixed, concentrated, and unhappy expres-sion. The music ends. Hearing the bell for the train, he suddenly looks to the right, then to the left, and slowly turns to face Claudia.*

238. MS: *Claudia, sitting still on the bench.*

CLAUDIA: I know it's hard. But going on like this will only make things harder. (*She gets up, starts walking toward the camera, then turns to the right, where Sandro is staring at the ceiling.*) Please don't look so solemn. (*Softly, even more pleading.*) And don't wait for the train. . . .

Sandro starts moving slowly to the left, looking at her and then down; the camera leaves her offscreen right. He passes some other posters which read "Technica." He hesitates, with his back to the camera, still looking at her. He turns, steps back toward the door, looks back once, then again.

239. MS: *Claudia standing against the wall, in front of the "Summer in Sicily" poster. She turns abruptly toward the wall, then turns around again.*
    CLAUDIA (*on the verge of tears*): Please. Go away.

240. MS: *a train, pulling into the station from background toward camera on the left, comes to a stop. A young man runs from right background to catch it, crossing over and going off-frame left foreground. As Claudia also emerges from the waiting-room door, walking briskly toward the train, a conductor steps off the train, shuts the door, and turns to the compartment behind him. The camera stays on Claudia as she comes into MCU and follows her as she moves toward the left, turns her back to the camera and boards the train. The door is shut behind her; she turns and stands by the window, looking toward the right. As the train begins to move slowly along in the foreground from right to left, Claudia, still staring back toward the right, is carried offscreen left. Voices of conductor and other railroad personnel are heard off.*

241. MCU: *Sandro, his back to the camera, emerges from left foreground and walks onto the platform just as the train begins to pull out. He stares after it for a moment, then turns around and starts to move back toward camera, pensively. Suddenly he turns around again and races after the train. The camera follows him as he turns toward the left, catches the last car, and pulls himself aboard. A boy, watching him, turns and walks toward the camera, glances at the train, then exits left foreground.*

242. MS: *Claudia, facing left in her train compartment, puts her bags on the rack. She closes the corner window, looks out, and then falls into the seat, leaning back and closing her eyes as if exhausted. She smooths her hair away from her forehead and lets herself be rocked by the train's motion, as if about to go to sleep. Suddenly she looks up, startled.*

243. MCU: *Sandro appears in countershot in the compartment doorway and stands silently, leaning against the door frame with a half-smile.*

244. MCU: *Claudia, looking directly into camera.*
    CLAUDIA (*ironically challenging*): I really want to see what we're going to say to each other now. Go ahead. (*Louder.*) Talk. (*She looks away for a moment, then looks back at Sandro again and speaks angrily.*) Sandro, I do not want you to come with me. I don't want to see you;

how else can I tell you that? (*She pauses, then looks away again, as if in exasperation. Then she speaks grudgingly.*) Why did you come?

SANDRO (*off, quietly*): I couldn't help it.

CLAUDIA (*staring into the camera, insistently*): But since we will have to help it, we might just as well . . .

245. MCU: *Sandro, as in 243. The camera, shooting from a low angle, follows him as he steps into the compartment. He moves toward the left.*

CLAUDIA (*off*): . . . make this sacrifice now.

Sandro sits down silently in the seat opposite Claudia and, a bit apprehensively, looks at her.

246. MCU: *Claudia sits with her right elbow propped against the headrest, staring at her hand in front of her chin, moving her fingers nervously. Her head rocks back and forth with the movement of the train.*

SANDRO (*off, softly but ironically*): Sacrifice . . .

247. *Reverse angle* MCU: *Sandro leans forward, looking intently toward the left.*

SANDRO: I have no intention of sacrificing myself. (*Angrily.*) It's idiotic to sacrifice oneself. (*Leaning forward, raising his voice.*) Why? For whose sake? (*Glancing out the window, softly.*) If Anna were here, I could understand your scruples. (*He looks at her again, then leans back and looks away, decisively.*) But she isn't.

CLAUDIA (*off, pleading*): Sandro!

SANDRO (*leaning forward, softly*): Forgive me.

248. MCU, *as in 246: Claudia looks at him in alarm. A bit of his head appears in extreme right foreground.*

SANDRO: I didn't want to seem cynical to you . . . (*He leans back, going offscreen.*)

249. MCU, *as in 247: Sandro, leaning forward.*

SANDRO: . . . but isn't it better to face things as they actually are?

CLAUDIA (*off*): For me, things are exactly the same as they were three days ago . . .

250. MCU, *as in 246: Claudia, her hand against her mouth.*

CLAUDIA: . . . when we met. (*Sadly, looking away to the left.*) Only three days ago. (*She glances back toward him.*) Can you imagine? (*She passes the back of her hand over her lips.*) And you and Anna . . . (*She gets up, then turns around, standing against the window, almost in torment.*) But no, things aren't like that. Is it possible that so little can make one change, forget?

SANDRO (*off, almost whispering*): It takes even less, much less.

CLAUDIA: But it's so sad. . . terribly sad. (*Shaking her head.*) I'm not
used to it. I'm not prepared for it. . . . (*Stroking her chest right below
her neck, as if to feel her pulse.*) Here, feel it. . . . (*Almost amused.*)
I've never, never been so confused in my entire life!

*Sandro emerges from right foreground, his back to the camera, and
comes close to her.*

CLAUDIA (*staring into his eyes*): Sandro, why don't you help me?

SANDRO (*pressing*): I think the only way to help each other is by being
together!

CLAUDIA (*clasping her shoulders and shaking her head*): No. No, I
don't believe that. Look, sit down. Sit there. (*She pushes him down into
his seat, so that he goes offscreen right foreground.*) And at the next
stop, get off.

SANDRO (*off*): And you?

CLAUDIA (*on the verge of tears*): I . . . I . . . I . . . (*Screaming,*

gesturing in exasperation, sobbing.) Leave me in peace! (*She quickly turns away and runs offscreen left.*)

251. MS: *the shoreline, seen from the train window, as the train races along. The camera pans back to the left inside the train, revealing Claudia, who is outside the compartment, leaning against the corridor wall. As she hears some voices coming from another compartment, she steps forward, listening with interest.*

YOUNG MAN (*off*): Excuse me, but since this train is going to Palermo, I wondered. . . . Are you[23] going to Palermo too?

YOUNG WOMAN (*off*): No!

YOUNG MAN (*off*): Then you're getting off at Tindari?

Claudia moves forward and stands next to the compartment door, watching and listening.

YOUNG WOMAN (*off*): No!

YOUNG MAN (*off*): You're going to Sant'Agata di Militello?

YOUNG WOMAN (*off*): No.

YOUNG MAN (*off*): Then you're going to Cefalù.

Claudia smiles, amused, and leans against the compartment door, looking in. Sandro emerges, coming down the corridor, and stands behind Claudia.

YOUNG WOMAN (*off*): How did you know?

YOUNG MAN (*off*): A friend told me.

YOUNG WOMAN (*off*): You see, I work in Catania, but I don't come from there.

YOUNG MAN (*off*): And this friend of mine knows you and has told me all about you.

Without turning, Claudia taps Sandro, who has squeezed next to her and is peeking over her shoulder. She points, still smiling, toward the compartment.

252. MCU, *high angle: a young man and a young woman are seated next to each other in the compartment. The young man, on the right, leans toward the woman.*

YOUNG WOMAN: Does she work in Cefalù?

YOUNG MAN: Yes. She's a gardener.

YOUNG WOMAN (*amused, opening a magazine on her lap and glancing at it*): Then she couldn't possibly know me. In the villa where I live, we have a male gardener!

YOUNG MAN: That doesn't mean anything. It just means he must have
   talked to my friend.
YOUNG WOMAN (*sitting up, turning toward him*): What did they say?
YOUNG MAN: Well . . . they said many things!

253. *As in 251.* MS: *watching the couple, Claudia and Sandro stand close*
   together, her back touching him. She throws back her head, laughing,
   then disappears left into her own compartment, next door, while Sandro
   remains there, smiling.
YOUNG MAN (*off*): They said you were very well brought up and that
you mind your own business . . . that kind of thing.
YOUNG WOMAN (*off*): We have a radio just like yours.
Sandro silently invites Claudia back out of her compartment and holds
her arm to help her. This time she stands with her left side close to Sandro.
She continues to watch the couple, smiling, but Sandro is looking at her
alone. He continues to hold her arm, then tries to take her hand, but she
shrugs him off.
YOUNG MAN (*off*): Like this? No, you don't.
YOUNG WOMAN (*off*): Why not?
YOUNG MAN (*off*): Because this one's Chinese.

254. *As in 252.* MCU *of the young man and woman.*
YOUNG WOMAN (*taking the radio and fondling it*): They're very practical, these little radios. I don't know . . . like, when you go out for
   a walk.
YOUNG MAN: Which comes first, d'you think, music or love?

255. *As in 253.* MCU: *Claudia is still watching the couple, but Sandro is*
   hugging her even more closely than before. Claudia turns toward him;
   her smile fades. Their faces are almost touching. She looks down, pen-
   sively, but does not try to escape his embrace.
YOUNG WOMAN (*off*): Oh, for me, music. You have to look for a husband, but a radio, you can always buy one.
YOUNG MAN (*off*): No. Love. I'm a man and I know how these things
   are: love first, then music.
Claudia looks nervously at Sandro, and quickly backs away. Behind him,
she crosses the corridor and leans out the window, her hair flying in the
wind. When she pulls her head in, he is still standing in front of her,
yearningly. She looks at him and leans out the window again.

256. MCU: *Claudia, on left, and Sandro, his back to the camera, on right.*

Sandro moves toward her again.

SANDRO: No, Claudia, listen to me. . . . (*He moves in front of her, to the left.*)

CLAUDIA (*now on right, pleading, looking at him intently and putting her hands against his chest, as if to hold him at bay*): Sandro, please, . . . as a favor to me, . . . promise you won't come after me. (*He takes her by the elbows and tries to embrace her. She struggles to get away, turning her back to the camera, raising her voice, almost crying, and beating her fists against his chest in desperation. They are now turned around; Claudia's back is to the camera, and Sandro faces it.*) You mustn't come after me again!

SANDRO (*still holding her, looking at her desperately*): But why, Claudia? Why? Listen, even if you send me away . . .

The train is coming to a stop; he glances out the window, then looks back at her. She pushes on his chest more gently, but still as if to keep him away. Then she tries to get away from him.

CLAUDIA: No.

Sandro clutches her two hands so that she can't push against him.

SANDRO (*getting closer, as if trying to kiss her*): Claudia . . . Claudia . . . Let's not wait any longer. . . . It will be too late after . . . (*On the verge of tears, shouting.*) Come away with me!

She holds his chin for a moment, then sighs and pulls away, running offscreen left. Sandro stares desperately in her direction, then quickly glances out the window.

257. MCU: *Claudia, on extreme left with her back to the camera, in the corridor; Sandro swiftly emerges from the compartment on the left, behind her, looking at her imploringly. She pushes him away with her open hand; he squeezes it, then throws it down, turns and exits through the compartment corridor door in right background. Claudia turns around, toward the camera, leans against the wall and sighs with relief as he goes out. The corridor door slams; she looks down and exits left.*

CONDUCTOR: Castoreale!

258. MS: *on the platform. Sandro, with his back to the camera, anxiously looks up at the train and calls: "Claudia!" A conductor quickly passes from right to left in front of him. As the train starts to pull out slowly toward the left, he turns toward the camera, walking alongside the train. The camera pans with him and the train as he begins to run. It finally reveals the full length of the train leaving the station. Sandro stops and*

stares at it, then slowly turns around. As he starts walking toward the
foreground, pondering, the camera follows him, keeping the long railroad
platform in deep focus. Sandro puts his hands in his pockets. He turns
around to look at the train once more, then lowers his gaze and exits left.
The camera stays fixed for a moment on the rails and the station in a
temps mort.

259. LS, *high-angle from above of a crowd of men running wildly down a*
     street in Messina, perpendicularly from left background to right fore-
     ground. Four jeeps full of police, sirens going, make their way through
     the crowd in the same direction.

260. LS, *high-angle from above of a large, noisy crowd gathered in front of a*
     building below an unlit neon sign. Only that portion of the sign contain-
     ing the letters "B," "A" and "C" is visible. Two jeeps stop and police-
     men pour out.

261. CU: *backs of men in the crowd, a policeman trying to make his way*
     through.

262. MS: *inside a bar. Two men, with their backs to the camera, raise the*
     closed shutters; the crowd starts to pour in. Amid the confusion, Sandro
     makes his way inside. He looks around, bewildered, and speaks to a
     journalist.
     SANDRO: Zuria! Where is Zuria?
     JOURNALIST (*impatiently*): Maybe inside, I don't know.

263. MS, *reverse angle. Inside the bar, amid the confusion, a sexy young*
     woman in a tight-fitting dress stands center, glancing around as if looking
     for someone.
     MAN (*off*): I called, Commissioner, because I think that the situation
       requires the intervention of the police. . . . They are smashing every-
       thing here.

264. MCU: *the same journalist in dark sunglasses, staring off to the left.*
     Sandro, on his left, taps him on the shoulder with a newspaper.
     SANDRO: Which one is he?
     JOURNALIST (*angrily, without looking at Sandro, gestures impatiently*
       to the right): There he is.
     The journalist quickly walks away, exiting frame left. The camera follows
     Sandro as he walks to the right, thus revealing a short, balding man in
     right foreground who is staring left with the same intensity as the
     journalist.
     SANDRO: Excuse me. Are you Zuria?

ZURIA (*glancing briefly at Sandro, sarcastically*): Until there is proof to the contrary. (*He resumes his rapt gaze in front of him.*)

SANDRO (*bending down slightly toward him*): I'd like to ask you something.

ZURIA (*getting up, in a tone of dismissal*): Wait a minute. I'm busy right now.

He moves off-frame left. The camera holds on Sandro as he stares after Zuria, as if quickly evaluating him, then watches the commotion in front of him.

WOMAN (*off*): I was looking for a dress shop . . .

265. MS: *the young woman in the tight dress in center background, surrounded by a crowd of reporters and photographers, who are jostling each other. One photographer kneels before her to take a picture. Zuria emerges from right foreground and stands among the others with his hands behind his back, seemingly entranced.*

WOMAN (*speaking Italian with a pronounced foreign accent*): . . . and suddenly I noticed this whole pack of men following me. Never seen anything like it.

Two men in the crowd try to make their way in, but they are pushed off right foreground. Zuria stands rapt in front of the woman, his hands behind his back.

266. MCU: *the woman, on left, talking; in front of her, Zuria, in right foreground and in profile; and behind him, the police commissioner.*

WOMAN (*in an innocent, naive tone*): So many men!

COMMISSIONER: But what do you[24] expect, dressed the way you are?

267. MCU, *reverse angle: the commissioner, on left, and Zuria, on right, both looking toward the left. Sandro stands behind them, craning his head to see the woman. The commissioner looks her up and down, not unappreciatively.*

WOMAN (*off*): But I go around the world dressed like this. . . .

268. ECU *of her upper left thigh, in profile, as she slowly caresses a split in the side-seam of her dress.*

WOMAN: Oh, not like this!

A cheer goes up from the noisy crowd.

269. MCU: *the woman, who is a head taller than the men surrounding her. Behind her, the glass doors of the bar, with the huge crowd of men pressing against them.*

WOMAN (*laughing assuredly, addressing a short man in front of her in left foreground, who smiles sympathetically*): My seam has split. That's why I was looking for a dress shop.

270. *As in 267. The commissioner, Zuria, and Sandro. The commissioner quickly moves offscreen left.*

271. MS, *slightly high angle: the woman stands, calmly leaning her elbow on a stool; behind her, the commissioner is trying to keep men away; in front of her, with their backs to the camera, Sandro (in extreme right foreground) and Zuria (in extreme left foreground) looking at her.*

COMMISSIONER (*pushing people away*): Stand back!

ZURIA: How old are you?[25]

WOMAN (*looking toward him, rocking back a bit, as if reciting a lesson, in a childish, coquettish tone*): Nineteen. I'm married. My name is Gloria Perkins, and I've been a writer for the past year. I write in a kind of a trance, you see . . .

272. MCU: *Zuria, on right, and Sandro, on left, looking toward Gloria and*

still listening intently.

GLORIA (*off*): . . . and I'm usually in touch with dead people . . .
Tolstoy, for example . . .

Zuria and Sandro glance at each other. Sandro smiles, amused, but hides his smile behind his hand.

273. CU *of Gloria, on right; she smiles naively, looking to the left. Several men, shorter than she, look her over.*

GLORIA: . . . or Shakespeare. But I'm also interested in a film career.

274. MS, *as in 270. Zuria moves forward and to the left, passing Sandro, who is leaning against a counter.*

ZURIA (*slyly*): And in Palermo? What kind of reception did you get there?

275. MS: *Sandro, with his back to the camera, in extreme right foreground; Zuria, in front of him, leaning against the counter, facing left but with his head turned toward Gloria.*

GLORIA (*piqued*): In Palermo, I was with my husband. (*Stepping forward, posing as a camera flashes.*) Now I'm on my way to Capri, to write an article about tourism.

ZURIA (*over his shoulder to Sandro*): It was just the same in Palermo. Worse.

COMMISSIONER (*emerging amid the crowd from left foreground, his back to the camera*): If you care to return to your hotel, miss, we are here to escort you. (*Stepping toward the camera*)

GLORIA: Thanks.

276. MS, *high-angle: the crowd rushes toward the door in the background, passing Zuria and Sandro, who stand in the middle with their heads turned toward the door behind them.*

MANAGER (*standing by Zuria and Sandro, shouting at the crowd*): Out! Get out! Out!

Noise of the crowd shouting.

277. MS, *from above: Gloria, escorted by the policemen, leaves the building, walking triumphantly from left to right through the hysterical crowd of men. The camera follows her as she makes her way, waving and blowing kisses. A police car stands waiting to take her away. She climbs in, then turns, waving to the crowd.*

278. MS: *inside the bar. The camera follows Zuria, who guides Sandro to the door, moving from right to left. They walk out and join the crowd, their*

backs to the camera, watching the spectacle in front of them.
ZURIA: It's shameful.
279. MCU: *Gloria finally enters the car. Tumultuous cheering.*
280. LS, *high-angle: the car pulls away slowly, disappearing into right fore-ground. The crowd remains cheering after it.*
281. MCU: *Sandro and Zuria emerge through the crowd, walking toward cam-era, peering after the car. Zuria, on left, turns toward Sandro.*
ZURIA: Do you like her? (*He holds up five fingers.*) Fifty thousand.
SANDRO (*looking at him, in disbelief*): No!
ZURIA (*amused, while Sandro turns his head back to the spectacle*): Yes.
What do you think all this fun is for? Just a way of getting people to
notice her, that's all. If people fall for it . . . you're made. (*He starts to
walk slowly toward camera. Sandro follows, looking down pensively.*)
If fifty thousand weren't all I earned a month . . . (*Glancing at Sandro
with a sigh.*) . . . I assure you, I'd have a go at her myself. What did
you want to tell me?
They begin to walk slowly across the street, the camera tracking with them.
SANDRO: I read your article about the girl who disappeared. (*Stopping,
turning toward Zuria.*) I'm her fiancé.
ZURIA (*stopping, turning toward him*): Ah, would you like to tell me
the story of that disappearance with all the details?
SANDRO: Look, if I had any information, I wouldn't be here. (*Aggressively, challengingly.*) But I see you don't have much of anything,
either!
ZURIA (*calmly*): Not at all—on the contrary. I've had lots of people
calling. (*Gesturing, waving his thumb up, as if counting.*) One says
he's seen her in a car with a Rome license plate; . . . (*They move
on across the street, turning to the right.*) . . . another's seen her at
the harbor talking to a group of foreign sailors. . . . And what if she's
gone off on a boat under an assumed name?
They stop in the middle of the street, Sandro looking intently at Zuria.
SANDRO: Is that what happened?
ZURIA (*starting to walk in the middle of the street, toward camera*):
How should I know? Someone else says he saw her in a drugstore in
Troina. . . . (*He stops, turning toward Sandro.*) In fact, now the drug-
gist himself says a girl who more or less fits the description came into
his place to buy tranquilizers, in Troina.

SANDRO (*looking up, pensively*): Is it far from here?

ZURIA (*pointing down the street, toward the camera, then turning to Sandro*): About thirty miles. I can give you the name of the druggist if you want.

282. MCU: *Sandro, looking intently at Zuria, whose head alone is visible in extreme left foreground.*

SANDRO (*considering*): Yes. . . . Yes, why not. . . . (*Decisively.*) But you should publish this in your paper tomorrow. It's the Palermo paper you work for, isn't it? I mean, a paper with a big circulation . . .

283. MCU: *as in 281. Zuria begins to cross the street, leaving Sandro off left. A bus is passing behind him.*

ZURIA (*gesturing impatiently*): That's right, but the story's stale now. No interest. (*He turns back toward Sandro.*) They won't publish it.

SANDRO (*emerging from left foreground with his back to the camera, coming up to Zuria*): No, no, no. You have to do me this favor.

ZURIA (*looking down at the hand Sandro is waving in front of him and clutching it, smiling*): Don't be offended, but why should I do a favor for you?

SANDRO: Let's say for business reasons, then. To round out your salary. *Zuria laughs knowingly and takes Sandro by the arm. The camera stays on them as they walk off, arm in arm, down the street.*

284. MLS, *high angle: the terrace of the Princess Montalto's villa, near Monreale.*[26] *The princess, Claudia, and Giulia, their backs to the camera, are seated at a little table. Patrizia sits in profile at the left side of the table. The young prince, Goffredo, is standing behind a chair on the other side. A servant enters left frame and pours drinks.*

CLAUDIA (*sadly*): I've looked all over the islands.

PATRIZIA: That must have been really tiring.

CLAUDIA (*softly*): Useless, most of all.

285. MS, *reverse of 284: in extreme left foreground, Patrizia, her back to the camera; in front of her, Giulia, sitting behind the table, watches Claudia, sitting next to her; in right foreground, the servant stands and serves them; on extreme right, the princess also watches Claudia. As the servant moves away, Claudia reaches for her drink, but is too restless to remain sitting. She gets up.*

CLAUDIA: I can't stand it any longer.

The camera pans left with her as she walks away from the table toward a

*jalousie door. But she doesn't go into the villa; she stands at the edge of
the terrace, facing the wall, her back to the others. Goffredo pensively
crosses the terrace to the other side of the doorway. Corrado and Ettore,
Patrizia's husband, emerge through the door and walk toward the table.*

GIULIA (*turning toward the men*): How can you stand heavy discussions
in this heat?

CORRADO (*approaching her and then leaning over the back of her chair,
in mock solemnity*): When you get to be over fifty, my dear, all you can
feel is cold.

*Ettore stops and glances at Claudia, still standing aside, then turns and
speaks in an irritated voice.*

ETTORE: And what's this?

286. CU *of Patrizia, looking half-right.*

PATRIZIA: It's Claudia—Anna's friend. (*She turns her head a bit more,
addressing Claudia.*) You haven't met my husband, have you?

287. *As in 285.* MS: *Ettore turns toward Claudia and takes her hand.*

ETTORE: Ah, good.

*Claudia turns slightly toward him and then remains standing, facing the
wall, immobile.*

GIULIA: Imagine, she just came back . . .

ETTORE (*turning to Corrado, abruptly*): By the way, did you call him?

CORRADO: Who? Sandro?

288. *As in 286. Patrizia, looking up.*

PATRIZIA: But didn't he say he would be coming here?

289. MCU: *Ettore, on right. On left, behind him, Claudia is still standing with
her back to the group.*

ETTORE (*looking down, pondering*): Of all the things that had to happen . . . (*Looking up toward the right, irritated.*) Among other things,
I need him. How can I keep these negotiations going if I don't have the
facts, the figures?

290. *As in 287.* MS: *Ettore stands with his hands in his pockets, looking at
Corrado, still behind Giulia's chair. Giulia gets up and stands between
the two men, her back to the camera, and addresses Ettore.*

GIULIA: Personally, I take it as a good sign that he hasn't gotten in touch
with us. (*She turns around.*) D'you want to bet he has found Anna?

291. MCU, *reverses 290. Claudia, facing camera, in left foreground, her back
to the rest, looks very unhappy and lost. Behind her, in right background,*

Corrado and Giulia listen to Ettore, whose back is to the camera.

ETTORE (*sententiously*): After all, some forty thousand people disappear annually in Italy.

Claudia turns toward them as she hears this.

ETTORE: Forty thousand. More or less the San Siro stadium when it's full, eh![27]

As he chuckles, Claudia turns around, clasping her arms in anguish.

292. MCU *of the princess. She holds a cigarette in her right hand and looks toward the left.*

PRINCESS: I don't know this Sandro. What kind of a person is he? He couldn't have done away with her himself, by any chance?

293. MCU *of Claudia. She stares emptily, listening to the laughter of the others, who are offscreen. She opens her mouth as if horrified by their callousness.*

294. MS: *the others. Giulia stands in center, in profile; Corrado stands smiling on the right; behind him are Ettore and Patrizia; the princess sits on the extreme left.*

GIULIA (*her hands joined together, as in prayer*): My God! Here we are, joking about a thing like that! (*She turns around to the princess.*) We should be ashamed of ourselves.

The princess gets up, adjusting her shawl on her shoulders, while Giulia remains standing, staring toward the left.

PRINCESS: Are you all coming?

As the princess exits left, everybody rises. Ettore and Patrizia pass behind Giulia and exit left after the princess. Corrado, his hands in his pockets, passes in front of Giulia, turns around and peers closely at her face. Giulia returns the look. He looks toward the left, then back at Giulia. He shrugs his shoulders and exits left after the others. Giulia steps slowly toward the camera, looking coyly toward the left.

CORRADO (*off*): Why don't you[28] sell this villa, Princess? I could convert it into a fine clinic for people suffering from nervous breakdowns.

PRINCESS (*off, chuckling*): It already is one.

295. MS, *reverse angle of 294: the princess, Ettore, Corrado, and Patrizia are moving inside, through the door in right background. Giulia, however, stands in center foreground with her back to the camera, facing Goffredo, who gets up from a chair in front of her. (We now suspect that he was the subject of the interchange of glances and Giulia's coyness in*

294.) Giulia laughs softly and turns around and starts walking toward camera, while Goffredo follows behind her, obviously attracted.

GIULIA (*looking toward the right and pointing at Goffredo, behind her, as she addresses Claudia, who enters right*): Goffredo is the princess's grandson. (*She stops in* MCU.) Seventeen years old, lucky boy . . . (*She turns toward Goffredo, then back to Claudia, looks at her smilingly and speaks in an intimate tone.*) . . . and just think [29]—he paints!

GOFFREDO (*standing back, looking at Giulia, modestly*): Anyone can hold a brush. All you have to do is buy the paints and start working. Even Titian started out that way.

Giulia laughs coquettishly, clasping her chin with the tip of her fingers and glancing at Claudia almost conspiratorially. She turns around, still laughing to herself, and takes Goffredo's arm. They walk off toward the door.

GIULIA (*softly, to Goffredo, as they leave*): And your paintings—are they abstract?

GOFFREDO (*softly*): No.

GIULIA (*almost whispering to him*): What do you [30] feel when you're painting?

GOFFREDO: A shudder.

As they disappear into the door on left, Claudia, still with her back to the camera, moves slowly toward the door.

Dissolve.

296. MS: *Claudia, wearing a cocktail dress and with her hair up, is sitting on the bed in her room in the Montalto villa. The rich, lacy sheets and bedspread are pulled back. She playfully tries on a series of rings that she takes out of a white box, holding her hand out in front of her and admiring the effect. Playful music, scored for French horn, clarinet, flute, and strings (continuing through 303). Melancholy again, Claudia puts the rings back in the box, throws it behind her on the bed, then gets up and stares aimlessly at the bed. Then she hears the noise of an approaching car, and she rushes to the window and leans out. She turns around and runs off left.*

297. MS: *Claudia crosses right toward a french door which opens onto a large, white rooftop terrace. In the far background there is a beautiful tree and a mountain. She leans over the balustrade to see who it is. The camera remains stationary inside.*

298. LS *over Claudia's right shoulder and from her point of view. Music*

*intensifies. High-angle shot of a chauffeur getting out of a car in the
driveway below. He is holding a box, which he carries into the house. As
the chauffeur disappears inside, Claudia sees Giulia and Goffredo enter
from right. As they pass the car, Giulia takes Goffredo's arm excitedly.*
GIULIA (*excitedly, as they walk away*): May I really see your work?
      I admit, I'm curious. Come on, let's go.
They both walk off, going into another door.
299. *As in 297, camera inside Claudia's room with* LS *of Claudia out on the
      terrace. She turns around, toward camera, and slowly returns to the
      room, obviously disappointed.*
300. MS: *Patrizia enters left foreground and stands in profile in front of a
      vanity mirror. She wears a blond wig and hangs another, a black one,
      on the corner of the mirror. She looks at herself in the mirror, adjusting
      her wig. The music becomes even more playful. Claudia slowly enters
      through a door in right background. She moves toward Patrizia and,
      regaining her good spirits, stands smiling behind the mirror, only her
      head visible above it.*

PATRIZIA (*looking into the mirror*): Are you ready? I'm not. This dinner was all we needed. The vitality people have is so annoying. . . .
Claudia notices the black wig, picks it up and comes around the mirror into the foreground, holding the wig in front of her. She stops for a moment in profile, in front of Patrizia.
PATRIZIA (*referring to her own wig*): How do I look?
CLAUDIA (*looking at her, moving left and going off-frame, she responds routinely*): Divine.
PATRIZIA (*sourly, her eyes following Claudia*): You're just saying that to compliment me. (*She returns to her own image in the mirror.*)
CLAUDIA (*off*): Is that a compliment?
As the real Patrizia sits in extreme left foreground, her back to the camera, her mirrored image dominates the frame on the right. The mirror reveals not only Patrizia's critical self-inspection, but also, behind her, the bare back of Claudia, in her low-cut dress. Claudia's head is obscured by the reflected image of a lampshade.
PATRIZIA (*adjusts a curl of the wig on her cheek, scans her image, and then says in an ironic tone*): No! (*She laughs.*)
301. MCU, *reverse angle: Claudia is standing in center wearing the black wig, touching it here and there and evaluating its effect in the mirror in front of her. The ornate edge of the mirror is just next to the left frameline, and we assume that the mirror stands at a sharp right angle to the camera plane. Behind her, in left foreground, Patrizia is still sitting with her back to the camera in front of her own mirror. Having taken the blond wig off, she is readjusting her hair. She stands with the back of her left hand caressing her cheek and her head cocked coyly, as if posing. She seems to be admiring herself half-ironically and half-seriously. Patrizia gets up, moves toward the camera, and then exits left, presumably behind the mirror. Claudia laughs, amused, and strikes another pose, her right hand behind her head, as if playfully taking a sophisticated, haughty, and seductive posture. Then the camera follows her as she moves to the left. Suddenly we realize that from the beginning of the shot we have been watching not the real Claudia, but rather her reflected image. The camera pans left to reveal Patrizia (not her mirrored image), looking left at the real Claudia, whose back emerges, unexpectedly, to the left, not the right, of Patrizia.*
PATRIZIA (*smiling sympathetically*): You look like a different woman.
The camera follows Claudia to the left, leaving Patrizia offscreen right.

Claudia moves playfully toward the bed, slinging a shawl across her shoulder. She puts on another ring, poses with her arm stretched out, then walks jauntily toward Patrizia, who reappears as the camera pans right. The jocular music continues, underlining Claudia's teasing smile. They both turn their backs, proceeding to the door. Claudia takes her dark wig off and stands looking at Patrizia, who turns and affectionately touches Claudia's hair here and there.

PATRIZIA (*smiling at Claudia, leaning on the doorknob*): Shall we go?

302. MS: *the hallway. Patrizia and Claudia emerge from a door on right, but walk off in opposite directions.*

CLAUDIA (*moving toward camera*): I'm going down, okay? (*She walks into the foreground, wig in hand; then, suddenly realizing she still has it, she turns around and gives it to Patrizia.*) Oops. Here, you take it. (*Claudia starts walking toward camera again, then crosses in front of it to the left. She stops, standing with her back to the camera, at the entrance to a door that leads to a staircase.*)

303. MS: *Giulia and Goffredo are coming up the staircase; Giulia is laughing and bouncing as she climbs. The camera moves back as they reach the top, encountering Claudia, in right foreground, her back to the camera. Giulia smiles girlishly yet knowingly at Claudia, then turns to look at Goffredo. She bursts out giggling, holding her purse against her mouth. Goffredo, looking sheepish, exits left. Giulia stares offscreen left after him.*
   GIULIA *(turning to Claudia, whose back is to camera):* He wants to show me his paintings. *(Glancing again offscreen left, then back at Claudia, preening.)* He simply won't leave me alone. Poor thing, he must have a crush on me.
   The camera follows her slightly to the left, leaving Claudia offscreen right.
   GIULIA *(with a pleading look):* Please, come with me, won't you?
   She turns her back to the camera, moving toward the background and dragging the reluctant Claudia by the hand back onscreen and down the hall.
   CLAUDIA *(as Giulia disappears into a door in right background):* But why do you want me . . .
304. MCU: *Giulia walks forward through an outside hallway or gallery with windows on the right, followed by Claudia. The camera moves back with them.*
   GIULIA *(excited, glancing back at Claudia as she walks, unable to stop smiling as she speaks):* You mustn't leave me alone with him. He's capable of . . . I don't know. . . . Have you noticed his eyes?
305. MS, *reverse angle. They walk down the gallery, away from camera. As they get to the far background, Giulia begins skipping, then stops in front of a door, turns toward Claudia, and makes a quick curtsey.*
   GIULIA *(excitedly):* Here we are.
   They both go in.
306. MS, *reverse angle. They walk toward camera into an alcove.*
   CLAUDIA *(stopping in the doorway, protesting):* But Giulia, what am I coming for?
   Giulia turns around, goes back, and pulls her along by the hand. Claudia sighs and goes with her. They cross in front of camera toward the background, where they meet Goffredo, who appears standing in the doorway of his studio.
307. MS, *reverse angle. Goffredo stands at the door with his back to the*

camera as Giulia enters, followed by Claudia, who stops in the doorway. Giulia looks around the room, giggling, then glances at Goffredo, giggling again, while Claudia moves behind her to the right and off. Sexy, bolero music, scored for saxophone and woodwinds, begins (and continues through 316). The camera follows Giulia as she moves left, while Goffredo closes the door and remains offscreen right.

GIULIA (*stopping with her back to the camera in front of a sketch on an easel*): Claudia, come and see. A nude!

Goffredo reenters from right, walking slowly.

308. MCU: *Claudia, in extreme left foreground, her bent back to the camera as she flips through canvasses standing stacked against the wall. The camera moves left, tilting up as she stands erect in profile in front of the paintings.*

CLAUDIA (*slowly turning toward camera*): But they're all nudes, if I'm not mistaken.

Behind her on the wall is a large abstract painting of African masks, their big eyes seeming to follow her as she moves off-frame right.

309. LS: *the view from a window onto trees and mountains takes up most of the screen. Claudia enters left foreground, leans out the window, and looks out.*

310. MS: *Giulia, with her back to the camera, on left, and Goffredo, on right in profile, scratching his chin as if sizing her up.*

GIULIA (*slowly circling around the easel and turning around, as Goffredo moves closer, facing her*): You're really good! . . . But why paint only women?

GOFFREDO (*moving closer to her, putting his hands in his pockets, languidly*): No landscape is equal to a woman's beauty.

She smiles coquettishly and then moves toward the camera, so that they both face each other in profile.

GIULIA (*looking at him, playfully*): And the models? Where do you find them?

GOFFREDO: Oh, they're easy enough to get.

GIULIA (*slowly turning her back to him, looking toward the left*): I thought using models was old-fashioned. (*Turning right and looking up.*) Don't you think so, Claudia?

311. MCU: *Claudia, as in 309. She seems startled and turns toward Giulia,*

murmuring: Ah, what? *She nods, lost in her own thoughts, and returns to the window, as if looking for something or someone.*

312. MCU: *Giulia and Goffredo, as in 310. Giulia slowly walks away, exiting left; Goffredo looks Giulia up and down, pensively, then follows her offscreen. The music becomes more exotic.*

GOFFREDO (*exiting left*): It's strange how . . .

313. MS: *Giulia's back. She turns her head to the right as Goffredo talks.*

GOFFREDO (*off*): . . . women enjoy displaying themselves. It almost seems to be a natural disposition.

Giulia giggles and quickly moves to the right and stretches out on a chaise lounge, as if posing.

GIULIA (*her left elbow on a cushion, her hand propping her head provocatively, knees slightly bent, her right arm resting on her lap*): But how can they pose that way? I couldn't. (*She gives a kittenish sigh.*)

GOFFREDO (*off, except for his arm and hand*): Why don't you[31] try?

As if responding, Giulia stretches her legs out and sinks back into the chaise, lowering her eyes with artificial modesty. She gets up, giggling; the camera moves right with her, past Goffredo, who is leaning against a dresser, his chin on his folded arms. Giulia passes behind the nude sketch and stops at the right to look back at Goffredo. Goffredo then passes behind the nude sketch on the easel and emerges on the right, joining Giulia in MCU *as she stands gazing at three sketches on the wall.*

GOFFREDO: Try.

GIULIA: Me? (*Turning her head toward him, in mock anger.*) Goffredo, are you crazy? (*Turning back a bit and addressing Claudia, she laughs nervously.*) He's crazy.

314. CU: *Goffredo is in right foreground, biting his lips and gazing intensely at Giulia. Claudia stands in left background, her back to the camera.*

CLAUDIA (*turning toward camera*): Not really.

She smiles knowingly at Goffredo, who turns his head toward her; she says "Ah!" as if they understand each other. He quickly turns back toward camera, and she returns to a contemplation of his paintings.

315. MCU: *Giulia, against a painting, turns to the right, smiling as if posing, then walks in profile toward the right. She turns around, facing left, standing against—and as if within—a dark painting mounted in a white frame.*

GIULIA: And men? Don't you ever paint them?

GOFFREDO (*coming onscreen from the left and standing in profile, facing her*): Answer me. Why don't you try posing too? (*He puts his hand up on the wall above her head and leans forward, lowering his voice.*) I'd make a . . . marvelous portrait of you.

GIULIA (*staring at him in wonder*): But why me? Why don't you ask Claudia? She's much more beautiful than I am. (*She steps toward camera into* CU, *staring emptily ahead, while Goffredo remains behind her, looking at her back.*)

GOFFREDO (*coming up closer from behind her, softly*): It's you I want to do. You say . . . somehow you say more to me.

Giulia turns her head toward him, smiling, then turns back toward the camera and giggles. The camera follows her as she moves slightly to the left.

GIULIA (*in a provocative tone*): Do I say more to you?

Now in extreme left foreground, she quickly swings around, turning her back to the camera and facing Goffredo, who is right, and a step behind. He nods; she moves closer to him, laughs nervously, and then throws her arms around his neck. They kiss and embrace passionately.

316. MS: *Goffredo and Giulia embracing, partially hidden behind the easel. They knock the easel over, and separate, startled. (The music ends.) Giulia laughs nervously, retreating to the left, but Goffredo grabs her and forces her backward against a table. They embrace, Goffredo with his back to the camera. He bends her back over the table. Objects fall noisily onto the floor. Claudia enters left foreground and stands watching them. Goffredo runs his hand down Giulia's side.*

317. MCU: *Claudia, in center, looking toward the right and smiling slightly, then laughing indulgently. But then she becomes shocked, and speaks reproachfully.*

CLAUDIA: Giulia!

318. MCU: *Goffredo's back completely covers Giulia. Giulia, panting, pushes him up and to the left, but continues to stare provocatively at him. Goffredo, on left, looks at her calmly and seriously. They both glance toward the left, in Claudia's direction. Giulia turns to the right, and the camera follows her (leaving Goffredo off) as she moves decisively toward the door, opening it for Claudia to leave. As Giulia leans against it,*

*Claudia enters left. She pauses and stops to the right of Giulia, her back
to the camera.*

GIULIA (*looking defiantly at Claudia*): If Corrado's looking for me, tell
  him I'm here. And tell him that my little heart is beating fast, fast . . .
  (*Raising her voice.*) . . . and that's all that matters to me right now. Do
  I make myself clear?

CLAUDIA (*calmly*): Very. (*She goes into the hall and turns back to look
  at Giulia.*)

GIULIA (*with her back to the camera, standing by the door in extreme
  left foreground, facing Claudia*): And now what must I do to be left in
  peace?

CLAUDIA (*drily*): All you have to do is to close the door, Giulia.

*Giulia shuts the door firmly on Claudia and then turns around, leaning
against it with a half-smile.*

319. CU: *from behind, the back of Claudia's head as she faces the other side*

of the closed door. She turns around slowly, pensively, and walks down the corridor, toward camera. Suddenly she hears the noise of a car. She quickly turns, exiting right. The camera rests for a moment on an urn in the corridor.

320. MS: *she runs down the corridor toward the background, her back to the camera, then turns right, disappearing around a corner. The camera goes outside and pans to the right, down the gallery. Claudia is visible at intervals through the large windows of the gallery as she runs to the right. She bumps into a chambermaid, but doesn't stop.*

321. MS: *Claudia, from behind, going down the ornate staircase. At the bottom, she turns right and goes off-frame.*

322. MS: *the staircase landing with a high, arched ceiling. Claudia descends stairs on right and sees herself in a large mirror hanging on the wall of the landing. She stops as if startled by her own image, moves closer to it and checks her hair, then turns around and exits right.*

323. MS: *Claudia hesitantly enters a doorway, which is symmetrically framed by urns and putti. She leans against the outside door, peers out and sighs, trying to catch her breath. She looks disappointed. She moves forward, the camera tracking with her.*

RAIMONDO (*off*): He wasn't at the hotel . . .

324. MS: *Corrado, in profile, and Ettore, with his back to the camera, are talking to Raimondo, who sits in a sportscar right behind them.*

RAIMONDO (*as another car quickly drives by in front of them and Claudia comes into right foreground, standing with her back to the camera*): . . . and he probably wasn't in Milazzo, either. The porter said he'd asked if he could rent a car. (*Raimondo gets out of the car as Claudia enters right.*) I'm going to change.. I'll be back soon. (*Corrado and Ettore turn around, and Raimondo quickly passes in front of Claudia. Nodding to her, he says:*) Ciao.

Raimondo exits right foreground; Claudia stares at Corrado and Ettore, then turns and quickly moves away, exiting right. Corrado shuts the car door.

ETTORE (*turning to Corrado, as they both start walking away from the car toward the right*): Anyway, tomorrow we'll try to find him.

325. LS: *Claudia stands with her back to the camera in left foreground, watching Ettore and Corrado, who are walking slowly toward her.*

ETTORE: He must be in Milazzo, or somewhere.

Patrizia enters right foreground and approaches Claudia.

PATRIZIA (*turning to Claudia*): Shall we go, Claudia?

CLAUDIA (*without moving*): I'm not coming.

PATRIZIA (*surprised, moving closer to her*): Then why did you change? *Claudia walks away, exiting left foreground; Patrizia watches her, puzzled, then exits in the same direction.*

ETTORE (*his voice in the distance*): Send a car to pick him up. It must be ninety miles.

CORRADO: All right, we'll send a car.

Giulia and Goffredo enter right foreground, walking toward the car with their backs to the camera. The camera follows them as they walk past the two men, who come into MCU; *as they pass, Giulia glances tauntingly at Corrado. Corrado stares at them, then turns toward Ettore.*

CORRADO (*to Ettore, coldly*): Giulia is like Oscar Wilde. (*Turning and going toward the car with Ettore, as Patrizia emerges from left foreground and follows after them.*) Give her the extras, and she'll do without the necessities.

ETTORE (*to Corrado, putting his hand on his shoulder as they go to the car, where Giulia and Goffredo are waiting*): There you go again! You would die if you didn't quote somebody. (*He stops, waiting for Patrizia, and takes her by the arm as the others get in the car.*) Even in business meetings, he throws those names around. . . .

PATRIZIA: Who?

ETTORE: Corrado!

A servant comes around and opens the car door, while Patrizia laughs.

326. LS *from the other side of the car. Ettore gets in the driver's seat and the car moves off, exiting left. The servant stands watching, then moves away, exiting right. In the distant background, Claudia walks slowly back into the house.*

Dissolve.

327. *A pharmacy in Troina, Sicily.* CU: *a woman, the wife of the druggist, sits with her back to a large window overlooking a landscape of mountains and valleys. Sho looks intently toward camera.*

DRUGGIST (*off*): Please be patient!

328. MS: *Sandro stands on the right, gesticulating with his newspaper. The druggist stands with his back to the camera in left foreground. The druggist's wife watches them from another room in the background.*

SANDRO (*to the druggist, who closes a cabinet on extreme left*): What do you[32] mean, "patient"? You remembered she bought a tranquilizer, didn't you? There's no point in pretending you can't remember now.

As the druggist walks past Sandro, moving to right foreground, his wife comes in from the background; Sandro turns toward her, and she takes the newspaper from him.

WIFE (*reading from the newspaper*): "A foreign girl who looked like the girl who disappeared came into my drugstore . . . (*She glances up toward her husband, then continues reading.*) . . . the afternoon of the day. . . .*" She came and left. (*She addresses Sandro, but her eyes are on her husband, who stands still, with his back to the camera.*) With him. But this he doesn't say. (*She moves away toward the background, putting the newspaper down, upset; at the doorway to the other room, she stops and turns around, looking at her husband.*) If you think I didn't know . . .

As she walks away, the druggist follows her, while Sandro remains standing, looking down and frowning, then leans against the wall on the right, his hands in his pockets, watching the two of them.

DRUGGIST (*standing in front of his wife, his back to the camera, protesting*): But if I had planned anything with her, why would I have told the newspapers?

WIFE: That's just what I would like to know.

Sandro turns toward camera, frowning. The wife disappears momentarily in the other room, then comes back, standing in the doorway.

DRUGGIST (*gesturing with his right hand*): Well, then, that makes two of us who'd like to know! Or three, including this gentleman.

An old woman walks in and stands in center foreground, with her back to the camera.

DRUGGIST (*turning around toward her, gesturing*): And you,[33] donna Amalia, do you wish to know why I told the newspaper about the person who came in here a couple of days ago and then disappeared?

DONNA AMALIA: Disappeared? Who? When?

DRUGGIST (*sarcastically, angrily*): That makes four of us. (*To his wife.*) Anyone else? (*He turns and moves to the right, going around the counter.*)

329. MCU: *Sandro, on left, leans insistently toward the druggist, who turns to face him.*

SANDRO (*as the druggist's wife walks back in and stands angrily in the background watching them*): Listen, you have to be precise. Did this girl come into your drugstore or didn't she?

WIFE: She did!

Sandro glances at her, then turns back toward the druggist.

SANDRO (*to him, softly*): And was she blonde or brunette?

DRUGGIST: Dark.

WIFE: Blonde.

Sandro glances at her, annoyed, then addresses the druggist again.

SANDRO: And how was she dressed?

DRUGGIST (*calmly*): That I don't remember. Bright colors, I think.

WIFE (*leaning against the wall, provokingly*): He doesn't look at the clothes, he looks at what's underneath.

Sandro looks at her impatiently.

SANDRO (*to the druggist*): Has anyone else come in here to ask about this girl?

DRUGGIST: No, I don't think so.

SANDRO: Thank you.

He leaves quickly, exiting left. The druggist and his wife remain onscreen. He stares pensively after Sandro; she looks at her husband, grimacing sarcastically.

330. LS: *a sunny square. Ettore's car drives in, crossing frame from right to left, and stops behind Sandro's car.*

331. MS: *Sandro is standing outside in the foreground, against the wall, watching the car. The druggist emerges in the doorway on left, behind him. Underneath the drugstore's sign is the painted symbol of the MSI (Movimento Sociale Italiano), the Italian neo-fascist party. Also painted on the wall, at Sandro's left, is the word "Vote."*

332. LS: *the car pulls to a stop. In the background, two cows are being led offscreen right. Claudia gets out of the car on the left; a chauffeur gets out on the opposite side and goes over to help her, but she starts to walk decisively toward the foreground, crossing the square. As she comes into* MCU *in left foreground, Sandro enters left and stops on extreme left, his back to the camera.*

CLAUDIA (*calmly*): Any news?

SANDRO (*softly*): It's full of contradictions, but there are some clues.

Claudia turns around and moves away; the camera follows her, leaving

Sandro off, as she walks thoughtfully toward the background, swinging her purse.

333. MS: *Sandro, in right foreground, looks toward the right after Claudia. The druggist comes running from left background up to Sandro, who turns toward him as Claudia reemerges in right foreground and crosses in front of Sandro, her back to the camera. Sandro turns around to listen to the druggist.*

   DRUGGIST (*to Sandro*): Listen . . . in the paper, they forgot to say that when the girl left from here . . .

334. CU: *the druggist, on right, looking toward the left.*

   DRUGGIST: . . . she took the bus to Noto. (*Casting his eyes down, perhaps to look at Claudia's legs.*) It leaves from the square over there. (*He points to the left and glances in that direction, then casts his eyes down again.*) I noticed it, because I watched her walk off. . . .

335. MS, *as in 333: Claudia, in left foreground next to Sandro, on right, both with their backs to the camera; the druggist stands in front of them with his hands in his pockets.*

   DRUGGIST: Beautiful girl. (*Stepping toward Claudia.*) Lovely legs. (*To Claudia, taking out a pack of cigarettes.*) Do you smoke?

   As he takes out a cigarette and puts it in his mouth, his wife, who has emerged from left foreground and come to stand just behind him on left, glares at him resentfully, then turns toward Claudia.

   WIFE (*smiling sadly at her*): You are from Rome, aren't you? I knew it right away, because I'm from Viterbo. (*She glances toward her husband, who is smoking, his back to the group.*) He was doing his military service there, and so. . . . (*She looks down.*) You know. I don't like it here.

   CLAUDIA (*kindly*): How long have you been married?

   WIFE (*sighing, looking away to the right*): Three months.

   DRUGGIST (*gesturing toward her with the cigarette*): Go back inside.

   He walks back to the store, in left background, followed by his wife.

   SANDRO (*yelling after him*): Thank you! Thank you for the information! (*Turning toward Claudia, ironically.*) Charming couple, aren't they?

   He turns away, exiting right foreground. Claudia remains standing, watching the couple as they enter the shop in left background. The druggist's wife glances back at Claudia before disappearing through the door.

336. MS: *the car that brought Claudia is in the foreground. Sandro, who glances at Claudia, is in left background. Claudia turns around, and they stare at each other for a moment. Cowbells and mooing can be heard. Then Sandro opens the car door and says something to the chauffeur, who is sitting behind the steering wheel, in extreme right foreground. Sandro pulls Claudia's suitcase out of the car and walks back toward her. As they stare at each other silently for a moment, the chauffeur enters right, crosses foreground, and walks around the car, closing the door that Sandro left open. Both Sandro and Claudia turn toward him.*

SANDRO (*stepping toward him*): Tell[34] your mistress that we'll continue the search, and that Miss Claudia will get in touch with her, somehow.

CHAUFFEUR: Certainly.

The chauffeur returns to the car. Claudia and Sandro remain standing, watching him.

337. MS, *reverse angle: Sandro, on left with his back to the camera, stands watching as Ettore's car leaves, then moves toward the right; the camera follows him as he puts Claudia's bag into his convertible in extreme right foreground. As the other car drives off into the background, he looks toward the left, smiling, and exits slowly left foreground. Claudia suddenly emerges from the left and stares in his direction. Her expression is serious. She gets into the convertible, looking up as she shuts the door. Sandro comes around the back of the car and gets in on the right side, smiling at her, then starts the motor. The expression on Claudia's face is concealed by the frame of the car windshield.*

338. MS: *the countryside, seen from the moving car.*

CLAUDIA (*off, then the back of her head coming onscreen as the camera slowly pans to include her*): What's the name of this place?

SANDRO (*coming onscreen as the camera continues to pan left, so that they are both shown, from the back*): Noto.

CLAUDIA: And Anna . . . ? Where are we going to look for her?

SANDRO: In a hotel—there's only one, the Trinacria.

339. LS: *the hilly landscape, then the car enters, in distant right background, driving onto a bridge on the left. The camera pans left to follow the car as it proceeds across the bridge, toward the camera.*

SANDRO (*as the car passes a small tower*): This can't be Noto, can it?

CLAUDIA: Let's ask someone.
The camera follows the car as it comes into center foreground and drives past a white, modern-looking house, tightly shuttered.

340. LS: *the car continues into the town, the camera panning to reveal a small, modern church and other buildings.*[35] *The street is deserted.*

341. LS, *high angle, over the empty town square. The camera pans slowly to the right across the square and focuses on the church's three round-arched windows on right frame edge. The only sound is that of cicadas. Sandro's car enters and stops in the middle of the square. Sandro and Claudia get out; Sandro leans against the car and Claudia walks toward the left.*

342. LS, *low angle: Claudia walks from left foreground up to a white building, trying to see through the white-shuttered windows. The camera follows her toward the right; then she turns, walking back toward the building in the background, while Sandro enters left, his hands in his pockets in* MCU. *He looks both right and left in a puzzled way.*

343. MCU: *Claudia's back in right foreground, as she tries to see through the jalousie shutters. The fingers of her left hand are spread out against the shutters. She turns her head to the left and calls inside:*
CLAUDIA: Anyone here? (*Her voice echoes dully, as if the room were empty. She puts her left ear to the shutters and calls again. She turns toward the camera and addresses Sandro.*) Listen to the echo! But how come it's so empty?

344. *As in 342. Sandro is in the foreground, his hands in his pockets. He shrugs at Claudia, still standing at the window.*
SANDRO: Who knows? (*He turns, so that he is facing camera, and looks off to the left.*) And why did they ever build it, I wonder?
He turns and exits right foreground, while Claudia moves to another window of the house.

345. LS: *a valley below the town. Sandro enters left foreground and stands with his back to the camera, looking at a Sicilian town in the distance. He turns around, gesturing toward it.*
SANDRO: There's another over there.
He sits on a wall, facing Claudia, as she enters left with her back to the camera.
CLAUDIA (*looking over the valley*): This isn't a town, it's a cemetery.

(*She turns toward Sandro, who turns toward the right, and speaks pleadingly.*) My God, how dismal. Let's get out of here.

SANDRO: Let's go.

They both turn toward camera and exit right foreground.

346. LS: *Claudia and Sandro get into the car in the sunlight square, at the end of a dark, empty alley. The camera moves very slowly down the alley toward the square as the car backs around the corner, momentarily disappears, then reemerges before disappearing for good behind the church. The camera remains, in a* temps mort *on the deserted square with its modernist church and a campanile in center background. The noise of the motor fades away.*

347. CU, *low angle, of Claudia against the sky, laughing, her eyes closed, and hugging Sandro's head to her breast. Claudia laughs with pleasure. Sandro rises onscreen, his back to the camera, and kisses her. They walk off to the right, embracing. He kisses her again, very passionately, and they sink to the ground, disappearing below frame. The camera remains fixed, in a* temps mort, *on the deserted countryside, with the town in distant right background and a sunny but turbulent sky above.*[36]

348. CU, *from above: Claudia is lying on her back on the ground and looking at Sandro, on extreme right with his back to the camera. Sandro leans over and kisses her passionately. His back covers her almost completely. She responds with equal passion.*

CLAUDIA (*gasping slightly and whispering fervently*): My love, mine, mine . . .

Sandro kisses her hand and rests his face on her chest, as she closes her eyes ecstatically.

349. ECU: *Claudia from ground level, her face taking up the entire screen as she rises from below. Kissing Sandro, who lies underneath her, Claudia leans over him in high angle; they kiss and rub cheeks passionately. Claudia sighs with pleasure.*

350. ECU, *reverse angle, of the back of Claudia's head, her blond hair momentarily covering him. His fingers are clutching her head passionately. When she moves her head, we can see him smiling tenderly at her.*

351. *As in 349. Claudia gets up a bit and lovingly strokes Sandro's lips with her finger, as he gently smooths her hair from her face. She kisses his hand, and they continue embracing and kissing.*

352. *As in 350. They continue to embrace.*

353. *As in 349. Sandro's face in extreme foreground, Claudia leaning over him, her face taking up the entire screen as she smiles. She looks up into the sky, as if in wonder at it all. Then she bends down and kisses Sandro's neck.*

354. LS: *a freight train cuts across the valley, emerging from right background, the sea behind it. The camera slowly pans left to follow the train.*

355. MCU, *high angle: Claudia lying prone on Sandro, her arm around him, in the foreground. They are sprawled, quiet now, on the grass near the railroad tracks. The train passes behind them, a few feet away. Sandro looks up, startled, and leans on his elbow to watch it roar by and disappear. Claudia scarcely moves.*

 SANDRO (*softly, as if to wake her up*): Claudia. It's late. We have to go. *She murmurs and nestles against him. He lies back. She rests her face on his chest and closes her eyes. The camera stays on them for a moment. Dissolve.*

356. LS: *a street in Noto. Sandro emerges from the background, slowly walking in the middle of the street, looking around. The camera follows him as he comes into* MCU *and then walks across foreground toward the left, stopping with his back to the camera in front of Claudia, who stands next to a door, looking at the sign of the hotel "Trinacria." She turns toward him uncertainly. She glances back and forth at the door, then walks toward him, stopping next to him in* MCU, *on right.*

 CLAUDIA (*looking at Sandro, who is staring at the hotel door*): Sandro, it might be better if you went in alone.

 SANDRO (*turning toward her*): But you're joking!

 CLAUDIA (*calmly, sadly*): No. And don't think I want to spare myself the discomfort . . . the difficulty of this meeting. . . . (*Sandro glances down, then stares off pensively.*) That's not it. It's simply that there are certain things you can say more easily without me. Do try to understand. I'd feel I was there trying to influence you, that I was restricting you. (*Sandro looks back at her.*) That's what bothers me.

 Sandro looks at her for a moment, then starts toward the door. He turns around before he gets there and looks at her again. Claudia turns to watch him. Then Sandro goes in. Claudia steps closer to the door, standing with her back to the camera, watching as he walks up the stairs and disappears. Then she slowly turns toward the camera, sighing, and walks slowly across the square toward the right. Church bells ring. The camera

dollies with her until she stops, leaning against a stone stairway on right, and looks up. A man's voice can be heard muttering something.

357. LS: groups of men lounge about on the street and the stairway above, staring lasciviously at Claudia, who is standing in left background against the stairway. She slowly walks across the square toward the camera, attracting more attention, aware of the eyes upon her and of the murmured comments. The camera stays on Claudia as she makes her way through the men, coming into MCU and then stopping in center foreground, turning her back to the camera as she looks upward. The camera tilts up to the building's balcony, revealing a dozen more men moving to the railing to ogle her.

358. MCU: Claudia looking up at the balcony. Men of all ages loiter around her. She looks down, then right and left, oppressed by the men's attention. She turns to the right and walks across foreground with her back to the camera, stopping in front of the hotel door, while men approach her, staring. As Sandro comes quickly down the stairs and out the door,

followed by a woman, she turns around, running off in panic into left foreground. He rushes off after her.
359. MS: *interior of a store. Claudia backs in through the door at right, then turns and stands uncertainly. The shopkeeper approaches her from left.*
    SHOPKEEPER: What can I do for you, miss?
    CLAUDIA (*improvising*): A can of paint.
    SHOPKEEPER: What color?
    CLAUDIA (*shrugging impatiently and stepping forward, looking away*): Blue.
    The shopkeeper nods and turns away; the camera follows Claudia as she moves to the right, toward the window. She looks toward the door, standing in the foreground with her back to the camera as Sandro enters. The camera focuses on him as he walks toward her, leaving Claudia offscreen.
    SANDRO (*coming into* MCU, *with a concerned expression on his face*): But Claudia, what's happening?
360. MCU: *Claudia, huddling against some shelves. She keeps turning her face away as she talks.*
    CLAUDIA: Oh, Sandro—I'm so ashamed . . . ashamed. Did you see? I tried to hide. I feel so cheap. (*Almost sobbing.*) I hate myself.
    SANDRO (*off, coldly*): Do you enjoy saying things like that?
    CLAUDIA (*shaking her head*): No, no, I don't enjoy it at all.
361. MCU: *Sandro, looking intently at her.*
    SANDRO: So, why do you say them, then?
362. *Claudia, as in 360.*
    CLAUDIA: Because what I'm doing is so ugly. . . . Because if you were to say to me now: "Claudia, I love you," . . . (*In a desperate tone, on the verge of tears.*) . . . I'd believe you. . . . I would . . .
    The camera follows her as she turns away toward the left, crossing behind Sandro, whose back emerges in the foreground. He grabs her and holds her in front of him.
    SANDRO (*pleading*): Claudia . . .
    CLAUDIA (*looking at him intently*): No, let me say it. Or I would make you swear it, make you tell me so many things. . . . (*She pulls away from him and walks toward camera, while he turns around, staring at her from behind.*) And it's not right. . . . (*Almost crying.*) It can't be right. It's absurd.
    She turns her head toward him, and he steps closer to her, pleading.

SANDRO: Good. It's better if it's absurd. It just means there's nothing we can do about it. Do you understand?

Startled by a noise, they both turn toward the right.

363. MS, *reverse angle: in right foreground, with their backs to the camera, Sandro and Claudia face the shopkeeper, who stands on the left, holding several cans of paint.*

SANDRO (*as he moves away, following Claudia, while the shopkeeper comes up to them*): I am sorry, but we don't need it anymore.

SHOPKEEPER (*smiling, while Claudia rushes off, exiting right*): Don't worry about it.

SANDRO (*following Claudia*): I'm sorry.

SHOPKEEPER: That's all right.

364. MCU: *Claudia walks out of the shop and exits right. Sandro pauses in the doorway, staring after her, then slowly follows her. The camera moves with him, revealing Claudia leaning against a wall, staring emptily in front of her. He stops next to her, looking at her intently, putting his hands in his pockets.*

CLAUDIA (*without looking at him*): And when I think you must have said exactly the same things to Anna any number of times . . .

SANDRO (*leaning against the wall beside her*): Let's say I did. But I was as sincere with her then as I am right now with you. (*Claudia turns and stares at him in amazement.*) I've never known a woman like you—a woman who has to see everything so very clearly. (*He takes her arm.*) Come on. Let's take a walk.

He leads her toward the right, and they exit.

Dissolve.

365. MS: *a nun emerges onto a church roof, followed by Claudia and Sandro.*

NUN: How lovely up here! (*She turns her back to the camera, toward Claudia and Sandro.*) And to think I've never come here before. (*Sandro steps away from the door, standing to the left of Claudia.*) You can stay. I'm going back down.

Passing between Sandro and Claudia, she disappears through the door in the background. Sandro goes offscreen left as the camera follows Claudia to the right. She goes under the bell ropes and leans over the ramparts, then turns around toward camera.

366. LS: *the elaborate baroque buildings of Noto.*

SANDRO (*off*): What imagination! Look at all the movement. . . . (*He*

*slowly enters from right foreground, in profile, then turns toward cam-
era,* MCU, *looking at the view on the near side.*) They were interested
in the stage effects. Extraordinary freedom. (*He nods his head, turning
toward the camera and looking down, pensively. Then he turns toward
the right, leaning against the wall, his back to the buildings in the
background.*) I must make up my mind, decide once and for all to stop
working for Ettore. I'd like to get back to drawing up plans again. I had
some ideas, you know?
*He smiles, extending his hand to Claudia, who emerges from left fore-
ground.*

CLAUDIA (*standing next to him with her back to the camera*): And why
did you stop?

SANDRO (*looking down*): Hmm. (*The camera follows him to the right as
he walks away from her, leaving her offscreen. He stops and turns
around again, standing with his hands in his pockets, looking in her
direction.*) Why, why, why, why! Because it's not easy to admit that a

red floor looks nice in a room when . . . when you're convinced that it
doesn't. But the lady wants it red. Because there is always some lady,
or some gentleman. (*He shrugs.*) And then . . . (*He turns back, touching something on the low wall, then leaning on it.*) . . . then I was
asked to draw up an estimate—how much it would cost to build a
school. It took me a day and a half. I earned four million lire for it.
(*He shrugs again, glancing to the left, then staring again in front
of him.*) And from that day I went on drawing up estimates . . . for
someone else's plans. (*He looks half-defiantly toward Claudia.*)

367. MCU: *Claudia, on left, leaning against the wall with her arms folded,
    looking in his direction.*

    SANDRO (*off*): Why are you looking at me like that?

    CLAUDIA (*shrugging, in a serious tone*): Because I am convinced you
    could make very beautiful things.

    SANDRO (*emerging from right foreground, with his back to the camera,
    standing in front of her*): I'm not so sure. I just don't know. And what
    good are beautiful things now, Claudia? (*He looks away, toward the
    left.*) How long do they last? (*He leans against the wall closer to her,
    staring pensively in front of him.*) Once they had centuries of life ahead
    of them. Now—ten, twenty years at the most . . . and then . . . well . . .
    (*He goes down some steps to the left and ducks under the bell ropes,
    the camera following him in high angle, leaving Claudia off. He kicks a
    few pebbles, thoughtfully, then looks up.*) Claudia! (*She enters, stand-
    ing on the step above him, in extreme right foreground, her back to the
    camera*) Shall we get married?

368. MCU, *low angle, of Claudia against the sky and the bell towers of other
    churches.*

    CLAUDIA (*shocked*): What do you mean, get married?

369. MCU, *reverse angle, of Sandro.*

    SANDRO (*decisively*): Let's. You and I. (*He smiles, then looks down and
    smiles again, looking up.*) Answer me.

370. *Claudia, as in 368.*

    CLAUDIA (*upset*): Answer? But what can I say? (*Angrily.*) No. Not now,
    anyway. . . . I don't know. (*She moves right, lifting up one of the bell
    ropes and passing under it.*) I'm not even thinking about it at a time
    like this. (*She stops, the rope cutting diagonally across her face, and
    turns angrily toward Sandro.*) But why are you asking me?

371. MS, *reverse angle: Sandro walks forward and stares at her intently.*
     SANDRO: You look at me as if I said something crazy.
372. MS, *as in 370: Claudia stands bemused. Sandro enters from left foreground, lifting the bell rope. He comes close to her, his back to the camera.*
     CLAUDIA: But are you sure you want to marry me? Really sure . . .
     (*She steps toward camera, pulls down on the rope, looking down pensively.*) . . . that you want to marry me?
     SANDRO (*standing next to her, on left in profile, looking intently at her*): Since I'm asking you . . .
     Claudia leans against the rope and turns totally around, so that she holds the rope with both hands and leans her neck back against it.
     CLAUDIA (*pondering sadly*): But why isn't everything simpler? You say I want to see things clearly. (*She turns around again toward camera, holding onto the rope almost desperately, while Sandro turns away.*) I would like to be lucid . . . (*She taps her head, on the verge of tears, while Sandro turns back toward her. She speaks passionately, looking at the sky and shaking her hand to emphasize her point.*) I would like to see things clearly . . . (*She sighs.*) Instead . . . (*Angrily, she pulls hard on the bell rope, and the bell rings. She looks up, surprised, then to the left, then moves to the background and pulls another rope, ringing a higher-pitched bell.*)
373. MCU, *low angle, from behind Claudia. The huge bells in left background are rung as Sandro, off, pulls the ropes. Claudia glances toward the right as she hears the sound of another bell responding to theirs.*
     CLAUDIA (*joyfully*): They're answering. D'you hear them?
     SANDRO (*off*): From where?
     The camera pans right with Claudia, thus revealing Sandro, in right foreground, as he pulls a rope. She starts to climb the steps up to the balustrade.
374. MS: *Claudia, in left foreground from the back, looks out over the town at the other church.*
     CLAUDIA (*pointing*): From that bell tower over there.
     She turns toward camera, then, at the sound of another bell, she moves toward the right.
375. MS: *Sandro, in right foreground with his back to the camera, pulls on*

the bell ropes, ringing the bells. Claudia, clinging to the edge of the wall, moves from left to right background toward him. Bells answer in the distance. She passes behind and above him. Sandro goes to her, passing under the ropes, and looks up. She meets his gaze happily, her hair blowing in the wind.
Dissolve.

376. MS: *a sound van comes down the street toward camera. A man is standing up in the van, his head emerging from the sun-roof. The van turns right and passes the camera, then parks. People pick up leaflets distributed from the van. Loudspeakers extending from right and left of the van start playing recordings of popular music. A song begins with the bellowing notes of a baritone saxophone (and continues through 380).*

377. MS: *a bedroom. A woman's voice starts singing the song being broadcast by the van.*[37] *Claudia's head emerges from behind the bed (apparently she has been lying on the floor). She is mouthing the banal words of the song, her lips synchronized with the voice on the record. Still on her knees, she reaches across the unmade bed and picks up one of her stockings. She throws herself on the bed, the back of her head in the foreground, her right leg stretched up. She pulls the stocking on.*

SANDRO (*off, as the music continues, loudly*): Ready?

CLAUDIA (*rolling out of the bed*): Yes!

The camera pans right with her as she gets up and dances across the room toward Sandro, who comes onscreen. She throws her arms around his neck.

CLAUDIA (*playfully, theatrically embracing him while the song continues loudly*): Why am I so much in love with you?

SANDRO (*standing rather impatiently*): Come on. Hurry up.

CLAUDIA (*moving away, clowning around and rummaging wildly through drawers, cheerfully*): Yes, yes, yes . . . right away. . . . Where is it? Where? Where?

As the singer on the record sings "Si! Si!" ("Yes! Yes!"), she throws up both arms and starts to sing along again, as if she cannot resist the crude affirmation of the lyrics. She crosses the room in front of Sandro, who watches her indulgently. Dancing theatrically, she reaches the other chest of drawers. In mock despair at not finding what she wants, she throws clothes about the room. Then, leaning against the dresser, she smiles at herself in the mirror and poses foolishly, pushing her hair up in a mock-seductive way. She turns around, dancing sensuously to the song's rhythm.

SANDRO (*turning to the left, smiling as he exits*): Bye, bye. I'll see you later.

The camera follows Claudia as she rushes over to the left, crossing in the foreground and catching up with him at the door. Continuing to clown, she blocks his passage, dancing between him and the door and throwing her hands up in mock despair at his departure.

378. MCU: *Claudia, on left, blocks the doorway, posing with her right arm raised above her head as she leans against the wall; Sandro, on right with his back to the camera, is looking at her.*

CLAUDIA (*clowningly coy*): No, no, no. You can't leave me all alone in a hotel room.

The camera follows her as she turns seductively away from him toward the left, so that Sandro ends up, slightly amused, on the extreme right, in profile, looking at her. Claudia slides down the wall, in a mock fit of glassy-eyed, amatory bewilderment.

SANDRO (*smiling*): Come down as soon as you are ready. I'll be downstairs for sure, or out in the piazza.

CLAUDIA (*nodding, continuing to play the love-sick fool*): All right. But first you have to tell me that when you leave without me, it's as if you had only one leg. (*The camera stays on her, leaving Sandro off, as she moves toward the left, posing, staring playfully in front of her.*) Go, go and visit the city by yourself.

Sandro reemerges from right and sits in front of her, in extreme right foreground; only the back of his head is visible. A large, horizontal mirror hangs along the wall in the background.

CLAUDIA (*looking down at him, smiling*): You'll limp. (*She steps toward left foreground, hugging herself.*) You must tell me . . . (*She exits left foreground; only her back is visible, reflected in the mirror.*) . . . that you want to kiss my shadow on the walls.

The mirror reflects her image as she turns around to face it, still hugging herself. Only the very top of Sandro's head is visible on the lower right.

379. MCU, *high angle, down on Sandro, in center, who laughs, looking down, then rests his chin on his hands as he looks up toward camera. Around him, on the walls, the shadow of Claudia's arms move sensually as she*

dances to the soundtrack. Sandro's smile fades, and he becomes pre-occupied with his own thoughts.

380. CU: *the back of Claudia's head emerges from the right; she comes into the center, very blond against a dark drape. She turns toward the camera, her head sensually bent, resting on her right, raised shoulder, her eyes closed as she smiles dreamily.*

    CLAUDIA (*playfully*): And then you have to tell me . . .
    The sound van pulls away, and the music ceases. She suddenly straightens up, drops her right shoulder, and becomes serious as she looks intently left, in Sandro's direction.

381. MCU, *high angle, on Sandro, looking pensively down, from behind Claudia's left shoulder as she stands in extreme right foreground. He looks up at her, silent, unsmiling, as if distracted and perhaps even annoyed by her intrusion on his thoughts.*

382. MCU: *from behind a small portion of Sandro's face on extreme left. Only Claudia's torso is visible; then she kneels down and peers questioningly into his face.*

    CLAUDIA (*looking uncertainly at him, her voice broken, almost whispering*): . . . then you have to tell me that you love me.

383. MCU, *as in 381, slight high angle. Sandro looks pensively at Claudia, whose back is in extreme right foreground, then makes an effort to smile. The back of her blond head fills most of the right half of the frame.*

    SANDRO (*smiling more broadly*): You know I do. Why must I tell you?
    (*He brings his face closer to hers and kisses her perfunctorily.*)

384. MCU, *reverse angle, as in 382. Claudia is serious. She does not respond to Sandro's kiss as he moves his face away from hers.*

    CLAUDIA (*whispering, as if to herself*): Of course. (*She sits down on the floor slowly and looks up at him thoughtfully.*) Why . . .

385. MCU: *Sandro is smiling down at her, his face very much foreshortened by the low camera angle (the shot is distinctly from Claudia's point of view).*

386. *As in 384. Sandro, on extreme left, touches Claudia's hair with his left hand as she studies his face thoughtfully.*

    SANDRO: I'll see you later then.
    He gets up and exits from left foreground. From the floor, she watches him leave; she says nothing.

387. MS: *Sandro stops at the door and smiles. The camera holds on the door*

after it closes; Sandro's shadow can be seen through the translucent glass as he moves off.

388. MS: *Claudia continues to sit pensively on the floor. She looks down, then gets up on her knees, putting her hands in her large pockets, shrugs, stands up, and exits right. The camera holds for several beats, in a* temps mort, *on the empty room and the large window in the background.*

389. LS: *the piazza. A large cathedral occupies most of the frame.*[38] *A man in a dark suit is sitting in front of it at a table. He puts some papers down and gets up, crossing frame diagonally and going off left. Behind him, Sandro, in his light suit, looks at the papers on the small table, then turns and walks right, across the piazza. The camera follows him in* MLS *as he approaches the door of a large building. He goes up a few steps, looking up at the door and the sign next to it, looks at his watch, rings the bell, and knocks at the door. Getting no answer, he steps back and looks for signs of life in the building. Finding none, he turns around and leaves, the camera following behind him as he walks down the street toward a horse and carriage.*

SANDRO (*calling*): Hey, listen. . . .[39] (*The coachman comes over.*) Is there anyone here? A caretaker, somebody?

COACHMAN: He must be in the church.

SANDRO: But isn't this a museum?

COACHMAN: How would I know?[40]

390. MCU: *Sandro, on right, and the coachman, facing him in left foreground.*

SANDRO (*turning around and pointing at the door*): It says from 9:30 . . . (*He turns, pointing at his watch.*) . . . to 12:30. It's 10:00 now. . . . (*He steps toward camera, talking to himself, annoyed.*) A fine way of receiving tourists.

He passes in front of the coachman, moving to the left to look at an elaborate iron grillwork door, his hands in his pockets, his back to the camera. The coachman turns around, looking after him.

COACHMAN: Tourists? What tourists? . . . Last year some French women tourists came and went swimming down at the beach in their gip. (*Gesturing below his waist.*)

SANDRO (*turning toward him*): In their what?

COACHMAN: Gip.

SANDRO (*annoyed*): In a *slip!*[41]

The coachman giggles affirmatively.
SANDRO: And so?
COACHMAN: We let them know that they'd better leave. (*Gesturing with his hand.*) Go away. . . .
Sandro grimaces at the provinciality and walks away, exiting right foreground.
391. LS, *low angle, of the bell tower in an ornate baroque building. Sandro walks into left foreground and looks up. The camera follows him as he moves toward background, swinging his keys on their chain; he climbs up onto a low wall as the camera remains at the same angle, and thus his head and upper body go offscreen above. He is looking down at the small table (from shot 389); a bottle of ink, pen, and drawing paper are lying on it. Two men huddle together in conversation on the other side of the square, in front of a beautiful fan vault in the church wall.*
392. MCU: *the upper half of Sandro's body as he looks toward the men, then down at the drawing on the table. He continues swinging his key chain.*
393. CU, *from high angle, of a carefully executed drawing of the vault under a small, open, china ink-bottle, which functions as a paperweight.*
394. CU: *Sandro raises his head and turns his gaze toward the right.*
395. MS: *the actual vault in the building wall—the model for the drawing in 393.*
396. CU: *Sandro looks forward pensively, then lowers his gaze, as if evaluating the drawing, looks up thoughtfully once more, then down again.*
397. CU, *high angle, of the table with the drawing, ink, and pen. Sandro's keys swing back and forth across, dangerously closer and closer to the ink-bottle. Finally they strike the bottle, spilling ink all over the drawing.*
398. MS: *Sandro, from the back, moves from center to right foreground, still swinging his keys. The two men on the other side of the square walk quickly from left background toward him.*
SANDRO (*to them, turning to gesture toward the foreground*): Forgive me[42] . . . I . . .
YOUNGER MAN (*angrily, looking him in the eye*): But you did it deliberately.
SANDRO (*his back to the camera as he tries to placate the young man*): Deliberately! Why would I? No . . . No, really . . .
The young man lunges at Sandro, but his older comrade restrains him,

saying "Hey, come on!" The young man stops, his back to the camera, looking at Sandro, who is on the extreme right. Sandro looks down, embarrassed, and straightens his jacket. The older man stands between them, also looking at Sandro. Sandro looks up, somewhat sheepishly, and moves closer to the young man.

SANDRO: How old are you?[43]

YOUNG MAN (*as his friend smokes a cigarette, looking at him*): Twenty-three.

SANDRO: Twenty-three. Huh. (*He looks down, laughs without humor, and nods to himself. Then, aggressively:*) I was twenty-three once, too, and I got into more fights than you can imagine.

Sandro is distracted by something behind the young man, and looks over the latter's shoulder. Both the young man and his friend turn to see what Sandro is looking at.

399. MLS: *a long line of seminarians in black uniforms, flanked by several priests, files out of the church, crossing frame diagonally from right background toward left foreground.*

400. LS: *the piazza. On left, the long line of boys continues exiting the church; on right, in profile, stand Sandro and the two men, watching them. Sandro pats the young man's shoulder, but he is shrugged off. He turns, steps over a low wall, and walks toward the moving line of boys. He accompanies them down the steps, his white suit in high contrast to the boys' black uniforms.*

401. MS: *lobby of the Hotel Trinacria. In left foreground, a young maid is bent down, cleaning the keys of a piano, making sounds randomly. A squat woman, the owner of the hotel, enters quickly from a door behind her. The camera follows her, thus leaving the girl off, as she moves to the right.*

OWNER (*annoyed at the girl*): Go ahead, play, play . . .

She turns toward the background, pushes the button on the callbox, and is about to proceed down the hall. As Claudia enters right foreground, she turns around and calls to her. Claudia, turning her back to the camera, faces the hotel owner.

OWNER: Miss! (*She comes up to her, standing in* MCU *in front of her.*) Excuse me if I interfere, but I heard you say . . . everyone gets to know everything here . . .

402. MS: *Claudia, on right, looking at the owner, on left, with her back to the camera. The woman touches Claudia as she speaks; Claudia looks at the lady's hand, winces, and edges back uncomfortably.*
   OWNER: That girl you are looking for . . . why don't you try the Home for the Youth of Pergusa?

403. MS, *reverse angle. As the woman talks, the maid enters from left background and stands behind them, watching them and listening as she cleans the mirror.*
   OWNER (*gesturing, sure of herself*): Foreign girls who pass through usually end up there sooner or later.
   Claudia hears the sound of a door opening and turns abruptly around, toward camera.

404. MS: *the owner, in extreme left foreground, and Claudia, right in front of her, both with their backs to the camera; Claudia looks anxiously toward the door in right background. Sandro, smoking, comes through the door. The camera follows as she moves toward him, leaving the owner off.*
   CLAUDIA: How come you're back so soon? (*She walks past him as she prepares to leave the hotel.*) Shall we go?
   Sandro takes her hand and pulls her back into the lobby. As they come into MCU, Claudia stops in extreme right foreground, her back to the camera, as Sandro, still holding her hand, looks at her agitatedly.
   CLAUDIA: But Sandro . . . What's the matter?
   SANDRO (*looking down*): Nothing. (*He steps aside to let her through the door to their room.*) Sorry.

405. MCU: *Claudia enters their room and turns to Sandro. He closes the door behind him and stands in the center, puts the lit cigarette back in his mouth. The camera follows him as he moves closer, leaving Claudia offscreen left. He comes into CU on extreme right and stares toward the right in a preoccupied way, ignoring her presence. From the street can be heard the voice of a peddler yelling "Candies! Candies!" Sandro takes a troubled puff on his cigarette and walks off right. Claudia turns, in CU, and watches him, perplexed.*

406. MS: *the street in Noto, from the balcony of their room in the hotel. Sandro enters left foreground, in profile, onto the narrow balcony. He removes his jacket, then leans against the rail, smoking. The peddler is still hawking his wares. Sandro walks restlessly along the balcony toward the camera,*

coming into MCU. *He throws the cigarette into the street. The camera stays on him as he comes even closer, into* CU. *Then, as he turns around, the back of his head, now facing the camera, is in extreme left foreground. The full majesty and beauty of the piazza and the Immacolata Church are revealed directly across the street. Sandro moves to the center, his back to the camera, closes the shutters, and steps back inside the room. He turns around, so that only the left third of his face is visible against the closed shutters.*

407. MCU: *Claudia, in center, looks at him and smiles, though a bit guardedly. Sandro enters from right foreground, his back to the camera, and tries to kiss her. Claudia throws her head back, smiling but a bit reluctant. Sandro kisses her on the face and neck; she laughs as they struggle playfully, turning around.*

CLAUDIA: Ouch!

Feeling pressed, she pulls away and gasps, her back to the camera. Sandro looks frustrated and even a little desperate. He grabs her again and roughly throws her onto the bed.

408. MCU: *(cut on motion) Claudia falls back on the bed. Sandro gets on top of her.*

CLAUDIA (*protesting*): No, Sandro, please!

SANDRO (*trying to kiss her*): But why?

CLAUDIA (*struggling*): There doesn't have to be a "why."

He kisses her. She puts her hand on his cheek, pushing him back, pulling away and turning onto her side.

CLAUDIA (*still struggling*): What's wrong? (*He kisses her against her will.*) Wait a moment . . . just a moment. . . . (*She turns away, on her side, gasping for breath.*) I feel as if I don't know you.

409. MCU: *Claudia stares into the camera; Sandro's face is in upper right frame, behind her.*

SANDRO (*coldly, upset*): And you're not happy? You have a new adventure!

CLAUDIA (*raising her head slowly, glancing behind, shocked*): But what are you saying?

She sits up and moves back, so that the upper half of her body goes off left frame. Only her legs remain on screen as she sits with her knees up. Sandro's face fills the right half of the frame.

SANDRO: Just joking . . . (*Upset.*) It's impossible to joke with you. (*He moves forward and snuggles his cheek against her legs, stroking them, looking pensively in front of him.*) But explain to me . . .

410. ECU: *Claudia, only her hair, forehead, and eyes visible in the frame.*

SANDRO (*off*): . . . why you don't want to. Huh?

She slowly raises her face, so the rest of her features are visible.

CLAUDIA (*tender but exhausted, shaking her head slightly*): Oh, Sandro! I want what you want, but . . .

Sandro's head, from the back, emerges momentarily onscreen in the lower left foreground, then disappears again as he puts his head down on the bed.

SANDRO: But?

She slowly swings around and gets up, moving toward the window in the

*background, her back to the camera. Then she turns around, crossing her
arms on her chest, her head slightly bent, and looks down.*

CLAUDIA (*softly, but decisively*): Did the owner tell you about that place
near here?

411. MS: *Sandro is lying on the bed, spread out, his eyes closed. He rubs an
eyebrow restlessly.*

SANDRO (*annoyed*): Yes, yes, she started to—but I didn't feel like listening. . . . If we were to take all these rumors seriously . . .

He gets up and moves toward the camera, coming into MCU, *moving
restlessly.*

CLAUDIA (*off, hesitantly*): Yes, it's true, but . . .

*As Sandro moves into left background, his back to the camera, and begins
to put on his jacket, Claudia enters left foreground; the camera stays on
her as she walks toward the right, thus leaving Sandro off.*

CLAUDIA (*turning around toward camera, then pensively toward
right*): Besides, we haven't been in touch with anyone. (*Glancing toward left.*) Not even with Anna's father. . . . We should have called,
sent a telegram. . . . He must feel terribly alone, let's be fair. . . .

*As she turns left to speak to him, Sandro enters foreground; the camera
stays on him, leaving Claudia offscreen, as he crosses to the right.*

SANDRO (*impatiently*): Yes, sure, you're probably right, but we are the
last people who should be around him at this moment. (*Glancing down
to the left.*) And then . . . to call him. . . . Who knows where he is?
(*Adjusting his tie.*) Where?

CLAUDIA (*off, submissively, then almost imploringly*): As you
want. . . . But let's get away from here. Go pack your things.

*The camera pans very slowly left, leaving Sandro off, passing an old
armoire, which occupies the whole screen for a moment, then continues,
revealing Claudia, who stands there sadly, looking toward the right. She
quickly turns and walks toward the background.
Dissolve.*

412. LS: *Sandro's car emerges from a tunnel cut through a mountainside,
on left, and follows a curve on right toward camera.
Dissolve.*

413. MS: *the lobby of the San Domenico Palace Hotel in Taormina. On a
white wall, an old bell on an ornate, cast-iron stand; above it, a picture*

*of old ships and next to it, on right, a barometer. A small mandolin or-
chestra is playing dinner music (through 428). A bellboy enters from left
foreground, goes to the bell and rings it. The camera stays on him as he
turns around, walks back to the left and opens a door whose open wooden
bars on the top reveal Sandro and Claudia, walking side by side toward
the lobby. The boy opens the door; outside, a dark street lit by a couple of
streetlights. The boy bows as Claudia comes through the door, followed
by Sandro. As the boy shuts the door, Claudia sighs, as if in relief. A
middle-aged porter walks into right foreground.*

PORTER (*to Claudia, in center, and Sandro, who stands next to her,
   facing him in profile on the left*): Good evening. Good evening. (*To
   bellboy.*) Show the gentleman to the desk, please.

SANDRO: Thank you.

PORTER: You're welcome.

The bellboy moves to the left, and Sandro follows him.

SANDRO (*as he exits left, to Claudia*): Wait for me.

*Claudia steps forward, looking around. She seems unsure of herself. The
camera follows her as she starts moving toward the right, down the corridor behind an elegantly dressed man. The man bows to a middle-aged
lady in evening dress and says "Marchesa!" A short, bald man coming
the other way turns and eyes Claudia's legs as she continues down the
corridor. She turns the corner and exits right. The short bald man, in left
foreground, addresses a porter, who is offscreen left, pointing back down
the hall:* "Concierge! Who is that doll?"

PORTER (*off*): She just arrived; I don't know.

414. MS: *Claudia runs down a staircase, toward camera, into another hall; in
   the right foreground, a man sitting by a window, reading a newspaper,
   raises his head and also admires her figure as she passes in front of him.
   Claudia exits right foreground.*

415. MCU: *the back of a man on a small balcony contemplating the crowded
   room below. Claudia enters from left foreground, her back to the camera.
   As she looks down, she sees Patrizia below, on extreme left. She turns
   away, toward camera, as if embarrassed.*

PATRIZIA (*calling*): Claudia! Claudia!

*Claudia turns and exits right; the man on the balcony, who wears a
monocle, turns to watch her.*

416. MS: *Patrizia, in right foreground in a black evening dress, walks toward camera to meet Claudia. In the background, there are groups of people sitting and standing in the large, elegant hall.*

   PATRIZIA (*coming into* MCU, *smiling*): Claudia, here I am looking for the others, and I find you!

   As Claudia emerges from the left, her back in CU *to the camera, Patrizia kisses her.*

   CLAUDIA (*softly*): How are you?

   Patrizia examines Claudia's face closely, then laughs and turns away. She finds a chair and sits down. Claudia, her back still to the camera, follows her, standing in front of her. The two women look at each other silently while people walk around, crossing screen and strolling toward camera. Fragments of different conversations can be heard: "It is appalling . . ." "He is charming . . ."

417. MCU, *low angle: Claudia, on left, looking around at the people. Behind and above her, a middle-aged couple (the man with the monocle) lean over the narrow railing, talking loudly in a foreign language.*

   CLAUDIA (*looking up at the balcony, then down, toward Patrizia*): Why don't we see if we can find a quieter place?

418. MCU, *high angle, of Patrizia, sitting in center and looking up toward the left.*

   PATRIZIA (*smiling*): Quieter? (*Cheerfully, as she gets up.*) Yes, sure. *Claudia enters from left foreground, her back to the camera; the camera follows them as they walk toward background, moving through a large crowd of well-dressed people who are talking and dancing. The camera dollies after them. Patrizia takes Claudia's hand and they disappear into the crowd. The camera stays on the dancing couples. In the center, a man pulls a woman by the shoulder away from another woman, with whom she is having an animated conversation.*

419. LS: *Patrizia, followed by Claudia, emerges from left background into an adjacent room; they cross the screen diagonally and come into* MCU, *standing facing each other in the foreground for a moment; Patrizia sits down in an armchair on the right, and Claudia sits on the left.*

420. MCU: *Claudia, on right in profile, looks around and away, as if uneasy; finally she turns toward Patrizia.*

421. MCU: *Patrizia, in center, looks directly into the camera. She smiles slightly, as if she understands what is on Claudia's mind.*

PATRIZIA: You're looking well.

422. MCU, *reverse angle, of Claudia. She stares seriously at Patrizia, then smiles slightly, as if with a sense of relief that Patrizia understands everything.*

423. MS: *Patrizia, on right, and Claudia, on left. Sandro emerges from left background, walking toward them with his hands in his pockets.*
PATRIZIA (*looking up toward him*): Ah, here's Sandro.
He smiles, stops in the center between them, and kisses Patrizia's hand. Claudia looks up at him, and he glances at her.
PATRIZIA: Why don't you two go up and change?
SANDRO (*nodding and turning to Claudia, smiling*): Yes. Let's go.
Patrizia gets up, helped by Sandro; Claudia rises, and the two women walk toward left background, with Sandro following. As they leave the room, a waiter with a tray follows them out.

424. MS: *Patrizia emerges from right background, followed by Sandro and Claudia. They make their way through the room, crowded with dancers, toward camera.*
PATRIZIA (*over her shoulder to Sandro*): Were you able to get good rooms?
SANDRO: Not very, it seems!
PATRIZIA: We should have spoken to Ettore. He always manages to get what he wants.
As they talk, they come into foreground; then the camera tracks with them as they move forward, Patrizia on extreme left, Sandro in the middle, and Claudia on the right, looking away from them, not participating in the conversation.
SANDRO (*putting his hands in his pockets, to Patrizia*): Is Ettore mad at me?
PATRIZIA (*cheerfully, playfully, loudly, in order to be heard over the crowd*): Of course not. . . . And then, as you know, Ettore would forgive you anything as long as you admit that you drive worse than he does.

426. MS: *two elderly ladies, one on right, the other in center, look up smiling as the camera tilts up to show two English gentlemen in a serious conversation.*
ENGLISHMAN (*to his friend, who is smoking and looking in another direction*): What really matters between friends is achieving truth.

426. MS: *Patrizia, Sandro, and Claudia, continuing the track forward of 424.*
    CLAUDIA: How can you stand all this confusion? You always said that too many people annoy you.
    PATRIZIA: You people shouldn't always take me so literally. Actually, I'm quite used to it. First my mother, then my husband—both very dynamic.
    They start climbing some stairs.
    SANDRO (*smiling to Patrizia, as Claudia, preceding them, goes momentarily off left*): Your mother?
    PATRIZIA: Yes. Even I had a mother, you know. A bit of a Prussian, but I had her. My childhood was like a merry-go-round. I was always being whirled from one place to the next: here, there . . .
    Patrizia's back is to the camera as they climb the stairs; Sandro and Claudia smile at her.
    CLAUDIA: Mine, on the other hand, was a very prudent childhood.
    PATRIZIA: What do you mean, "prudent"?
    CLAUDIA (*turning her head back, toward Sandro, and laughing*): It means without any money.
    They all laugh as they reach the top of the stairs and move toward a doorway on left. An unsmiling, middle-aged woman passes them and descends the stairs.
427. LS: *led by the hotel manager, Patrizia, Claudia, and Sandro move toward the camera down a long hall. Two young men in tuxedoes follow them, talking.*
    YOUNG MAN: That idiot . . . cuckold . . .
    As the men disappear left, Sandro turns toward Patrizia.
    PATRIZIA: Until later, then.
    SANDRO: See you later.
    Patrizia turns back to her room. Sandro and Claudia hug, laughing, as they come down the hall, toward camera. The manager, with elaborate gestures, shows them the way. The camera follows them as they move toward the right, going down a stairway, along a white wall. At the end of the stairway, they pass a large, elegant window that opens onto another public room, where a crowd is milling and talking. Claudia and Sandro follow the manager to the right, turning their backs to the camera to enter the doorway of their suite.

428. MS: *camera from inside the suite. The manager enters the door in center background, gesturing with professional ceremony as he shows Sandro and Claudia in. He turns on the light and steps toward camera, coming into* MCU.

MANAGER: Please, please come in.

Again the manager waves his arm in elaborate invitation. The camera stays on the manager, leaving Sandro and Claudia off, as he crosses toward the left and prepares to open the draperies, with graceful if mechanical precision.

CLAUDIA (*off*): Leave them drawn, please.

The camera follows him as he crosses from left to right; the camera picking up Claudia and Sandro again on left.

MANAGER: As you wish, madam.[44] (*He checks the closet, presumably to see if there are enough hangers, and then turns around, bowing to Claudia on left.*) Do you need anything? Is everything all right?

CLAUDIA: Yes, thank you.

MANAGER (*stepping between them to leave the room*): Excuse me.

As he leaves, Claudia and Sandro turn around, watching him as he crosses the hall of the suite to open the other bedroom door. Claudia silently mimics his elaborate gestures and gait.

SANDRO (*looking at him, his back to the camera, with his arms crossed behind his back*): Thank you, thank you.

MANAGER: If everything is all right, then . . . with your permission . . . Good evening.

SANDRO: . . . Evening.

As he exits right, Claudia breaks into laughter. Sandro laughs also, turning to her.

SANDRO: They could have used a robot.

He moves toward her, takes her face in his hands, smiling tenderly as he is about to kiss her, but there is a knock at the door. He turns and says, "Come in!" Claudia turns to the camera, sighing, then turns around toward the background. A porter comes in with their bags.

SANDRO: Ah, yes, you can put that one here, the other one over there.

Claudia bends down to take one of the bags. Sandro puts his arm around Claudia's shoulder, sneaks a kiss, then goes to the porter, who has re-emerged from background, and tips him.

PORTER: Thank you.

The porter exits right; Sandro takes off his jacket and disappears into the door to his room, in center background. Claudia picks up the suitcase, holding it horizontally with both hands in front of her, and walks toward camera into her room. It is so heavy, and she is so exhausted, that as she comes through the door, she drops it.

429. MS: *Claudia kneels over the open suitcase, looks up with a sigh, and then throws her nightgown onto the bed and puts her slippers next to it. Sandro leaves his room, presumably on his way to the bathroom. The camera maintains its low level, so that only the bed, the nightstand, the lower part of the door, and Claudia's and Sandro's legs are shown as Claudia calls him. His legs stop and hers approach his.*

CLAUDIA: Listen . . .

SANDRO: Yeah . . .

430. MCU: *Claudia, on right, over Sandro's right shoulder.*

CLAUDIA (*leaning against the door, her head bent on her shoulder, looking at him with evident fatigue*): . . . try not to get too involved tomorrow.

431. MCU, *reverse angle: Claudia's head, from the back, now in extreme right foreground; Sandro, in front of her, on left, looking down aimlessly.*

SANDRO (*glancing at Claudia, changing the subject*): Aren't you going to change? (*He looks back down, pensively.*)

CLAUDIA (*softly*): Didn't you say you wanted to quit working with Ettore?

Sandro starts moving toward the bathroom on left, thus partially disappearing behind the door and a plant in left foreground. He turns on the bathroom light.

SANDRO (*stopping and stepping back into frame*): Yes, sure, I did say so.

He disappears into the bathroom; she follows and leans against the door, on extreme left, under the plant, her back to the camera.

432. *The wall and the bathroom door on right. Noise of running water. Claudia enters from left foreground in* CU, *crossing frame in profile, then turning toward camera as she leans against the door.*

SANDRO (*off*): Brr! It's ice-cold!

CLAUDIA (*looking down, pensively*): Sandro!

SANDRO (*humming off, cheerfully*): Yes?

CLAUDIA (*moving farther, to the extreme right. Her voice is sleepy*): I'm not coming down.

SANDRO (*off*): Why not?

CLAUDIA (*turning her gaze to the right, sighing*): Too sleepy.

SANDRO (*off*): Sleep is something one has to learn to overcome.

CLAUDIA (*smiling*): Have you?

SANDRO (*off*): Yes, I have. As a young man. I never slept. (*As he talks, Claudia turns her head to the right, smiling tenderly. She touches her lip with a finger then touches it to the door. She smiles and puts her cheek against the door.*) And I had friends who slept even less than I. The first one to go to bed had to pay a fine. We didn't do anything wrong. We'd go to a movie, and when it was over we'd go to a café, talk, . . . (*Claudia turns around and goes to her room. With her back to the camera, she begins to undress.*) . . . then just sit on a bench somewhere and listen to some drunk for a while, or watch bill-posters work, or a herd of goats. Then we'd run up to the market, or we'd wake up other friends or a girl by calling under her windows.

Claudia, on right, kneels down beside the suitcase, tries to find her nightgown, but, totally exhausted, curls up on the rug, her head resting on the open suitcase, and closes her eyes. (Offscreen, music for bass and mandolins begins; it is the same rustic, playful, but slightly mysterious theme which began the film. The music continues through 435.)

433. MS: *Claudia's room, with the door open in center background. In foreground, Claudia lies on the floor. Sandro enters background and stands in the doorway, drying his face with a towel. The camera tilts up to Sandro, leaving Claudia off, as he steps toward the foreground, smiling down at her.*

SANDRO (*the camera tilts down as he kneels next to Claudia*): Tell me, are you really so sleepy?

CLAUDIA (*without moving from her position*): Mmmmmmm . . .

SANDRO (*looking at her tenderly, stroking her hair with one finger*): What time d'you want to get up tomorrow?

CLAUDIA: Late.

SANDRO: Late, eh?

CLAUDIA (*in a sleepy voice*): Very late.

SANDRO (*putting his hands on her shoulder, helping her up*): Come on, then, let's go night-night.

She gets up slowly, leaning heavily against him; he puts his arm around
her shoulder and leads her to the door in the background. The camera
remains as before, so that they can now be seen in low-angle MS, from
the back, her head resting on his shoulder. He musses her hair affectionately; she exits left into the bathroom, and he goes back to his room.

434. MS: *Sandro crosses frame from right to left, coming into his room; he
goes to his suitcase, gets some clothes, turns toward camera in* MCU,
takes off his robe, and begins to dress.

SANDRO (*calling, smiling*): Do you know that when I was a boy I
wanted to be a diplomat? (*Turning to the right.*) Can you imagine me a
diplomat? (*He turns his back to the camera, putting on his shirt.*)
Strange, but I never imagined myself rich. I saw myself living in a
rented room somewhere . . . (*Gesturing, with irony.*) . . . full of
genius . . .

435. MS: *Claudia emerges sleepily from the door in the background in a long
white nightgown.*

SANDRO (*off*): Instead, I have two houses . . . one in Rome, the other in Milan. As for being a genius, I never got into the habit. What do you think?

CLAUDIA (*looking down, seriously, then taking off her wristwatch and winding it*): I have a different view. (*She turns her head as he enters through the door in the background, behind her, buttoning his sleeve. She turns quickly toward him, then to the left.*) In any case, it's better if we talk about it some other time. Would you mind turning that light out?

Sandro goes to the background to turn off a light, then comes back and looks at her; she gets into bed without looking at him. He tucks her in; the camera moves to the left so as to focus on Claudia's face on the pillow against the ornate iron bedstead. She watches him lovingly, with a playful half-smile, as he bends over her.

SANDRO: Good night, love. (*He bends down and kisses her.*)

CLAUDIA (*grasping his arm, looking at him intently. He sits down on the bed, in center foreground, his back to the camera*): Tell me you love me.

SANDRO (*after a moment of silence, seriously*): I love you.

CLAUDIA: Tell me again.

SANDRO: I don't love you.

The camera remains on Claudia as Sandro gets up and then goes out of frame.

CLAUDIA (*quietly, looking down*): I deserve that.

The camera stays on Claudia as Sandro touches her nose affectionately and says in assent, "Mmmm," then follows him to the right, leaving Claudia off, as he leaves the room, closing the door. The door remains shut for a moment, then opens very slowly. Sandro's face emerges and peeks around the door.

SANDRO (*smiling*): It's not true. I love you. (*He leaves, closing the door.*)

436. MS: *a small mandolin orchestra is playing (a different tune from that played offscreen in previous shots). The lounge is full of people. Sandro enters from left; the camera follows him as he crosses in front of the orchestra and stops at a bar on the right. Couples and waiters move in the foreground, walking away from the bar. Fragments of their conversation, in several languages, mix with the music. Sandro picks up a drink, downs it, and walks toward the foreground, lighting a cigarette. He stands in front of the orchestra, on left, looking the crowd over and*

smoking. Behind him, Gloria Perkins, the girl who caused the distur-
bance in Messina, enters left, crosses behind Sandro, and stops on the
right, where she turns and looks seductively at him. He turns around,
returning her gaze, then turns his back to her and exits left. She exits
right, while the camera remains on the orchestra and passing guests.
A tall woman in a black evening dress is drinking at the bar.
VOICE (*in English*): Hello, Mary!
TALL WOMAN (*turning around*): Hello!
437. MS: *a woman in left foreground, her back to the camera, is examining*
a large painting depicting an old man suckling the breast of a young
woman.[45] *Sandro, smoking, enters right in* MCU; *the woman turns to look*
at him, then turns back to the painting. Sandro glances at her and the
painting. She returns his glance and smiles. Then he looks toward the
left, and his smile fades as if he recognizes someone. He sets his jaw, and
exits quickly. The woman turns around and follows him with her eyes.
438. MS: *a drawing room, visible through a doorway. A group of people are*

*sitting around a little table. A waiter exits, bowing. Sandro enters right
foreground, his back to the camera, which tracks foreward with him.
Ettore gets up from his armchair and comes to meet him.*
ETTORE (*shaking hands with Sandro*): Ah, at last!
SANDRO: How are you?
ETTORE: Come, I'll introduce you to my friends.
SANDRO (*hesitating*): I'll catch up with you later. I want to take a look
  around first.
ETTORE: I assume you're going to be available from tomorrow morning
  on. If you don't give me some figures to work with, how am I ever to
  manage? See you later.
*Ettore walks back to his friends without waiting for Sandro's reply. Sandro
turns toward camera and looks around; fragments of conversation in
English are audible ("And what happened then?" "Oh, they seem to be
getting along very well."). Sandro turns to the right, and the camera
follows him. He passes below some french doors opening into a room
a half-floor above the lounge. Gloria Perkins comes into the doorframe,
behind a large, ornate vase, and looks around the lounge below her.
Sandro stops in extreme right foreground. They stare at each other.*

439. MS, *reverse angle: camera above Gloria Perkins's shoulder, her head in
    extreme right foreground as she looks at Sandro, below her, smoking,
    staring at her pensively. People move about; conversations in different
    languages are heard. Gloria Perkins exits quickly left frame. Sandro
    stands and watches her leave, then turns back slowly and disappears into
    the background. A woman's voice says: "Je suis en voyage de plaisir."
    The camera stays on the scene below: on the right, a dancing couple sits
    down; while on the left, another man helps a woman get up from her seat,
    takes her by the arm, and walks off with her. They are conversing in
    French.*

440. MS: *a dark, empty lounge with a television. A large window is in the
    background, through which an arcade is visible. Sandro enters left, his
    back to the camera, moving slowly into the room, smoking. He turns his
    head to the extreme left foreground. The flickering light from the tele-
    vision, offscreen, is reflected in his face. Explosions and other noises
    issue from it and mix with the mandolin orchestra music from the other
    lounge. He sits on a couch in the center and watches the television
    screen. Then he slaps his hands together decisively, as if having made*

a decision, gets up, and leaves the room, exiting right foreground. The camera stays on the empty room for a moment.

441. CU: *Claudia's right hand stretched diagonally on a pillow, a ring on her middle finger. The room is dark. Forlorn clarinet music begins off, not unlike that played during the search for Anna on Lisca Bianca (continuing to 443). The camera moves up to her head as she pulls the covers over her mouth and nose. Her eyes are open and look about blankly. She sits up, very slowly, turning her face from camera as she looks at the empty pillow next to her. Her head falls back as she looks emptily at the ceiling. A clock strikes the late hour. She pulls herself up for a moment, then lies down again.*

442. MCU: *Claudia lying in bed, from a different angle, her head on the pillow. The room is brighter. The music is heavier, more oppressive. She turns her eyes to the right, staring pensively, then restlessly throws her pillow on the floor. The camera tilts up slightly, thus revealing the ornate bedstead. On her stomach, Claudia stretches out and turns on the light. She looks at her alarm clock, puts it back, then falls back on the pillow, face down, as if unable to move, her right hand still holding the clock. Then she gets up, her back to the camera, opens the door, and goes to Sandro's room. She opens the door, leans against the wall in the doorway looking in, then walks inside. She looks around; he isn't there. From the open suitcase she pulls out one of his shirts. She lets it fall over her face, kissing it and hugging it. Then, in a change of mood, she throws it into the suitcase and wanders back to her room. The camera stays on her as she leans against the wall, in MCU, nervously tracing horizontal lines across the door with her fingers. She reaches a large mirror, and we see both the original and the reflected image of her face on the right. She stares at herself, raising her eyebrows and making funny faces. A church-bell strikes the time. Then, bored and upset, she turns her back to the mirror. From the reflection in the mirror, we see her return to the bed and sit down, bending her head and shoulders, as if in pain. She raises her head and turns off the lamp.*

443. MCU, *high angle: Claudia's head, from the back, in left foreground. She is holding her watch in her left hand, her arm propped on the nightstand. She has a magazine in front of her, and her right hand is writing on a page that shows the photograph of a woman.*

CLAUDIA (*counting aloud and writing in the magazine, as if trying to*

fall asleep): . . . Twelve, thirteen, fourteen, fifteen, sixteen, seventeen, eighteen, nineteen, twenty. (*She sighs deeply and scribbles through the picture, then drops the watch, puts the pencil down dejectedly, turns her head toward the camera, coming into* CU *on left. She props her head on her left hand for a moment, then lies back, nervously touching her lips, hair, and neck. She starts counting again, very slowly.*) One, two, three, four, five, six, seven, eight . . . (*Whispering, faster.*) . . . twelve, thirteen, fourteen . . .

444. LS: *daybreak through a french door opening onto the balcony; beyond, distant mountains in the ghostly light of dawn. Claudia enters from left foreground, her back to the camera, and slowly goes to the balcony and looks out. She turns around and returns slightly bent, her hands clasped together, as if she were in pain. The sound of train wheels clacking by on the tracks that run along the sea. The camera follows her as she moves to the right and goes out through another french door onto the balcony. From behind her shoulder we can see the quiet sea outside and a palm tree on the right. Claudia crosses in the foreground and exits right, while*

the camera remains for a moment in a temps mort *on the landscape outside the balcony window.*

445. LS: *a very long corridor in the hotel, with an arched ceiling, completely empty. Claudia emerges from the far background and runs the whole length of the corridor toward camera. As she gets closer, her footsteps ring more loudly on the tile floor. She stops at a certain door and goes in.*

446. MS: *Patrizia lies asleep in bed, in the dark. Noise of the door closing.*

CLAUDIA (*off*): Patrizia! Patrizia!

PATRIZIA (*sits up, holding the covers over her bare chest. She reaches for the light and turns it on, yelling*): Huh?

CLAUDIA (*abruptly entering frame left, her back to the camera, and leaning over toward Patrizia*): Where's Ettore?

PATRIZIA (*fully awake, looking at her*): He must be asleep in the other room.

CLAUDIA (*agitated, pressing*): Could you see if Sandro is with him? He's not in his room. Forgive me, but . . .

The camera stays on Patrizia as she gets out of bed, looking up toward Claudia without saying a word. She passes in front of Claudia (who is left off-frame) and proceeds to the door of the other room, smoothing her hair down. She opens it and goes over to the bed in left background. Claudia reenters from right and stands with her back to the camera in right foreground.

PATRIZIA (*leaning over the bed*): Ettore!

ETTORE (*off, sleepy*): What's the matter?

PATRIZIA: Nothing, nothing. I was looking for Sandro.

ETTORE (*off, impatiently*): And you're looking for him here? Ask Claudia.

PATRIZIA (*turning around, calmly*): Certainly.

As she hears this exchange, Claudia quickly goes behind the door, her hand over her mouth, upset. On the left side of the frame, Patrizia comes back toward camera, closes the door, and stands in front of Claudia.

CLAUDIA (*her hand over her mouth, looking at Patrizia, almost on the verge of tears*): Patrizia, I'm afraid.

PATRIZIA (*lightly, calmly*): Don't tell me about it. At night I have nightmares . . .

CLAUDIA (*nervously, playing with the collar of her dress, sighing*): No! I'm afraid Anna's come back. I feel she's come back. I feel they're together again.

PATRIZIA (*moving to the left, putting her hand on Claudia's shoulder*): What's gotten into you? We would have known if she were back. Sandro's probably out in the garden getting some fresh air . . . (*Claudia moves quickly away, exiting right; Patrizia turns toward camera, looking affectionately after her.*) . . . watching the dawn. (*Smiling.*) It would be amusing to discover . . .

447. MCU: *the top of Claudia's head, in profile and turned toward the left, her hair covering her face as she sits down, her chin on her hand.*

PATRIZIA (*off*): . . . that he's really a sentimentalist after all. (*Patrizia's hand enters frame right, patting Claudia's head.*) Listen, try not to get obsessed about this. (*As Claudia raises her head, her hand to her mouth, pensively looking toward the left, the camera moves slightly toward the right, thus revealing Patrizia on extreme right, in profile, as she looks affectionately at Claudia.*) Go and get some sleep. (*Both faces are in tight close-up.*)

CLAUDIA (*taking her hand away from her mouth, staring emptily toward camera*): A few days ago, when I felt Anna might be dead, I felt like I was dead, too. (*Patrizia looks down pensively. Claudia brings her hand to her mouth, still staring in the same direction, while her voice becomes colder, as if sadly facing the facts.*) Now I don't even cry. (*Patrizia leans her head on Claudia's shoulder, staring thoughtfully toward the left.*) Now I am afraid she might be alive. (*She turns her head slightly toward the right and nods to herself, in self-irony.*) Everything is becoming so damned easy, . . . (*She sighs.*) . . . even depriving myself of pain.

Patrizia nods and smiles sympathetically. Claudia gets up, quickly crossing in front of Patrizia and going off right.

PATRIZIA (*her head turned toward the right, reassuringly*): It never helps to be melodramatic.

CLAUDIA (*reentering frame from right, but now in the background, near the door*): You're right. (*She walks toward foreground, playing nervously with her hands.*) Why should I cry? (*Patrizia turns her head completely toward her; she turns around, standing in front of the door, looking down, on the verge of tears.*) I'm tired of being like this. (*She resolutely opens the door and leaves.*)

448. MCU to LS: *Claudia's head as she closes the door; the camera follows her as she starts walking back up the long, empty corridor. Suddenly, she begins to run toward the far background.*

449. MS: *a doorway and the stairs that lead into the large lounge. Claudia enters and walks down the stairs; the camera follows her as she walks through the lounge. It is deserted and messy from the night's festivities. Chairs are scattered about, ashtrays full, paper on the floor. She walks through a doorway in the far background, begins to run again, hesitates a moment, then turns and exits right background.*

450. MS: *another large room, empty, and in the same state of disorder. Pale morning light comes through the windows in the background. Claudia enters left, walks through the room, crossing frame to the right, looking around. The surf can be heard outside. She goes out onto the balcony in right background, looks out, then comes back into the room and starts to run, crossing the screen and exiting left. The camera stays on the empty room for a moment.*

451. MLS: *an immense dining room. Claudia enters from left foreground and walks along a very large table covered with a white tablecloth, toward background. The camera pans slowly to the right (thus leaving Claudia momentarily off), showing the austere room: a fireplace in the background, couches in front of it; some smaller tables scattered on the right, next to the huge table that dominates the left foreground. Claudia re-emerges in extreme left background, hesitating in front of the fireplace, as if she has heard something.*

452. MS: *over the back of Claudia's shoulder. She stands in extreme left foreground. A couple are making love on a couch in front of her. As the man is kissing the woman, he suddenly sees Claudia and looks up; it is Sandro. The woman turns her head toward Claudia; it is Gloria Perkins.*

453. MCU: *Claudia, staring aghast at them. She stumbles backward.*

454. CU, *slight high angle: Gloria, in the foreground, stares up at Claudia; behind her, on left, Sandro looks up with an expression of fear and then puts his face down, behind Gloria's, as if to hide. Gloria lies down. The nipple of one of her breasts is uncovered by the movement; she slowly covers it again.*

455. MCU, *as in 453. Claudia backs farther and farther away, shaking her head in disbelief, gasping, bewildered. She turns left and runs off.*

456. LS: *she runs through the dining room from left background toward camera, exiting left foreground.*

457. MCU: *Sandro is on right, still prone; Gloria, on left, lies leaning on her arm, looking in the same direction. Then she turns toward him and caresses his cheek.*

GLORIA (*seductively*): Dear . . .

Upset, he slaps her hand away. The camera stays on him (leaving Gloria off) as he gets up, brushes his jacket with his hand, and straightens his tie, still staring toward the left.

GLORIA (*off, except for her hand in extreme left foreground caressing his sleeve*): Aren't you going to leave me a little souvenir? Only a little souvenir?

He looks down at her coldly, looks up again, takes some money out of his pocket, drops it contemptuously, and walks off briskly, exiting left foreground.

458. MCU, *low angle: the money is lying on the couch between Gloria's legs, which alone occupy the frame, stretched out along the sofa. Her legs move sensually as she tries to pick up the money with her feet. The back of her head comes into frame as she pulls herself up.*

459. LS: *Claudia, in left background, runs toward camera out of the hotel courtyard through the entrance archway. She turns right, crossing left to right, running along the wall and exiting right.*

460. LS: *she enters right and runs across an elevated open square until she reaches the guardrail on the left side. She stops and leans against it. A figure is walking slowly up the road on the left; he stops and looks up at her.*

461. LS, *high angle: the bombed-out tower of the San Domenico church lies beyond the railing. A bench is on the right. Claudia emerges from the left and walks very slowly toward the right, holding onto the railing. She stops, her head bowed.*

462. MS: *from behind Claudia, who is standing with her back to the camera in extreme right foreground. She watches the trees blowing in the wind.*

463. LS *as in 459, but now it is Sandro who is coming out of the hotel courtyard. He walks through the archway, stops, and looks around. Then he turns to the right and starts walking along the wall.*

464. MCU: *Sandro walking toward camera along the old wall. He looks around, then down, disconsolate. The noise of a dog barking and a car driving off. He picks aimlessly at the bark of a tree in extreme left foreground.*

465. CU, *low angle: the sky and the ruined building on the right. Claudia's face emerges from the right, sobbing. She looks up, then down. She forces herself to stop crying. The noise of Sandro's slow, heavy steps can be heard, off. She breathes heavily in an effort to pull herself together.*

466. LS: *Claudia is standing with her back to the camera in center background against the railing, the ruined church beyond. Sandro emerges from left foreground and walks slowly toward the right. He doesn't have the courage to look at Claudia, behind him. He stops as he reaches the bench in right foreground, then slowly comes around it, looking downward, and slumps down. A boat whistle sounds in the harbor. Behind him, still standing in left background, Claudia turns toward him and very slowly moves toward the bench, coming up behind him.*

467. CU: *Sandro is bent over, weeping. As Claudia comes up behind him (with only the lower part of her body visible), Sandro half-turns toward her, but looks down again, sobbing.*

468. MCU, *low angle: Claudia looks down at him silently and compassionately. Sandro continues weeping, off.*
469. *As in 467. Sandro still weeping. He lifts his head and wipes away his tears with his knuckles. He tries to turn toward her, but cannot.*
470. *As in 468. Plaintive clarinet music can be heard over Sandro's sobs. Claudia lowers her eyes.*
471. CU *of Claudia's hand on the back of the bench. It opens and closes, as if trying to comfort Sandro, but fails to touch him.*
472. *As in 468. Claudia looks down as before. She moves her eyes to the right, then up, then down again.*
473. *As in 471. The hand tries again to comfort Sandro; it moves up, now without hesitation, and caresses the back of his head. The music becomes louder and more dissonant. Claudia's hand remains open on the back of his head, as if supporting it.*
474. LS *from behind them. Claudia stands on left by the bench, her hand still on the back of Sandro's head. Sandro is slumped over in grief. In the far background the enormous peak of Mt. Etna. The dissonant music gets louder, tympani marking its climax, as Claudia gently strokes his head. Fade out.*

END

Notes on the
Continuity Script

1. The apartment, on an islet in the middle of the Tiber, belonged to Lady Montague, who had been go-between between Princess Margaret and Peter Townsend. See Chiaretti's "The Adventure of *L'avventura*" (translated in the Grove Press edition), pp. 185–186.
2. This shot violates the "axis of action" or "180° rule": if the rule had been observed, Sandro should have been on the left, since he stood to Anna's left in the preceding shot. See the Introduction, above, p. 13, for a discussion.
3. Using the formal pronoun.
4. Still using the formal.
5. See Antonioni's reminiscence of the waterspout in "About Myself and One of My Films," "Contexts," below.
6. Using the formal form.
7. Using the formal.
8. Sandro addresses the old man with the second-person plural formal, a form characteristic of Southern Italian.
9. By convention, Sandro should have entered from the right, since he went off left in the previous shot.
10. The cut here is in the motion begun by Claudia in 175, except, of course, that the motion is reversed, too.
11. He uses the familiar form.
12. Using the formal.

13. Using the familiar form.
14. The Villa Grevina Palagonia of Bagheria was converted into a set for the purpose. See the description of its preparation in "The Adventure of *L'avventura*" (Grove Press edition, pp. 200–201).
15. The lieutenant paternalistically addresses the fisherman in the familiar form.
16. Using the familiar form.
17. Using the formal.
18. A noncommissioned officer in the Italian navy.
19. Using the familiar.
20. Using the formal.
21. For the first time, Sandro addresses Claudia in the familiar form.
22. Claudia also uses the familiar form from here on.
23. Using the formal.
24. Using the formal.
25. Using the formal.
26. The villa used as the set belongs to Prince Niscemi. The woman playing the Princess is actually Princess Lampedusa.
27. San Siro is a stadium in Milan, well known to Italian soccer fans. The reference suggests that Ettore is from Milan, a point which his accent, his "practical" outlook and attitude also seem to confirm.
28. Using the formal.
29. Using the familiar.
30. Using the familiar.
31. Using the formal. It is important to note that the difference in the form of address used by the two characters (Giulia uses the familiar second-person pronoun, Goffredo the formal) conforms to the general custom in which a younger person always addresses an older in the formal, whether or not he/she is being addressed in the familiar.
32. Using the formal.
33. Using the formal.
34. Using the familiar.
35. The "abandoned town" has been identified as one of the Cassa del Mezzogiorno towns near Caltanisetta, Sicily. See Joseph Bennett, "The Essences of Being," *Hudson Review* 14 (1961), 432–436.
36. This scene takes place near the tunnel of Santa Panagia.
37. A popular song of the Sixties. The lyrics go: "No! No! I'll never leave you. I'll be in the sweetest of torments, but I'll never lose you. No! No!

I'll never leave you. . . . I'll always hate you, but no, I'll never leave you. . . . I'll be in the sweetest torment."

38. The Chiesa Madre in Noto.
39. Using the formal.
40. The coachman has a strong Sicilian accent and occasionally uses dialect.
41. The coachman mispronounces "slip," which means "bikini" in both French and Italian.
42. Using the formal.
43. Sandro switches to the informal, confidential form.
44. Treating Claudia as the wife.
45. The theme of the painting is "Roman Charity." The old man is Cimon, who has been sentenced to death by starvation. He is visited in prison by his daughter, Pero, who suckles him to keep him alive (see Valerius Maximus, *Factorum . . . libri,* IX.5.4). Thanks are due to William Arrowsmith and Svetlana Alpers for helping me identify this theme, thereby correcting the erroneous interpretation that I offered in *Antonioni, or the Surface of the World,* pp. 100–101.

Variants and
Omissions
from the Shooting
Script

Since the shooting script of *L'avventura,* which was edited by Tomasso Chiaretti, has been translated and published in English, and since the Grove Press edition lists scenes omitted and varied in the actual film, it seems unnecessary to repeat that listing here. What is not available in English, however, and what must interest every student of Antonioni's work, is information provided by Chiaretti about preproduction intentions that were changed before the publication of the shooting script.[1] We summarize Chiaretti's account.

The film was originally planned to begin with a short scene introducing Claudia's home and family, visibly petty bourgeois, even a bit vulgarly so. For a variety of reasons, the decision to delete this scene seems wise: Anna must be the dominant female presence at the beginning of the film to being into sharper focus its major themes: the crisis in the moral life, the fragility of emotions, the idea of the double, the *giallo alla rovescia,* and so on.

From the inception of the film Antonioni had to defend against the strenuous demands of collaborators that some hint be given the audience about Anna's fate. At one point he actually agreed, reluctantly, to a scene in which Claudia, left alone by Sandro in her room in the Hotel San Domenico as he amused himself in the lobby below, was to receive a telephone call about the discovery of Anna's

---

1. Tommaso Chiaretti, "Postilla alla sceneggiatura," in *L'avventura,* 2nd ed. (Bologna: Cappelli, 1977), pp. 167–174.

drowned body. (Another possibility that was debated was that Anna should simply show up calmly at the San Domenico, and refuse to explain her absence.) A fortunate aesthetic consequence of the financial rescue of the company, left stranded on Panarea by the original producer, was that Cino del Duca, the new producer, supported Antonioni's original plan for a *giallo alla rovescia*—no culprit, no smoking gun, not even a body.

Chiaretti describes two scenes from the original screenplay that were actually shot but were not edited into the film. One was to have occurred in a dilapidated and abandoned fishing village, Santa Panagia. (This sequence perhaps corresponds to shots 338–346.) The second was to have occurred on the road to Taormina (hence just before shot 412): Claudia and Sandro were to have met a bizarre figure, a minstrel of some sort, who delays their trip by engaging them in a curious infantile game.

Other sequences, planned but not shot, included the following. After Anna and Sandro make love in his apartment, there was to have been a scene in which they are shown exiting the building (just after shot 33): Anna looks as morose as before, and Claudia and Sandro have a slightly sarcastic interchange. Then, on the road toward the south, as dusk falls and Sandro turns on the lights of his car, Claudia begs him to leave them off because the twilight is so beautiful. But that causes an accident in which they are almost killed: the car misses a curve and plunges through a hole in a wall that had been made by a previous collision. Claudia and Sandro are shaken up, but Anna finds the whole incident amusing.

In another unshot sequence, Sandro searches for Anna on a nearby island. There is no news, and he is advised that the current from Lisca Bianca can take twenty-four or more hours to arrive at the island. He goes to a barbershop and gets a shave. The carabinieri who have accompanied him find not Anna but rather a crate of contraband cigarettes beached on the shore. They confiscate it from the loudly protesting wretches who inhabit the island (the Grove Press edition lists this sequence as the alternative to shots 183–201).

Also unshot was a sequence involving an interview with a midwife reported to have talked with a nervous girl on the bus to Noto (alternative to shots 338–346).[2] The midwife is not very friendly, immediately denying that she did anything improper. She tells them that if she should see the girl again, she would warn her that they are looking for her.

2. The sequence is published in the Grove Press edition (1969), pp. 172–176.

The biggest change is the ending. In the original version, Sandro's betrayal was to have taken place under much seedier circumstances. The couple stop not at the luxurious Hotel San Domenico but rather at a third-class hotel, "isolated and poorly lit," some miles from Taormina. As in the film, they have two rooms and Claudia immediately goes to sleep in sheer fatigue. The femme fatale, however, is not the prostitute Gloria Perkins, but a relatively unattractive though lecherous chambermaid who comes to Sandro's room to replace a light bulb. At dawn, raucous voices and shrieks awaken Claudia; she goes to Sandro's room and finds his bed unslept in. A man tries to stop her from descending the stairs to see what is happening in the lobby, but she disregards his warning. As she reaches the stairs she witnesses below a sordid spectacle: three men—one of them Sandro—are having their papers examined by the police as three half-dressed women—one of them the chambermaid who replaced his light bulb—stand by angrily. The proprietor of the hotel is trying to persuade the police that he is not guilty of pandering, but the police are dubious. When the police officer sees the beautiful Claudia whom Sandro had left in their room for the tawdry allure of the chambermaid, he scratches his head in amazement. The rest of the sequence is like the actual film's ending.

Contexts

Contents

Two kinds of contexts are important for any complete edition of *L'avventura:* an account of the film's production history and the extensive remarks made by Antonioni about the film's intentions.

Production History

The fascinating and sometimes harrowing history of the production has been narrated in detail by the late Tommaso Chiaretti under the title "L'avventura dell'*Avventura*" ("The Adventure of *L'avventura*").[1] What emerges from this and other sources[2] amply justifies Antonioni's often-quoted remark that *L'avventura* was the most difficult and demanding of his films, even though in his earlier career he had become used to working under unfavorable conditions. Thanks to his old friend Gino Rossi, who had been instrumental in backing *Cronaca di un amore*, Antonioni had apparently secured ample financing from a Roman film company called Imera, with additional support from a Sicilian concern, Faro Film. The script (by Antonioni himself, with Bartolini and Guerra) was more or less completed by the end of the spring of 1959. Scheduled for July 18 of the same year, the first takes were shot only in September because of various difficulties. In the meantime, Art Director Piero Poletto had left for Southern Italy with a small crew in order to choose the locations and to prepare the settings (the fisherman's hut, for instance, was built on the deserted island of Lisca Bianca). Antonioni planned to shoot the movie in its actual narrative sequence: the departure from Rome, the cruise on the yacht, the stopover, Anna's disappearance, the search. When production started, the ending had not even been decided: the producers wanted either Anna's return or some positive evidence of what had happened, maybe just a phone call informing both the searchers and the audience that her dead body had been found somewhere. Antonioni insisted that the girl was to fade away in a mist of indifference and oblivion. But even in his own version, the final scenes differed from the conclusion as it now appears. With a slight alteration of the original plan, shooting began with the shots in Sandro's apartment, actually the Isola Tiberina apartment belonging to Lady Montague, who had granted permission for one day of filming—and who put up with an invasion that lasted much longer. After completing the dialogue between Anna and her father and the scene in the art gallery (another one,

1. See his edition of the shooting script: Michelangelo Antonioni, in collaboration with Elio Bartolini and Tonino Guerra, *L'avventura*, edited by Tommaso Chiaretti (Bologna: Cappelli, 1977), pp. 29–44. Most of this account appears in English (translated by Salvatore Attanasio) in the Grove Press edition of *L'avventura* (edited by George Amberg and Robert Hughes; New York 1969).
2. See Aldo Bernardini's *Michelangelo Antonioni* (Milano: "I 7," 1967), pp. 151ff.

taking place in Claudia's lower middle-class home and originally appearing in the script, was discarded), the crew left for the Lipari Islands, settling in Panarea (250 inhabitants, three churches, no electricity, no telephone, no hot water, only one small boardinghouse and a couple of primitive "restaurants"), from which they embarked daily to film on deserted Lisca Bianca. Transportation between the two islands was difficult, especially because the yacht promised by Faro and Imera did not arrive. Only an old rowboat was available to carry the actors, the crew, cameras, electric generators, and other equipment back and forth. Since the yacht was also essential for the cruise scenes, the first takes in Lisca Bianca were those of the search for Anna, followed by the scene inside the hut. Later the yacht materialized, but it was available for ten days only, just enough to shoot half of the necessary footage. What was worse, when the yacht left, so did all contact with Imera and Faro. Further, the weather conditions became more and more unbearable. One really wonders how production continued when the technicians went on strike because of the shortage of food and drinking water (to say nothing of their salaries) and the local innkeepers' refusal of further credit. When the steamers resumed regular service, some money (though much less than expected or needed) arrived from France, where *Il grido* had been a critical success. Further, a Parisian company, Cino del Duca Films, was willing to take over the production of Antonioni's new film. It wasn't easy, however, for the actors to swim or sunbathe in the middle of winter, and Lea Massari (Anna) left the island as soon as she could, claiming that she had suffered a heart attack. Others stuck it out: the total stay in Panarea and Lisca Bianca was nine weeks, though the shooting schedule had called for just six. The Sicilian scenes were completed between November 10 and January 15, with a two-day interruption at Christmas, in this order: the scenes in the customhouse (in the Villa Palagonia at Bagheria); in the Villa Montalto (the eighteenth-century Villa Niscemi); then in Noto, Palermo (for the remaining cruise section, with a different, bigger yacht), Messina, Santa Panagia (a love scene later to be cut), and the San Domenico Hotel in Taormina, selected as the setting for the end of the picture. Back in Rome, Antonioni worked on the editing and sound recording (score by Giovanni Fusco) during the months of February and March. In May, *L'avventura* was ready for the Cannes Film Festival.

The Italian premiere in Milan, on October 18, was opposed by an action of Milan's attorney, Carmelo Spagnuolo. Spagnuolo, together with Italy's attorney general, Pietro Trombi, was leading a "moral" crusade against "pornographic" pictures, first banning and then effecting savage cuts in such films as Visconti's

Rocco and His Brothers, while leaving all sex-comedies and soft-core productions undisturbed. Withdrawn by an order of the Milanese court on October 26, *L'avventura* was censored, and about eighty meters were cut in the love scene near the railroad tracks and in the one with the American callgirl, while other scenes were "obscured" with a masking device before circulation was permitted again. Antonioni himself was charged with obscenity and immorality (and acquitted three years later).

Two Statements by Antonioni about the Film

Though a very private man, Antonioni has often written and spoken about his films, and particularly *L'avventura*. The two most important of his remarks are separated by twenty-three years. The first is the famous "Cannes Statement," made at a press conference at the Cannes Festival just after the premiere of the film in May 1960. It is one of Antonioni's most forceful critical pronouncements, in many ways unprecedented in its clear articulation by a filmmaker of his aesthetic intentions. The second—"Vi parlo di me per raccontarvi un film"— was published in 1983 at the invitation of Antonioni's friends in the journal *Cinema nuovo*. It is a much more private piece, a reminiscence of the ardors and joys of filming *L'avventura*. The very title demonstrates Antonioni's reticence—he is only willing to speak about himself because it might be relevant to our interest in the film.

Cannes Statement
Michelangelo Antonioni

Today the world is endangered by an extremely serious split between a science that is totally and consciously projected into the future, and a rigid and stereotyped morality which all of us recognize as such and yet sustain out of cowardice or sheer laziness. Where is this split most evident? What are its most obvious, its most sensitive, let us even say its most painful, areas? Consider the Renaissance man, his sense of joy, his fullness, his multifarious activities. They were men of great magnitude, technically able and at the same time artistically creative, ca-

From "A Talk with Michelangelo Antonioni on His Work," *Film Culture,* no. 24 (Spring 1962), 50–51. Originally published in *Bianco e nero* 22, nos. 2–3 (February/March 1961), 69–95.

pable of feeling their own sense of dignity, their own sense of importance as human beings, the Ptolemaic fullness of man. Then man discovered that his world was Copernican, an extremely limited world in an unknown universe. And today a new man is being born, fraught with all the fears and terrors and stammerings that are associated with a period of gestation. And what is even more serious, this new man immediately finds himself burdened with a heavy baggage of emotional traits which cannot exactly be called old and outmoded but rather unsuited and inadequate. They condition us without offering us any help, they create problems without suggesting any possible solutions. And yet it seems that man will not rid himself of this baggage. He reacts, he loves, he hates, he suffers under the sway of moral forces and myths which today, when we are at the threshold of reaching the moon, should not be the same as those that prevailed at the time of Homer, but nevertheless are.

Man is quick to rid himself of his technological and scientific mistakes and misconceptions. Indeed, science has never been more humble and less dogmatic than it is today. Whereas our moral attitudes are governed by an absolute sense of stultification. In recent years, we have examined these moral attitudes very carefully, we have dissected them and analyzed them to the point of exhaustion. We have been capable of all this, but we have not been capable of finding new ones. We have not been capable of making any headway whatsoever toward a solution of this problem, of this ever-increasing split between moral man and scientific man, a split which is becoming more and more serious and more and more accentuated. Naturally, I don't care to, nor can I, resolve it myself; I am not a moralist, and my film is neither a denunciation nor a sermon. It is a story told in images whereby, I hope, it may be possible to perceive not the birth of a mistaken attitude but the manner in which attitudes and feelings are misunderstood today. Because, I repeat, the present moral standards we live by, these myths, these conventions are old and obsolete. And we all know they are, yet we honor them. Why? The conclusion reached by the protagonists in my film is not one of sentimentality. If anything, what they finally arrive at is a sense of pity for each other. You might say that this too is nothing new. But what else is left if we do not at least succeed in achieving this? Why do you think eroticism is so prevalent today in our literature, our theatrical shows, and elsewhere? It is a symptom of the emotional sickness of our time. But this preoccupation with the erotic would not become obsessive if Eros were healthy, that is, if it were kept within human proportions. But Eros is sick; man is uneasy, something is bothering him. And whenever something bothers him, man reacts, but he reacts badly, only on erotic impulse, and he is unhappy.

The tragedy in *L'avventura* stems directly from an erotic impulse of this type—unhappy, miserable, futile. To be critically aware of the vulgarity and the futility of such an overwhelming erotic impulse, as is the case with the protagonist in *L'avventura,* is not enough or serves no purpose. And here we witness the crumbling of a myth, which proclaims it is enough for us to know, to be critically conscious of ourselves, to analyze ourselves in all our complexities and in every facet of our personality. The fact of the matter is that such an examination is not enough. It is only a preliminary step. Every day, every emotional encounter gives rise to a new adventure. For even though we know that the ancient codes of morality are decrepit and no longer tenable, we persist, with a sense of perversity that I would only ironically define as pathetic, in remaining loyal to them. Thus moral man who has no fear of the scientific unknown is today afraid of the moral unknown. Starting out from this point of fear and frustration, his adventure can only end in a stalemate.

About Myself and One of My Films

Michelangelo Antonioni

An author can talk about his films only by talking about himself. But what the director says about himself and his work does not help to understand the latter. It is best, therefore, to limit oneself to an episodic narration. Of that time, for example, when a tornado arrived while we were filming *L'avventura* and Monica Vitti got scared.

There are many ways to talk about a film, and there are many people who can do it. Critics, writers, philosophers, psychiatrists, viewers, even painters and architects. But there is only one way for the author: to talk about himself. This can be easy or difficult. For me it's impossible. Moreover, I am convinced that what a director says about himself and his work does not help anyone understand his work. Even less so if we are dealing with an old film. In that case, what's best is an episodic narration of what was happening around the set during the shooting. Although fragmentary and incomplete, perhaps it's more explanatory. Is this how films are made? No, it isn't. It was so that time, the time of *L'avventura*.

I could start from the waterspout that pranced on the sea, shaded up high like a very tall mushroom with its hat lost in the clouds. I yelled to the cameraman to bring the camera, right away, and to shoot. But Monica Vitti was afraid, and so one of the fishermen who was working for us told her that he knew how to "cut" the waterspout (his father had revealed the magic words to him in church one Christmas night, years back), and in fact he pronounced them, and the waterspout vanished. And I got angry because the waterspout was exactly what I needed to give mystery to the island; it was tremendous plastic material. The next day I wanted to fire the fisherman, but I couldn't; he had wrapped a bandage around his head to protect his cheek from the Aeolian wind, and it was all swollen up like a balloon, a sudden toothache, God's punishment because the fisherman had taken His place by "cutting" the waterspout. Maybe I should say that all this was happening in Panarea, in the Aeolian islands, and that every

From *Cinema nuovo* 32, no. 284/5 (August/October 1983), 4–6. Translated by Seymour Chatman.

morning we went with a boat to shoot on a rock called Lisca Bianca, twenty minutes from Panarea. When the sea was calm we could see puffs of steam come out of the water and dissolve into many tiny sulfurous bubbles. But it was never calm. The storm was constant: wind force eight, nine. In that short distance, to get to Lisca Bianca meant literally risking our lives. I think I have hated it, the sea.

The liners had stopped service, and we were eating carobs and moldy cookies. There were wild rabbits on the island, but they were sick. No cigarettes. And no paycheck either. At one point the workers went on strike and decided to go back to Rome as soon as the ship resumed service. We were forced to hire some others who would arrive on that same ship. This took place, if I'm not mistaken, a month later. But on the ship the two groups met, and when the second one learned from the first how things were, they didn't even disembark. There were six or seven of us left: the actors, the cameraman, the production manager, and my helpers. We had learned to load the cameras on our shoulders and to build practicable sets above the sheer drop from the cliff to the sea. One night the sea didn't allow us to go back to Panarea, and we were forced to camp out on the rock. While we were trying to get on board, a wave tore a raft from its moorings and set it adrift with two men on it. I spent the night looking at that hell which was the sea, with the nightmare of those two at its mercy. I was hearing the waves breaking against the cliff and seeing their spray, lit up by the moon, rise up to me, eighty meters high. The raft was found at dawn, with the two exhausted men. The sky was clear, the sun shining, the sea force eight.

I remember also the crossing to Lipari to examine, after two months of shooting, the first footage. We were watching, as if from the bottom of a valley, the waves coming, and it seemed impossible that such a small boat as ours could climb up there. And yet it managed. Wave after wave, like a car taking turns. We saw the footage. It looked horrible.

From Panarea we could call, that's true. There were two radios, American war surplus. The motor supplying energy to these devices had a manual starter, like old cars. The mail clerk often had his arm in a sling; he would break it starting the motor. But when he was well we could communicate. It happened that anyone on the island who had a portable radio could tune in on the wavelength of the transmitter and listen to the conversation. Thus the whole company's feelings were broadcast; the little streets of Panarea resounded with love phrases at full volume. Or with insults. Mine, to people in Rome who were slow finding a new producer. The original one, in fact, had disappeared during the first difficulties, and there was nobody left to back us. But I didn't care. I had twenty thousand meters of film with me; I could still go on shooting. My problem was another: how to tell the truths of the film while "silencing" the other ones that were swarming on the margins, that were pressing on us so forcefully. To take the first ones as a measure for the others? Naturally, I would have preferred to save my colleagues from worry and bitterness and the dejection I felt that they had to endure that absurd way of living and working. If this were cinema, what was cinema?

There are pleasant films and bitter films, light films and painful films. *L'avventura* is a bitter film, often painful—the pain of feelings which fade away, or reveal to us their eventual disappearance the moment we first perceive them. All this narrated in a language that I've tried to keep free of effects. They say that the film is "articulated in a relaxed rhythm, in spatial and temporal relationships which adhere to reality." These words are not mine. I myself do not have the words to say such things. I give an example. Everyone asks after seeing the film: what happened to Anna? There was a scene in the scenario, later cut (I don't remember why), in which Claudia, Anna's friend, is with the others on the island. They are speculating endlessly about the girl's disappearance. But there are no answers. After a silence someone says: "Perhaps she only drowned." Claudia turns suddenly. Everybody looks at each other in dismay. There: this dismay is the connotation of the film.

Reviews and
Commentaries

Reviews and Commentaries

On the evening of May 15, 1960, *L'avventura* was shown at the Cannes Film Festival. The audience at the Palais de la Croisette loudly yawned during the search for Anna on the island, booed and hissed during the scenes when Giulia and Goffredo make love and when Sandro spills ink on the young architect's work. The ending was drowned by a wave of laughter and catcalls. But the following morning thirty-seven intellectuals, including Roberto Rossellini and André Bazin, sent an open letter to Antonioni, apologizing for the behavior of the festival audience and proclaiming the film a masterpiece. It was given a special award by the Jury "for its remarkable contribution toward the search of a new cinematic language." The French critic Robert Benayoun, in a report from Cannes, called it "the most important film since World War II after *Citizen Kane.*" François Mauriac and Françoise Sagan also reviewed the film favorably. In England, critics were no less enthusiastic. The film got excellent reviews from tough-minded American critics like Stanley Kauffmann, Dwight Macdonald, John Simon, and Andrew Sarris.

On September 13, *L'avventura* opened in Paris; at the same time, the Cinémathèque programed a series of Antonioni's films. Notwithstanding the censorship issue (or perhaps thanks to it), the film was a financial success in Italy. In two years it grossed over 300 million lire, not a bad return for the time. It also collected awards— the critics' Silver Ribbon for best music (Giovanni Fusco), Foreign Press Award for best acting (Monica Vitti),

Best Foreign Film and Best Foreign Actress (Vitti) at the Académie Française du Cinéma, Saraceno d'oro for best actors (Vitti and Ferzetti), Best Film at the Vancouver Film Festival, and special mention at the Salonika Film Festival in Greece. The London opening (November 11, 1960) led to a celebration at the British Film Institute, where Antonioni was granted the Sutherland Award as the most original director of the year. In New York (Beekman Theatre, April 4, 1961), the movie was a critical success, though reviewers of the daily papers were initially perplexed. The following year it shared the New York Critic's Circle Award (with Vittorio De Sica's *Two Women*). In 1962 it was judged the second best film of all time by a British Film Institute poll of critics. It still appeared on the ten-best list twenty years later.

L'avventura and the Critics

Guido Fink

Since so many critics have sung the praises of *L'avventura* from so many different perspectives, it is difficult to attempt a summary assessment. It is easier to begin with the few dissenting views. For instance, when the film opened in Italy, there was a predictable flow of sermons from both the Right and the Left blaming Antonioni for his "cynical" lack of ideals, his shameless aestheticism, and his indifference to people and religion. And when *L'avventura* opened in New York the most influential local critics, Bosley Crowther (*New York Times*) and Paul Beckley (*New York Herald Tribune*), openly wondered what the cinematic "puzzle" was trying to say, and where that girl had disappeared to (Crowther suspected her fiancé of having pushed her off a cliff). Crowther and Beckley both discussed *L'avventura* again in the Sunday editions, but in more respectful terms—obviously they felt somehow uneasy about their previous criticism. They still claimed, of course, that *L'avventura* was "going too far," and that it compared unfavorably with other "modern" films, as well as with the works of other Italians like Fellini (Beckley).

Such academic or literary quarterlies as the *Hudson Review* and the *Yale Review* printed long, challenging essays by Joseph Bennett and Simon Lesser (see below); William S. Pechter jokingly referred to the *Hudson*izing of *L'avventura* while he himself was *Kenyon*izing it (*The Kenyon Review,* Spring 1962).

The original, Italian, Antonioni underground felt both pride and chagrin. Now Antonioni had ceased to belong to a small coterie. Was his work going in the right direction? Guido Aristarco answered "yes" and "no" in a dense, appreciative essay in *Cinema nuovo*. Antonioni deserved maximum credit for his "earnestness," for the maturity of his expressive style, for avoiding those tricks or pseudo-mystical shortcuts marring, for instance, Fellini's *La dolce vita*. At the same time, Aristarco felt, Antonioni had mistakenly identified the bourgeois condition in capitalist societies with the human condition in general. In Marxist terms, his works showed no "perspective," no dynamic or dialectic hope of real change. He was the cinematic heir of Gustave Flaubert and the "decadent" avant-garde writers of the early twentieth century (James Joyce, Franz Kafka, André Gide), instead of the great realists, Honoré de Balzac or Leo Tolstoy. For

Aristarco, *L'avventura* and *La notte,* while being great movies, were not as great as Luchino Visconti's "progressive" *Rocco and His Brothers:*

> Such reduction of man's possibilities to a merely subjective level is one of the key aspects of Antonioni's work. Loneliness means lack of communication, and it results in the general idea that every man is a stranger, that each of us is a stranger to himself.[1]

Domenico Tarizzo, a psychoanalyst interviewed in *Cinema nuovo,* went well beyond Aristarco in criticizing *L'avventura:* "Muddled and obscure in the psychological analysis of his characters (. . .), Antonioni is quite close to that cheap and vulgar existentialism which we find nowadays . . . in the dull and pointless production of the so-called *école du regard.*"[2]

Only Italo Calvino's answer (reprinted below) vindicated Antonioni's work. Today's readers may be disturbed, even in this beautiful and perceptive statement by Calvino, by the insistent, almost exclusive concern with the meaning, or meanings of *L'avventura.* Its very novelty and unconventionality obviously led critics to speculate about its content, in philosophical or sociological terms. Words like *alienazione* ("alienation") and *incomunicabilità* ("incommunicability") were such commonplaces in all discussions that they ended by becoming the butt of jokes and parodies. Umberto Eco's brief essay, "Antonioni 'impegnato,'" had the merit, among others, of reminding us that Antonioni's films were important as organic metaphors of our world because of their narrative structure and organization.[3] On the other hand, it was only natural that in a period of dramatic and long-awaited changes in the country (industrialization, opening to the political left, economic boom), Italians found in Antonioni's mature pictures, beginning with *L'avventura,* a good basis for discussing the difficulties that most people felt at the time—lack of communication between the generations, for instance, or the obsolescence of family values, or the feeling of estrangement. Accordingly, the longest and perhaps most challenging Italian essays devoted to *L'avventura* by Piero Amerio, and Ludovico Zorzi and Lucio Aromando, followed, like Lesser's, a psychoanalytical approach. Nor was this phenomenon limited to Italy and America: even Ian Cameron's long essay

1. Guido Aristarco, "Cronaca di una crisi e forme strutturali dell'anima," *Cinema nuovo,* no. 149 (January–February 1961), 43.
2. Domenico Tarizzo and Italo Calvino, "Quattro domande sul cinema italiano," *Cinema nuovo,* no. 149 (January–February 1961), 24–27.
3. Umberto Eco, "Antonioni 'impegnato,'" in *Michelangelo Antonioni,* ed. Carlo di Carlo (Rome: Edizioni di Bianco e nero, 1964), 67–71.

of 1962, after devoting many pages to a formal analysis of various scenes in *L'avventura*, concluded with the suggestion that the picture advocated a "necessary bridge" between Marx and Freud, more or less in consonance with Jean-Paul Sartre's views.[4]

Full-length descriptions of *L'avventura* in specifically visual terms were less frequent, limited to talk of a "dreamlike" quality (Alberto Moravia), or of the difficulties of "looking," or of finding semantic relevance in visual appearances, shapes, objects (Agostino Pirella, Gianni Scalia). But its relations to contemporary trends in painting, such as abstract expressionism, were abundantly mentioned in passing: John Simon compared Antonioni's composition to that of Pierre Bonnard and Henri Matisse, and Dwight Macdonald, going even farther back, saw in his cinema a combination of Joyce and Paolo Veronese. The reference to the author of *Ulysses* may prove a valuable indication of another frequent trend in the film criticism of the early Sixties: the use of literary terms of comparison as a way of improving upon cinema's still rather doubtful reputation. Although some felt that if transposed into different media the "plot" of *L'avventura* could have been banal or meaningless (Galvano della Volpe), that its strength lay "in its incorruptibility, its single-minded insistence that, even in cinema, truth and style must win" (William Whitebait), others, like William S. Pechter, called *L'avventura* "the best new novel I have encountered in the past few years," and literary references were more abundant than pictorial ones. Penelope Houston wrote that *L'avventura* reminded her of *The Wings of the Dove* and *Tender Is the Night*, the latter being, of course, one of the two books that Anna leaves behind (the other is the Bible).[5] F. Scott Fitzgerald was also considered a possible influence by Tommaso Chiaretti and, more exhaustively, by Franco Valobra in a long essay on the relationship between the American writer and Italian film. Albert Camus, Paul Claudel, André Breton, Arthur Rimbaud, and many more were summoned by Claude Perrin.[6]

4. Piero Amerio, "Antonioni: appunti per una psicologia dell'irrelevant," in *Michelangelo Antonioni*, ed. di Carlo, pp. 45–51; Ludovico Zorzi and Lucio Aromando, "Antonioni: *L'avventura*," *Comunità* (January 1961), reprinted in ibid., pp. 379–390; Ian Cameron, "Michaelangelo [*sic*] Antonioni," *Film Quarterly* 16 (Fall 1962), reprinted in Cameron and Robin Wood, *Antonioni*, rev. ed. (New York: Praeger, 1971).

5. William Whitebait, "L'avventura," *New Statesman* (November 26, 1960); Penelope Houston, "L'avventura," *Sight and Sound* 30 (Winter 1960–1961); both reprinted, like Pechter's essay, in the Grove Press edition of *L'avventura*.

6. Franco Valobra, "Fitzgerald e il cinema italiano contemporaneo," *Centrofilm* (June–July 1961); Claude Perrin, "L'univers fragmenté de *L'avventura*," *Etudes cinématographiques* 36–37 (1964), 40–46.

It may seem, looking back, that contemporary critics have seen too many things in *L'avventura,* instead of looking at the text itself, or at what was not to be seen in its texture. After all, the film is the story of a disappearance. Someone is absent: hardly an apt situation for classical *neorealismo* which, as Pierre Sorlin would later remark, was mainly concerned with an extension of filmic visibility. Once again, French critics and scholars were the first to use such words as "lack," "absence," "emptiness," but without the usual negative connotation. (See Marie-Claire Ropars's insightful review, below.) Bernard Pingaud wrote, in an essay entitled "Antonioni et le cinéma réel":

> [Anna's] disappearance creates a sort of final vacuum, which, however, will be immediately filled up. It is this very vacuity that is made somehow visible, thanks to the other characters' embarrassing search, while it deepens and thickens in front of them. Their pain and failure expresses that "passage to emptiness" which is the central theme of the picture. I have seldom seen images that were so capable of conveying a physical feeling of annihilation, of escape, as the ones showing the lonely searchers continuing their quest and knowing in advance that it will be fruitless and vain. They look at each other, they reach, they touch, they separate, always without any hope or belief. This moment, when they begin to forget the one person they must look for, is what I call *temps mort*—more precisely, the time of death.[7]

Sixties' commentaries may look dated or distorted today, but the many readings and even misreadings of the film provide evidence of the tremendous importance that *L'avventura* has had in our time, and not only in the context of Italian cinema.

7. Bernard Pingaud, "Antonioni et le cinéma réel," in *Preuves* (Paris, 1960), p. 117.

L'avventura

Marie-Claire Ropars-Wuilleumier

Because it is literary without recourse to literature, difficult on the difficulty of loving, enduring and slow on the impossibility of enduring, *L'avventura* at first seems a film of contradiction and ambiguity. However, Antonioni has spelled out his intention: "The characters in the film live an emotional adventure—it involves the death and the birth of a love—a psychological and moral adventure which makes them act in contradiction to the established conventions and the criteria of a now outmoded world." But this statement, too, is ambiguous insofar as it implies both a psychological analysis and an attempt at criticism: telling a story and showing the failure of feelings, or rather their inadequateness to the world. And the ongoing conflict between these two themes may explain the spectators' uneasiness as they search for a meaning, as they alternately look to the film's length and to the beauty of its images to justify, without understanding them, their reticence and their enthusiasm.

Here neither the exploration of [its use of] time nor a study of the film's form can function as first references. Unlike *Hiroshima mon amour*, *L'avventura* is not a film *about* time, but *in* time; it tells us less about the difficulty of being than about the impossibility of enduring; and its refusal of drama, its *temps morts*, the interminable drawing out that betrayed in the characters of *Hiroshima* the very anxiety of being, here take on significance only through the basically psychological perspective of the film. Indeed, because of the subject, of the way the story, "triggered by the interior mechanism and not by the facts," unfolds, *L'avventura* belongs to the tradition of the psychological novel, where the evolution of feelings does not bump into obstacles other than those of other feelings: and hasn't Antonioni told us he had put his characters in a bourgeois environment so that their feelings, freed from material needs, could appear in their naked truth?

If Antonioni's analysis is not, from a literary point of view, new, it raises a problem of language that *is* new: finding the cinematographic equivalent of a

From *Esprit* 12 (December 1960), 2080–2084, copyright © Editions du Seuil, 1970. Translated by Seymour Chatman and Renée Morel.

gradual internal change that words cannot describe; this is why the characters do not say anything important; usually their most decisive words are nothing but the confused and painful result of an anxiety—"No, things are not that way"; "Well, what do we say now?"—or a fleeting delusion: "I had gotten used to being without you. . . . I don't feel you anymore." The rest is small talk offering only the trivial and the useless. Thus, much of the dialogue and many of the events present a mere surface, and the truth of the characters appears not *in* the acts nor in the words, but *through* them.

Antonioni's perspective might explain one of the apparent contradictions in *L'avventura:* if this film about [emotional] fragility ("Is it possible that so little can make me change?"—"Even less") cannot but be a slow film, if the less dramatic scenes are those that are the most drawn out, it is because slowness is altogether the temporal sign and the rhythmical equivalent of the fragile duration. During the endless search on the island, Antonioni's camera, the only mobile thing in apparently immobile scenes, moves along with the characters, progressively illuminating, little by little, through a look, a gesture, encounters, silences, even absences, the moment when Claudia and Sandro forget Anna and become aware of their mutuality, and gradually move from a search for Anna to a search for their own selves. The music signals the beginning of the adventure which, throughout the film, gets confused with the search. For this search is not the kind where one finds something, but rather where one is constantly becoming someone else in the process, and it never achieves any repose, any stability. This is where Antonioni's art reveals itself as an art of duration: through the mobility alone of his camera, which follows the internal itinerary of the characters, through the slow unfolding of places that never appear twice, he succeeds in creating a time dimension which is not that of memory; and if certain images echo the themes from the beginning, they suggest, in the viewer's mind, the present moment and not the past, thus making the viewer aware of time, which passes and modifies human beings though nothing is apparently happening.

To grasp this motion of time and of souls through the film's sequences requires from the spectator an effort of detachment that can only be achieved because the film has rejected dramatic effect and a purely realistic rendition. For each scene takes place on two levels: the level of facts, immutable or insignificant, and the level of feelings, shifting and often belying the facts. If the long scene [at the beginning] in which Anna and Sandro meet and kiss endlessly in silence causes a growing uneasiness in the spectator, it is because of the discrepancy between what takes place on the screen and what takes place in the soul; and the very beauty of the images makes the discrepancy even more acute. Yet this feeling of uneasiness may enable the viewer to grasp Antonioni's second perspective: the level of critical analysis. For him, [emotional] fragility is not the only reason for failure; if Aldo in *Il grido* (*The Cry*) goes as far as suicide, it is because he can't stop loving; and in *Le amiche,* the very possibility of love is called into question. *L'avventura* shows only one aspect of a broader problem: people are not happy because their feelings originate in myths that have no relation to the modern world.

Indeed, this theme can be seen in the attitude of each character and in the relationships uniting them. The discord between lovers, the impossibility of communicating or even of staying together, which Anna and Sandro as well as Sandro and Claudia have to contend with, does not stem from a specific misunderstanding: it is the consequence of a more general malaise whose reflection they find both around them and inside themselves. A second meaning then appears, embodied in another dimension of the film: whereas the analysis develops through time, the critique operates within each frame and each second; every scene in *L'avventura* is constructed in depth, built on several planes, never presenting the protagonists alone, but also their reflections and their opposites. Psychological analysis may bear on the level of their feelings alone, but the critique inevitably reintroduces the world that feelings would like to ignore, yet that nevertheless confronts them.

The presence of the world makes itself felt at the most immediate level, and first of all through the presence of others: when Anna and Sandro meet [at the beginning], Claudia is there too, waiting, available. Claudia and Sandro are not alone, either, when they look for Anna: the island scenes are constructed like frescoes in which individuals separate and meet at different levels, and where Claudia and Sandro keep running into other couples who act as reflections and omens. Likewise the groups of men standing motionless in a square and looking at a woman passing by or the stampede of a crowd, triggered by a girl who wants publicity, are signs of a generalized and hopeless malaise.

Antonioni did not choose a Sicilian setting by chance or just because of its beauty. The constant presence of men [in the streets], of towns and of landscapes plays a double role: the environment is interposed to extend and modify the sense of duration, and it also plays up the discrepancy theme. The Sicily depicted by Antonioni consists of desolate and breathtaking landscapes, but ones where a helicopter appears suddenly; ruins and amphoras, but also trains and cars; a magnificent palace turned into a police station; streams of seminarians and displays of collective eroticism. For Antonioni never shows Sicilian landscapes or monuments for their intrinsic beauty, but always in reference to what may contest or deny that beauty. And art in Sicily is baroque: in other words, movement, instability, the constant search for an impossible balance, like the spiral of the fountain in front of which Sandro lingers and becomes gloomy. All these elements creep into the images, modifying them or giving them their true significance. In Antonioni's work the world is never merely a setting or a symbol; it is part of the narration; the adventure of a man and a woman ill at ease with their love takes place in a country that seems ill at ease with their story.

Consequently the structure of *L'avventura* is based on a counterpoint: the profundity of the image constantly modifies the way the images are linked. Because Antonioni's style refuses fascination, beauty for him is always second (which does not mean secondary), and the constant dialectic of time which passes and of space which contests this passing invites the spectator first to detachment and then to understanding.

Understanding does seem to be the end of *L'avventura*. Claudia's and Sandro's unhappiness arises from the fact that they are constantly overtaken by their own selves; their development is always faster than the lucidity they seek through modifications, reflections, and uncertainties. It is a search leading nowhere, until the last frame, which is finally immobile, finally solitary, when Claudia lays her hand on Sandro's shoulder, a gesture that seems finally to bring them to rest and light. For if Antonioni's style draws its inspiration from [Cesare] Pavese, it is not certain he has adopted that author's tragic view. Of the three characters involved in this adventure, only one may have chosen the same solution as Pavese, who wrote: "He who cannot save himself cannot be saved by anyone." Anna has saved herself through death or escape, no one knows, since her salvation is bound up with her absence. Whereas Claudia and Sandro remain together, as witnesses.

But what did they see? And what kind of rest is it? The kind brought by resignation to failure? This is where Antonioni's world seems questionable or at least locked in the ambiguity it wanted to elucidate. For what are we to understand? That the absolute is not possible and that we must nevertheless get beyond this impossibility, accept the mess and the ugliness? Until the very last image the malaise gets worse; this may be because there is no common ground between Claudia's high idea of love and Sandro's weaknesses and shortcomings (he alone is to blame, or so it seems). It is necessary, says Antonioni, to invent a new dimension for our feelings; but Claudia and Sandro do not seem to comprehend the problems a modern couple has to face. Claudia's understanding does not distinguish itself very clearly from forgiveness; and invention, here, does not always seem far removed from a return to tradition; at any rate, the answer remains ambiguous.

This may very well be where the great beauty of *L'avventura* lies: the story raises a question, but does not answer it. If Antonioni traces his way through his story as if it were a labyrinth, where one must follow every twist and turn to arrive at an exit, it is not so much for the sake of [achieving] that exit as for [examining] the itinerary covered. In Antonioni's world, unlike [Robert] Bresson's, the adventure does not lead to a liberation; each moment of the film is above all a meditation on the need for understanding, and this call is addressed to the disoriented spectator as to anyone in search of authenticity.

Remarks on *L'avventura*

Italo Calvino

The most challenging aspect of recent poetical work (especially as far as painting and prose writing are concerned) amounts to an analysis of humanity's relationship to the external world, and to its own possibilities of expression, judgment, and action. Often the conclusions reached by such analysis are negative or depressing, resulting in failure or defeat; nonetheless, the issue is very important. This analysis seems to be the only possible starting point for any action that may prove morally and historically positive. Therefore, I consider *La noia* (one of the most serious and beautiful books by [Alberto] Moravia) and Antonioni's *L'avventura* as the greatest cultural events of the year. The theme of *L'avventura* is the faculty of people to choose and determine their own behavior, out of the chaos of casual gestures, instincts, careless or contradictory words— not people in general, but certain people, since the milieu is that of the idle and the affluent. . . . Nothing is demonstrated, nothing is clearly stated; the viewer receives no help or satisfaction; narrative style is barren, with no ornament or digression; the spectators are forced to make the same efforts and judgments they normally do, or ought to do, when confronted by reality. The script is uneven— sometimes rich in exquisite detail, sometimes rough and approximate. This is bad: in such a picture, one would expect faultless economy. (*La noia* is the exact opposite: as perfectly constructed as a clock, it is too dogmatic in defining its own meaning, which by the way is often wrong.) The plot in *L'avventura* stems from an apparently unquestionable, definite event—the disappearance of a girl. And it shows how practically everyone succeeds in questioning or forgetting it. Then the movie shows signs of narrating a love story—but it soon unwinds this story casually and gropingly. The two main characters are a man with a mushy personality and no willpower (out of regret for betraying his own profession) and a woman who would and could have consistency and sincerity and earnestness but is always forced down into the mire where everybody else is. It is a pessimistic picture that does not try to gild or sweeten the pill, that does not want to

From "Quattro domande sul cinema italino," *Cinema nuovo,* no. 149 (January/February 1961), 33–34. Translated by Alessandra Calanchi.

moralize or to reform the bourgeois way of life and manners as do the radicals or the leftist Catholics. You are in the mire, and there you stay: this is the only serious moral stance. . . . It is a picture of great, unsparing severity, of keen morality, because it is firmly grounded in today's humanity, not in gratuitous or literary abstraction. . . . As a description of society *L'avventura* is just perfect. Its Southern Italian setting, for instance—the inferno of underdevelopment contrasted with the affluent inferno—is the most truthful and the most impressive that ever appeared on the screen, without the least indulgence to populism or local color.

Shape Around a Black Point

Geoffrey Nowell-Smith

There is one brief scene in *L'avventura,* not on the face of it a very important one, which seems to me to epitomise perfectly everything that is most valid and original about Antonioni's form of cinema. It is the scene where Sandro and Claudia arrive by chance at a small village somewhere in the interior of Sicily. The village is strangely quiet. They walk around for a bit, call out. No reply, nothing. Gradually it dawns on them that the village is utterly deserted, uninhabited, perhaps never was inhabited. There is no one in the whole village but themselves, together and alone. Disturbed, they start to move away. For a moment the film hovers: the world is, so to speak, suspended for two seconds, perhaps more. Then suddenly the film plunges, and we cut to a close-up of Sandro and Claudia making love in a field—one of the most ecstatic moments in the history of the cinema, and one for which there has been apparently no formal preparation whatever. What exactly has happened?

It is not the case that Sandro and Claudia have suddenly fallen in love, or suddenly discovered at that moment that they have been in love all along. Nor, at the other extreme, is theirs a panic reaction to a sudden fear of desolation and loneliness. Nor again is it a question of the man profiting from a moment of helplessness on the part of the woman in order to seduce her. Each of these explanations contains an aspect of the truth, but the whole truth is more compli-cated and ultimately escapes analysis. What precisely happened in that moment the spectator will never know, and it is doubtful if the characters really know for themselves. Claudia knows that Sandro is interested in her. By coming with him to the village she has already more or less committed herself, but the actual fatal decision is neither hers nor his. It comes, when it comes, impulsively: and its immediate cause, the stimulus which provokes the response, is the feeling of emptiness and need created by the sight of the deserted village. Just as her feel-ings (and his too for that matter) are neither purely romantic nor purely physical, so her choice, Antonioni is saying, is neither purely determined nor purely free.

From *Sight and Sound* 33, no. 1 (Winter 1963/64), 15–20.

She chooses, certainly, but the significance of her choice escapes her, and in a sense also she could hardly have acted otherwise.

The technical means by which all this is conveyed are no less interesting, and give further clues about Antonioni's general attitude to life and to the cinema as a means of expression. When the first shot of the village comes up, one expects it to be what is generally known as an establishing shot—that is to say something to set the scene, to establish the location and atmosphere in which the scene will develop. In fact, however, the shot *is* the scene, not an introduction to it, and the location is not just somewhere for the event to take place, but synonymous with the event itself (equally the event is the location and not just something that happens there). Antonioni does not cut away from the background to concentrate on the characters, at least not immediately. He holds his shot, all his shots, just that bit longer than would be strictly necessary for them to make their point, if there were a point to be made. He holds them in this case for as long as it takes for the spectator to become aware not only of the background, but of the characters themselves becoming aware of the background. There are no ellipses: screen time and real time virtually correspond. But although the camera is subjective in matter of time, in that the audience's sense of time follows that of the characters, the general impression is of extreme objectivity. The spectator is never put in the character's place and encouraged to feel what the character is supposed to be feeling. On this occasion he will no doubt react in much the same way to the sense of absurdity and desolation put across by the landscape; but the important thing is not this, but rather that he should watch, with the camera, dispassionately and almost scientifically, the reactions of the characters themselves.

He has no certain guide to what they are feeling or thinking except their purely exterior reactions, fragments of behaviour; and in Antonioni films this behaviour will often seem at any given moment arbitrary and unmotivated. As a result the meaning of the film is forever in a state of flux. The behaviouristic form of observation suggests an initial determinism; somewhere in the background there is a basic pattern of cause and effect. But in practice everything is disconnected. There is something almost capricious in the way people behave; directions are always uncertain until it is too late; and the sense of an event is never clear until after it has happened, and something else has occurred to define the significance of what went before.

A world in which everything is surrounded by a faint halo of indeterminacy is going to be insecure in other ways as well. Empiricism has always been the agnostic's epistemology, and Antonioni is a radical agnostic. In his films there is never any certainty, any definite or absolute truth. The meaning of single events is often ambiguous, and cumulatively these events add up to a picture of a world from which order, value, and logic have disappeared. This should not be taken in too metaphysical a sense. The characters in Antonioni films do not go around, like the followers of Sartre or [Maurice] Merleau-Ponty, earnestly trying to put back the essences into existence. They are simply faced with the business of living in a world which offers of itself no certainty and no security, at least not in the immediate present. And when a character does seem to have assured himself somehow, through his job or through his relationship with another person, his security is probably (though not necessarily: again Antonioni is not Sartre) an illusion, for which he will have to pay before long.

This sense of fundamental insecurity which affects the more lucid of Antonioni's characters (the stupid ones are generally more or less immune, and probably happier as a result) is no doubt largely subjective. Their particular existentialist inferno is very much of their own making. But in a less acute form the same general malaise can be seen to affect the whole of society, and to be reflected in the physical environment which modern man has created for himself and in which he has chosen to live. The deserted village in *L'avventura* is a perfect example. Visually it recalls instantly the vacant surfaces and deranged perspectives of Chirico's *pittura metafisica,* and it means much the same thing. This civic townscape, devoid of citizens, dehumanised and absurd, in which two people come together and make love, acts in a sense as a symbol, or a parable, for the whole of modern life. Man, it seems to say, has built himself his own world, but he is incapable of living in it. He is excluded from his own creation, and his only refuge lies in fortuitous encounters with another being in the same predicament. In a word, he is "alienated." . . .

L'avventura: A Closer Look

Simon O. Lesser

Except in a few notable books, such as *From Caligari to Hitler* by Siegfried Kracauer and *Movies* by Martha Wolfenstein and Nathan Leites, and, more recently, in the criticism of Norman Holland, the knowledge of the unconscious now at our disposal has been largely ignored in the criticism of movies. The neglect is scarcely surprising. Despite all the rather tiresome (because in most instances merely opinionated) talk about whether such knowledge *should* be used in literary criticism, it is honored there more in the breach than in the observance—and when used is often applied either gingerly or rashly, with a second-hand, inexact, and incomplete knowledge of the concepts upon which it is supposed to be based. Movie critics have less incentive than their colleagues who discuss books to acquire the formidable body of background knowledge needed for making profitable use of what is known about the unconscious. They may feel that their readers prefer superficial commentary, and except where certain kinds of films are concerned (and perhaps then only if the critics have a relatively sophisticated audience or unusual gifts for simplification) this feeling is probably correct. Critics for dailies, and even weeklies, may also be deterred, and are certainly handicapped, by the need for working under short deadlines. The most valuable insights about what a work of art is communicating at the unconscious level are often slow in presenting themselves.

However understandable, the indiscriminate neglect of depth psychology in movie criticism is regrettable. As I have suggested in my book *Fiction and the Unconscious,* novels and short stories probably register on our minds to an unappreciated extent in terms of sense impressions, chiefly visual ones. But movies are cast in these terms from the very beginning; they are "written" in the very language of our dreams and fantasies. Theoretically, movies are in a better position than any other genre to bypass the conscious intelligence and communicate with the unconscious with little or no mediation. Perhaps the chief reason this is not better appreciated is that until recently few makers of movies were aware of

From *Yale Review* 54, no. 1 (October 1964), 41–50, copyright © Yale University.

the potentialities of their own medium. They concentrated on superficial subjects which could be conveyed through conventional symbols and which evoked ready-made responses, created or reinforced by popular literature. More sadly, even in dealing with promising material directors were usually overexplicit and heavy-handed, perhaps because they assumed that the understanding of images requires more intelligence than in fact it does, perhaps simply because they lacked visual imagination. But the possibilities of the medium have always been there and they have occasionally been realized—most often, perhaps, until recently, in movies with no trace of "artiness," such as comedies and melodramas. A Hitchcock thriller, *Vertigo,* will serve as an example. Though it seemed to be concerned with a purely external thing, a man's fear of heights, at the latent level it explained his fear, and showed how he was defeated by the clever exploitation of more hidden and encompassing personality weaknesses.

Vertigo, however, had an exciting, clear-flowing story to tell, and thus lent itself with at least apparent ease to customary ways of using the medium. Today a number of directors are emerging who recognize that movies can be utilized for more complex narrative purposes: to tell stories where the action is disjunctive, negative in character, or so elliptical that there may seem to be no story; to project the inner feelings of characters, complex interrelationships, even the moods, unverbalized and perhaps not even verbalizable, which may engulf, say, a couple or even a large group. And these new directors, of whom Michelangelo Antonioni and Ingmar Bergman are the supreme exemplars, accomplish these things not by finding unobtrusive ways of working in an unusual number of verbal cues but by making fuller and more imaginative use of the screen's natural visual idiom.

Besides using more and fresher symbols, Antonioni and Bergman frequently employ overdetermined ones, so that, like novelists for example, they can suggest additional implications of the story they are telling. To the extent that they do this they must resort to symbols which cannot be too easily penetrated, for the more hidden level or levels of meaning are nearly always ones that would arouse anxiety or revulsion in viewers if consciously perceived. Occasionally, moreover, again like their colleagues who depend upon words, they will tell a story which is not intelligible or perhaps even interesting on the basis of its manifest level of meaning, a story which is not likely to be affecting, much less enjoyable, unless it is apprehended unconsciously.

It is when one deals with films of these two kinds that one most keenly regrets the neglect of depth psychology in movie criticism. It must be assumed that these films are intuitively understood by most of the large number of people all over the world who evidently enjoy them; the enjoyment of films of the second kind in particular is inexplicable unless one assumes that they are unconsciously understood. But precisely because they are understood in this fashion, it seems unlikely that many viewers can *account* for their response to the films; to do so, in the face of strong internal resistance, they would have to formulate what has been grasped only subliminally and nonverbally.

It may be surmised that one of the most powerful factors impelling these viewers to read movie criticism is the hope of finding commentary which will help them to understand their own reactions. Unfortunately, most reviewers share the helplessness of their readers and are unable to satisfy these desires. What is worse, and less apparent, is that—more or less inevitably—they often mislead their readers. *Something* must be said, and if a critic lacks the skill to explicate below-the-surface meanings and is not content to be vague, he is likely to stumble into misinterpretations. Nor does the harm which results from the lack of psychological knowledge always end there. Because of a natural tendency to bring one's judgment of a work of art into line with one's intellectual formulations about it, the misinterpretations may sometimes lead to inaccurate appraisals. Unable to decode the meaning of a picture, a critic may conclude that it has none and write a review which fails to do justice to his own immediate, and more correct, reactions.

These tendencies are in evidence, it seems to me, in some of the press and magazine commentary on Michelangelo Antonioni's cinema masterpiece *L'avventura*. For example, Bosley Crowther of the *New York Times* shows respect for Antonioni's artistry, but declares that in watching *L'avventura* he felt he was trying to follow a picture of "which several reels have got lost." Even in a piece written long after his original review he refers to the picture's "deliberately garbled story-line." As I shall try to show, the story-line is, on the contrary, tight and faithfully adhered to. A review by Edith Oliver in *The New Yorker* may be an example of the second, and more regrettable, kind of critical failing. She dismisses *L'avventura* as tedious as well as incomprehensible. Still, she refers to evidence "that Mr. Antonioni has something in mind," and at another point writes, "One reason I am so angry and harsh is that there are also indications, here and there, that some original ideas—Mr. Antonioni's own ideas—have gone to waste." Evidently Miss Oliver felt baffled when she tried to explain *L'avventura,* but such comments, I like to think, may be vestigial remnants of an intuitive initial recognition of the picture's stature.

The idea for *L'avventura* may have come as a phrase: *"There is a search. But one has forgotten for whom one is searching."* The idea, even in its more impersonal forms, stirs reverberations. You go into a room to find something and realize you have forgotten what you were looking for. Then you remember, but perhaps feel some vague sense of dissatisfaction: "Was that really it?" This sense of bafflement is likely to be keener when you plan a day, a month, a career. The goals and purposes of life, which in youth may have seemed self-evident, in adulthood seem impossible to define; it goes without saying that the route to one's destination, whatever it may be, is unmarked also. This is one of the themes of Kafka's *The Castle*.

In the erotic life of man the situation seems, if anything, more difficult. How can you possibly find her whom you seek? Her image is blurred. At one time it may seem impossible to find her because there are so many women among whom to choose. At other times it may seem impossible because there are so few. Either way, the essential difficulty remains the same: how can you recognize your long-sought beloved when her image and her qualities are so indefinite and indistinct? How can you know love itself and distinguish it from its innumerable partial embodiments and counterfeits? After a time the hope of success may all but disappear. Because of need, the search may continue, but be pursued with a growing sense of futility and disillusionment.

L'avventura is, among other things, the story of one such compulsive, interminable quest for someone whom the hero does not really expect ever to find. But *L'avventura* is not all story—it is part poem and part essay as well—nor is this all it has to say. The movie makes a sweeping, it could almost be said an encompassing, statement about the erotic life of modern man. It is doomed from the start, the movie asseverates: doomed because the quest for the beloved is hopeless and because its hopelessness breeds disenchantment, cynicism, and self-hatred; doomed because sexual fulfilment is so often unsatisfactory and guilt-ridden; doomed because sex is used, wrongly, as solace for frustrations and defeats, as an anodyne for the soul-sickness which afflicts us because of our own compromises, weaknesses, and corruption, and as an outlet for angry, destructive feelings which besmirch it; doomed, finally, because despite all this the quest goes on and must go on, though joyless, sterile, and, after a time, devoid of any prospect of success. Eternal restlessness and frustration are the inescapable conditions of our erotic life.

From first to last *L'avventura* is a story of baffled search. It is important to note that Anna and Claudia, to say nothing of the movie's minor characters, are searching for something, just as Sandro is. Anna's father is aware that his daughter is desperately looking for something, but warns her that she will not find it with or through Sandro. She is herself half aware of this. Her sulkiness is only partly explained by the need to choose between father and lover. One senses that to a far greater degree it is a product of her own doubts—about her lover, their relationship, and something in herself.

At the beginning Claudia is left to one side, unexplained and almost unnoticed, but in retrospect it is easy to see that she, too, is searching, and that her search is no less desperate than Anna's. At the beginning, in fact, she is in the unenviable position of searching *through* her friend. She has no lover herself, and no unattached male has been invited on the cruise as a possible partner for her. Nevertheless, she accompanies Anna. It is not an accident that time after time—beginning of course with the lovemaking of Anna and Sandro very early in the picture—she is forced to witness "primal scene" material. She is the observer—the outsider, the third party, the child watching the parents—of the weary, paid-for lovemaking between the Princess and her paramour, of the hostility that is the only link between Giulia and Corrado, the only married couple on the yachting party, and, later, of the exultant, vengeful lovemaking between Giulia and the young Italian "artist." Toward the end there is the more poignant confirming scene where she finds what she has been unconsciously searching for, her father-lover entwined in the limbs of the wanton he found at the Princess' party. Here she can feel her grief more fully, more poignantly, and, as it were, more justifiably, for she has at once recreated and reversed the prototype situation: she is still the outsider, but now in part a betrayed outsider, the mother from whom the envious daughter has stolen the father. It is chiefly through Claudia, whether as jealous daughter or, as in the last scene, part daughter, part wronged mother, that we are reminded that love almost invariably involves competitiveness and a sense of taking from someone else, one of the reasons it is tainted by feelings of guilt. Claudia has reason to know—not only because she has apparently failed to work out her jealousy of her mother but also because, even though Anna is evidently dead, she has the feeling of having stolen Sandro from her. At some level his infidelity is not only an expected and familiar pain but a warranted punishment, one reason she is able to forgive him.

It is upon Sandro's search, however, more than Anna's or even Claudia's, that *L'avventura* chiefly focuses. Gabriele Ferzetti is able to suggest that his restlessness long antedated his relationship with Anna, confirming the doubts her father's warnings have already implanted in us. While we are not fully prepared for Anna's physical disappearance, we are prepared for the fact that Sandro's search will not end with her.

The failure to explain what happened to Anna is undoubtedly one source of the complaint that *L'avventura* does not tell a coherent story. At first glance the criticism may seem justified, for Anna's disappearance is one of the most dramatic external incidents in the movie. But *L'avventura* is nowhere concerned with external events for their own sake; certainly it is not a mystery story in which our main concern should be, "What happened to Anna?" It is a psychological story of the quest for love and the beloved.

Once this is remembered—and Antonioni never forgets it—it seems clear that this incident is treated with the same sureness as everything else. An explanation of Anna's disappearance would be not only superfluous but distracting. The discovery of her body, for example, would call for additional reactions from everyone and in all probability would raise further questions. The movie confines itself to what is relevant: Anna disappears. She vanishes from Sandro's life and, very quickly, from his consciousness also, as in one way or another she was bound to. And she disappears while herself searching for something—or perhaps fleeing from something, which is another aspect of the same thing.

Except as a reproach, she soon disappears from Claudia's consciousness also. From the beginning Claudia has envied Anna and wanted her lover, who, we sense, is attractive in part because he is her lover. The scene toward the beginning when she is compelled to wait outside, with feelings we can divine, while Sandro and Anna make love is only one of the things that whisper this to us. We sense it also from the readiness with which she borrows her friend's clothing both before and after her disappearance, from the scene in which she dons a brunette wig, and from her immediate sensitivity to Sandro's desire for her. Though she makes no overt gesture of enticement, it is significant that the first physical contact between her and Sandro occurs as a result of her stumbling as she tries to pass him. Speedily enough she reaches the point where she confesses that she no longer cries for her lost friend but fears that she may be alive.

The more difficult and audacious thing *L'avventura* achieves is to make Sandro's quick acceptance of Anna's disappearance so understandable that we do not refuse to identify with him. Here we have little to go on except the longing for Claudia which quickly manifests itself (and this would arouse revulsion if we were not in part prepared for it) and what Gabriele Ferzetti has been able to suggest about Sandro's character and inner feelings. In part because we do not have to be given an explanation but simply reminded of one, this is sufficient: we intuitively realize that Sandro has no real desire to find Anna. Before her disappearance, we sense, the relationship was played out. Anna had already been exposed as a surrogate, one of a long succession of women who had to be possessed and then renounced because none was the one for whom Sandro was searching. This is another reason why psychologically it is better that Anna's fate should be left in doubt: the search for her is at bottom a pseudosearch. It is engaged in to save face and to relieve guilt rather than to find Anna.

Such sorrow as Anna's disappearance does arouse in Sandro, it may be surmised, is due to what it does to recall the disappearance of the original love object, the mother. At the very deepest level the failure to account for Anna's disappearance rings true psychologically because it recapitulates that earlier experience, which cannot be explained in terms of the love object's being alive or dead. She has "disappeared" because she has been thrust into the unconscious and can no longer be sought for *in propria persona:* she is taboo.

What we sense about Sandro's real feeling for Anna, and all the nameless women who have preceded her in his life, helps us to work our way to the core of Antonioni's picture. It can almost be regarded as a dramatization of a text from Freud:

> . . . when the original object of an instinctual desire becomes lost in consequence of repression, it is often replaced by an endless series of substitute-objects, none of which ever give full satisfaction. This may explain the lack of stability in object-choice, the "craving for stimulus," which is so often a feature of the love of adults. ("The Most Prevalent Form of Degradation in Erotic Life")

We know in advance, and Claudia knows, that Sandro's feelings for her will be subject to the same vicissitudes responsible for his easy acceptance of the loss of Anna. Claudia is a surrogate also, as we are reminded by Sandro's infidelity with the prostitute he finds at the party. It is a virtue of *L'avventura* that even though the relationship between Sandro and Claudia survives this, no assurances are given that it will endure indefinitely; the picture ends on an uncertain note. Indeed, far from trying to dissipate the melancholy impressions conveyed by the first part of the picture, the latter part deepens them. The relationship of Sandro and Claudia seldom escapes the burden of guilt which has encumbered it from the start. He is never able to feel any happiness, and some of the things which occur after the search for Anna becomes no more than an excuse for him and Claudia to travel together help to explain why this is so.

In one of the towns to which their search brings them Sandro leaves Claudia and goes for a walk. He chances upon a drawing in which a young man, evidently an aspiring architect, has faithfully reproduced the beauty of a detail of a nearby building. The drawing is at Sandro's mercy; the young man who has made it has walked some distance away to chat with a friend. Sandro lets his keyring dangle ever closer to a bottle of ink near the drawing; in the end he cannot resist the impulse to ruin the drawing by knocking over the bottle.

He rushes back to his hotel full of inarticulate grief about his act and the cluster of feelings responsible for it. We know that the impulse to sully the young man's work was born of the angry realization that he has sullied his own. Precipitately, brutally, impersonally, he tries to compel Claudia, who is well aware that at the moment he is scarcely aware of her, to have sexual relations with him. He seeks to use her, and sex, to console himself for the dreams he has forsaken. Antonioni is in effect asking a rhetorical question: what chance does sex have to give us happiness or even pleasure when it is misused in this fashion? Taken as a whole, moreover, his picture tells us that sex is likely to be so misused, particularly in our time.

But there is nothing condemnatory about Antonioni's attitude. He is not indicting sex, or his characters, or, like *La dolce vita,* with which *L'avventura* has been mistakenly linked, an age or social system. Tears are a purge also, and the Sandro who weeps at the end of *L'avventura* feels genuine sorrow—sorrow for the suffering he has caused his beloved and sorrow for his own unhappiness, for the restlessness and richly rewarded mediocrity to which he perceives himself to be doomed.

Dear Antonioni . . .

Roland Barthes

Dear Antonioni . . .
   In his typology, Nietzsche distinguishes between two figures—the priest and the artist. As for priests, we have more than enough of them: inside established religions, or even those outside. But what about artists? Dear Antonioni, I take the liberty of examining some aspects of your work so that I might focus on three forces, or, if you prefer, three virtues that, I believe, constitute an artist. I will name them: vigilance, wisdom, and, the most paradoxical of all, fragility.

As opposed to the priest, the artist wonders and admires; his gaze can be critical, but it is not accusing; the artist does not know resentment. It is because you are an artist that your work is open to the *Modern*. Many regard the Modern as a battle flag raised against the old world and its compromised values; but for you it is not the static term of a facile opposition. Rather it is the active difficulty of following the changes of the Times, no longer merely at the level of History on the grand scale, but also within a "smaller" History of whose existence each of us is the measure. Begun shortly after the war, your work developed step by step along a course of double vigilance, about the contemporary world and about yourself; each of your films has been a historical experience on a personal scale—that is, the relinquishment of an old problem and the formulation of a new question. This means that you have experienced and treated the history of the past three decades *with subtlety,* not as material of an artistic reflex or an ideological commitment, but as a substance whose magnetism you had to capture in every work. For you, content and form are equally historical; dramas, as you have said, are indifferently psychological and plastic. The social, narrative, and neurotic aspects are only levels, relevances (in the linguistic sense) of the *total world,* which is the object of every artist: there is a succession, not a hierarchy, of interests. To be precise, contrary to the thinker, the artist does not evolve. Like a sensitive instrument, he follows the successions of the New which his own

Originally presented as a homage to Antonioni at a retrospective of his work in Bologna, 1979. Published in French as "Cher Antonioni," *Cahiers du cinéma* 311 (May 1980), 9–11. Translated by Nora Hoppe.

history presents to him. Your work is not a fixed reflection, but a moiré [water-patterned silk] over which appear, according to the inclination of the eye and the solicitations of time, the forms of the Social or the Passional and of formal innovations, from narrative method to the employment of Color. Your concern for this era is not that of the historian, the politician, or the moralist, but rather that of the utopian who seeks to perceive the new world in precise terms, because he wants that world and he wants to be a part of it. Your vigilance as an artist is an amorous vigilance, a vigilance of desire.

I invoke the wisdom of the artist not as an ancient virtue, still less as a mediocre discourse, but, on the contrary, as that moral knowledge, that acuity of discernment which permits the artist never to confuse *meaning* with truth. How many crimes has humanity committed in the name of Truth! And yet this "truth" has never been anything more than a meaning, an interpretation. How many wars, reigns of terror, acts of genocide and repression have there been for the triumph of a meaning! He, the artist, knows that the meaning of a thing is not its truth; this knowledge is a wisdom, a foolish wisdom, one might say, because it removes him from the community [but also] from the company of the arrogant and the fanatic.

Not all artists, however, have this wisdom: some hypostatize meaning. This terroristic operation is generally termed "realism." Thus, when you state (in an interview with [Jean-Luc] Godard) "I feel the need to express reality in terms that are not completely realistic," you exhibit a just feeling for meaning: you don't impose it, but you don't deny it either. This dialectic bestows upon your film (and I shall use the same term again) a great subtlety: your art consists in always leaving the road to meaning open and as if undecided—out of scruple. It is in this way that you accomplish with great precision the artist's task greatly needed in our time, a task that is neither dogmatic nor insignificant. Thus, in your first short documentary on the Roman street cleaners, or on the fabrications of nylon in Torviscosa, the critical description of the social alienation of bodies at work wavers, without disappearing, without becoming a more pathetic, more immediate sentiment. In *Il grido*, the strong meaning of the work consists, if one can say, in the very uncertainty of meaning: the aimless wandering of a man who can nowhere confirm his own identity and the ambiguity of the conclusion (suicide or accident) lead the spectator into uncertainty about the message.

This escape from meaning, which does not imply its denial, allows you to undermine the psychological fixtures of realism. In *Deserto rosso*, the crisis is no longer a crisis of emotions, as in *Eclisse*, because the emotions involved are sure (the heroine loves her husband): everything gets tangled and causes pain in a second area where affection—or rather a malaise of affection—escapes the armature of meaning that constitutes the code of passions. Finally, your latest films carry this crisis of meaning into the heart of the identity of events (*Blow-Up*) or people (*The Passenger*). On the whole, in the course of your work, there is a constant painful and demanding critique of that profound trace of meaning that one calls destiny.

This vacillation—or rather, to be more precise, this syncope of meaning—is expressed through the technical ways of the film medium (decor, shots, montage) that lack of competence keeps me from analyzing. I am here, rather, to talk about how your work engages, beyond the confines of cinema, all the artists of the contemporary world: you strive to render *subtle* the meaning of what man says, tells, sees, or feels, and this subtlety of meaning, this conviction that meaning does not crudely limit itself to the thing said, but goes on, ever further, fascinated by what is beyond meaning, is the very conviction, I feel, of all artists, whose object is not one or another technique, but this strange phenomenon of vibration. The object represented vibrates, to the detriment of dogma. I think now of what the painter [Georges] Braque once said: "The picture is finished when it has obliterated the idea." I think of Matisse, in his bed, drawing an olive tree and then observing the empty spaces between the olive branches, and discovering that, with this new way of seeing, he has left behind the habitual image of the object drawn, the cliché of the "olive tree." Matisse thus discovered the principle of Oriental art, which always chooses to paint the void, or rather, which grasps the representable object in that rare moment in which the whole of its identity falls brusquely into a new space—that of the Interstice. In a certain sense, your art is also an art of the Interstice (*L'avventura* would be a most obvious example), and thus, in this way too, your art has some relation to the Orient. It was your film on China that made me wish to travel there; and if this film was at first rejected by those who should have comprehended how its *force d'amour* was superior to any form of propaganda, it is because it was judged according to a reflex response of power and not according to a demand for truth. The artist is powerless, but he does have a certain bond with the truth; his work, always allegorical if it is a great work, grazes it; his work is the Indirect of truth.

Why is this subtlety of meaning decisive? Precisely because meaning, once fixed and imposed, once no longer subtle, becomes an instrument, a stake in the game of power. To make meaning subtle is therefore a secondary political activity, as is any attempt to deplete, disturb, and undo the fanaticism of meaning.

This is not done without risks, however. Thus, the third virtue of the artist (and I mean the word "virtue" in the Latin sense) is his fragility. The artist is never sure of living, of working—a simple, but serious premise—his obliteration is always possible.

The artist's primary fragility is this: he is part of a changing world, but he, too, is changing. This is banal, but for the artist it is dizzying, because he never knows if the work he is proposing is a product of the changing world or of the changing of his own subjectivity. You have always been aware, I think, of this relativity of Time, declaring, for example, in an interview: "If the things we speak of today are not those spoken of right after the war, then it means that the world around us has changed, and that we too have changed. Our demands, our purposes, our themes have all changed." The fragility here is that of an existential doubt that gradually possesses the artist as he moves through his life and his work; this doubt is difficult, even painful, because the artist never knows whether what he wishes to say is a truthful testimonial about how the world has changed or whether it is the simple, selfish reflection of his own nostalgia or desire: an Einsteinian traveler, he does not know whether it is the train or space-time that is moving, whether he is a witness or a man of desire.

Another explanation for the artist's fragility is, paradoxically, the resoluteness and the insistence of his gaze. Power, of whatever form, because it is violence, never gazes; if it were to gaze a minute more (a minute too long), it would lose its essence as power. He, the artist, pauses and gazes closely, and I can imagine that you became a filmmaker because the camera is an eye, that is, constrained by its technical nature to gaze. What you add, as do all great filmmakers, is to gaze at things radically, to the point of exhausting them. On the one hand you take a long, close look at what you were not asked to look at by the convention of politics (the Chinese peasants) or by the narrative convention (the *temps mort* of an adventure). On the other hand, your favorite hero is he who gazes (photographer or reporter). This is dangerous, because gazing at something far longer than you were asked to (I insist on this supplement of intensity) upsets the established order in whatever form, since the extent or the very duration of the gaze is normally controlled by society. Whence—if the work escapes this control—the scandalous nature of certain photographs and certain films, not the most indecent or the most aggressive ones, but merely the ones that are the most "posed."

The artist is therefore threatened, not only by the established power (the list of martyred artists censured by the State throughout the course of History would be desperately long), but also by the collective feeling, always there, that a society can get on very well without art. The artist's activity is suspect because it upsets the comfort, the security of established meanings, because it is at once extravagant and gratuitous, and because the new society, in search of itself through various systems, has not yet decided what it must think, what it shall have to think of *luxury*. Our fate is uncertain, and this uncertainty does not bear a simple relation to the political solutions that we can imagine for the troubles of the world. Our fate depends on this monumental History that determines, in an almost inconceivable manner, no longer our needs, but our desires.

Dear Antonioni, I have tried to communicate in my intellectual language the reasons that make you—and not only in the realm of cinema—one of the artists of our time. This compliment is not simple, as you know, because being an artist today is no longer a profession supported by the comforting consciousness of a great sacred or social function; it no longer means tranquilly taking one's place in the Pantheon of the Guiding Lights of Humanity. It means, with each work, having to face in oneself those specters of modern subjectivity which are—since we are no longer priests—ideological lassitude, bad social conscience, the attraction to and distaste left by facile art, the trepidation of responsibility, and the incessant scruple that tears the artist apart, between solitude and gregariousness. It is therefore necessary that you take full advantage of this peaceful, harmonious moment in which an entire assemblage comes to recognize, admire, and love your work. Because tomorrow the hard work begins once again.

Antonioni's Response to Barthes

Dear Friend,

Thanks for La chambre claire, *which is at once a very beautiful and a luminous book. It astonishes me that you say in Chapter Three that you are a "subject bandied back and forth between two languages, one expressive, the other critical," and that you confirm that opinion in your extraordinary first lecture at the Collège de France.*

But what is the artist also if not a subject bandied back and forth between two languages, one which expresses and one which does not?

It is alway like that. The inexorable and inexplicable drama of artistic creation . . .

Antonioni wrote the letter [in italics] to Barthes, but it arrived too late. The letter and the rest of the text were added to Barthes's homage in the *Cahiers du cinéma* 311 (May 1980), 11.

I was in the process of writing this letter when the news of the death of R. B. came by telephone. I did not know that he had had an accident and I felt the breath knocked out of me and an acute sadness. The first thing that came to mind was this: "So, there's a little less sweetness and intelligence in the world now. A bit less love. All the love which, *through living and writing,* he put into his life and his work."

I believe that the longer we proceed in this world (a world which regresses brutally), the more we shall miss the virtues which were his.

The Disappearance (On Antonioni)

Pascal Bonitzer

From *L'avventura* to *L'eclisse* a search for formal richness deepens in Antonioni, a search which seems to exhaust the possibilities of black and white even before the turn to color in *Deserto rosso*. Antonioni is a painter in the sense that, for him, white, black, grey, and the various colors of the spectrum are not merely ornamental, atmospheric, or emotional, but are veritable ideas which envelop characters and events. *La notte* is not only a film *in* black and white, but a film *about* black and white, a giant chessboard on which the characters move by themselves or are moved by chance, to which they have offered up a desire gone dead. White connotes the absence, the disaffection, the emptiness that paralyzes Antonioni's characters. Thus it is that in the trilogy formal richness—always suspect—has as its pretext (but is it only a pretext?) a thwarted love relationship, which either fails to take root (*L'avventura, L'eclisse*) or withers (*La notte*). This miscarriage contaminates the narrative fabric. The narrative is assaulted by an essential unfulfillment, as if the "disaffection" of the lovers is matched, in a slightly different sense, by a "disaffection" within the narrative itself. Morally speaking, the protagonists resemble the locales through which they disenchantedly move: deserted, disorganized, defamiliarized spaces, doubtless testifying to the dramatic change in the landscape, in the urban fabric, at the beginning of the Sixties. Disoriented, the characters are trapped in a world that offers them no point of reference, but only the blind reflexes of their deteriorated mental universe (for "the external is a mirror reflecting the internal"—Witold Gombrowicz, *Bokakai*). We note incidentally that there is no nostalgia in Antonioni (unlike Visconti or Fellini) for any sort of past, no moral, ethical, or sentimental point of view. On the contrary, what characterizes Antonioni's cinema is a positive interest in deserts of a new sort—spaces that are amorphous, discontinuous, empty; spaces constituted by the undifferentiated fabric of urban mutability. Antonioni's characters are drawn to the limit by emptiness, by frigidity, by

From *Michelangelo Antonioni: Identification di un autore,* ed. Giorgio Tinazzi (Parma: Società Produzioni Editoriali, 1985). Translated by Chris Breyer, Gavriel Moses, and Seymour Chatman.

abstract spaces which absorb and swallow up the human figure, the beloved face, the forms of our fellow creatures. The adventure they live is a disappearance.

L'avventura is ostensibly the story of a disappearance, but a disappearance whose importance and density evaporate little by little, until the very structure and form of the narrative are perilously contaminated and impaired; what happens in reality is *the disappearance of the disappearance* of Anna (which, however, does not mean her return). An odd story. *A Woman Disappears:* such a title might as easily suggest an exciting chase.

We note that many of Antonioni's other films have for their argument an inquest, a police-style investigation (this holds as well for *Identificazione di una donna,* the very title of which recalls the world of the police). In many Antonioni films something or someone disappears, but this disappearance is such that the tension appropriate to the police investigation, to the chase, to suspense, tends to vanish as well. Thus, in *L'avventura,* the disappearance of Anna underlines, insidiously, another disappearance, more secret and harder to make out, which haunts and misleads the remaining characters, preventing them from concentrating on the search for the missing woman. Antonioni has never been forgiven for the absent-mindedness that seems to overcome his characters—and perhaps *even* his camera—and that fractures his narrative. Anna's disappearance opens an unhealable wound in the characters' very hearts. Their drama becomes from then on something different from what is typical of many films: that of finding or definitively losing a missing person (note that the question becomes moot at some point simply because it loses its meaning). Their drama is rather that of not being able to put themselves together again.

Plastically, narratively, and ontologically, Antonioni's is a world in pieces, and "putting the pieces back together," which neatly represents both the task of the police and the unattainable goal of the lovers in crisis, is precisely the operation abandoned by Antonioni's derailed, alienated characters.

Hence everything happens as if the disassembled puzzle interests Antonioni more than its eventual reassembly. This is doubtless why his characters—even if they find themselves in a police story—act like detectives, but without a purpose and out of context. There is never a question (even if at first we believe there is) of finally recovering in its integrity the face of the beloved or the hidden truth, because the scattering, the explosion, the fragmentation of the world will not suffer the sentiment of love or belief in any truth to remain unique and whole. After all, Antonioni's characters seem prey to a gnawing "Who cares?" attitude, lending his films that inimitable touch of melancholy that has provoked such resistance. Nonetheless, we should not limit ourselves to this ethico-psychological question, as if it were the fundamental concern of the filmmaker. For everything points to the contrary, most of all Antonioni's formal inventiveness, an inventiveness that expresses a *positive* adventure, through (of course) moral and psychological—virtually physical—decomposition, which leads us to a nonhuman, nonfigurative universe that amounts to an abstract apotheosis. The universe expands, scatters, and cools, but within this entropy we find a secret happiness, the informal felicity of random spots (as in abstract paintings). Beyond the basically human point of view incarnated in the protagonists, there is another point of view. That abstract point of view is picked up in a nonhuman way by the camera in random movements—explosions, clouds, Brownian motions, spots, indeed, a neutral space filled with any movement whatsoever within which the flow of Antonioni's film comes to rest.

Antonioni, modern artist, modern painter, is interested in random forces, forms born of happenstance. We find, in his perambulating characters (people walk a lot in Antonioni's films), an insistent fascination with the amorphous, the formally abstract, the self-hidden, self-erased figure slipping into nondifferentiation. Is this the aesthetic manifestation of the death wish? In *L'avventura,* there is Gabriele Ferzetti's gesture of overturning an inkwell on the academic sketch of an ornamental fan vault done by a young architect. Although he pretends it was done inadvertently, the movement (a pendular motion [of his keychain] which lengthens "by itself") is subject to at least two contradictory readings. One is psychological and negative. The character is bitter, weary; he no longer believes in anything. His gesture can be explained as the resentment of a middle-aged man, full of self-disgust, against the freshness of a young architect who is ingenuously interested in ornamental vaults. But the gesture can also express a sort of aesthetic detachment, or perhaps even an aesthetic vertigo, the vertigo of the aleatory or random spot, which is more profoundly childish than the academic drawing which it destroys. As with anything to do with the random, there is ambiguity here, between destruction and creation, chaos and cosmos. To overturn an inkwell on a half-finished sketch is to destroy the sketch, but it is also to splatter on the paper, in place of the sketch (the dry academic copy), a wild ink-flower.

In the same way the art of the cinema inextricably contains a priori forms (the *mental object* which the *mise-en-scène* must bring forth on the screen) and raw images offered by the real world. The sketch disappears, but this disappearance is not a simple erasure; we shall never recover in its primal freshness "the virgin page defended by its whiteness." The inkblot signifies the entropy, the degradation, the irreversibility of events, but it is also the creation of a unique though shapeless and nameless image. How can we avoid seeing, in this "shapeless and nameless" mark, the adventure itself, the desired and completed destiny of Antonioni's heroes?

In *L'eclisse*, what sort of eclipse are we dealing with? What is eclipsed? What sun is hidden? No less than the characters of the film, vanished from their very meeting places, a place now empty which the camera revisits at the end of the day—and the film. This emptiness is an emptiness of the city, of anonymity, of insignificant encounters, and of the night which envelops everything. But since cinema, like the unconscious, does not know negation, emptiness in Antonioni exists positively; it is haunted by presence. There is no more beautiful moment in an Antonioni film (and each seems structured to reach this end) than that in which his characters, his human beings, are cancelled, only so as to leave behind, it seems, a space without attributes, a pure space, "a space which remains uniform unto itself whether it expands or contracts." Empty space is not a void: full of mists, of fleeting faces, of evanescent presences or of random movements, this space represents that final point of being finally freed from the negativity of intentions, of passions, of human existence.

Antonioni, *L'avventura,* and Waiting

Gianni Celati

fter many years it seems that Antonioni's *L'avventura* is one of those works whose effects can be seen everywhere, as a world-vision that is no longer merely individual, but collective and of our time. For example, without this vision, the cinema of Wim Wenders and of Jim Jarmusch would be unthinkable, as would be many other films and stories that employ slow descriptive rhythms, rhythms of hesitation without the prospect [of some narrative resolution]. It is here that a form of epochal understanding has been admitted to the canon: a kind of waiting that is no longer at the mercy of expectation, no longer deceived by expectation.

Seeing *L'avventura* again, I began to think about this new kind of waiting the moment that the girl disappears on the island. The bare island, those wandering or stationary characters, the low sky, the grey and sidereal view—like any desert they uncover the kingdom of the indeterminate, where the pretensions of culture quickly crumble. The views of the island are never offered as finished descriptions, but rather as pauses within the landscape, as tarries which produce dead moments, *temps morts.* The characters move up and down without a destination; they are simply forced to wait. As for the expectation of finding the girl, of discovering the truth, of making the event determinate or explicable, all that seems to collapse almost immediately into an enormous abulia or apathy.

Back in 1960, and perhaps even now, all this has often been related by intellectual discourse to a "collapse of values" in European culture. But clearly such discourse presupposes that before the collapse the so-called values of art, culture, and morality had a foundation. The simple unveiling of values as an empty order, without points of reference to be found outside the discourse that continuously justifies and defines them, comes to be an experiential truth that culture can never acknowledge. All attestations of the "collapse of values" are nothing but the anxiety of self-definition *specific* to our culture and the growth of this anxiety typical of the modern view of the world.

From *Cinema & Cinema* 14, no. 49 (June 1987), 5–6. Translated by Guido Fink.

If Antonioni's film participated in such [ideological] poverty, we probably would not be able to keep on seeing it. All we would find in it, over and over, would be the very same presuppositions of the intellectuals who may seem to have inspired it, and a view of the world, a series of statements, which dictate what we must understand.

But from the moment on the island when the girl disappears there begins a process of undermining expectations—the expectations generated by the narrated events combined with those produced by the values of culture, of art and morality, which are discussed at length in the film. That the manifestations of these values are gradually replaced by abulia seems to me the liberating aspect of this new type of adventure, in which the characters no longer manage to kill time. In other epochs, adventure was precisely a race amid dangers so as to kill time, to cheat the convention of waiting through the arousal of expectation: but what happens when time is presented as something that can no longer be cheated?

Let me point out just one aspect of this epistemology. In the films of Antonioni, as in the films of Wim Wenders, the frontal view permits delays without anxiety, which are often really *temps morts* along the thread of narration. The frontal view exploits orthogonal symmetries, and thus constitutes an orderly and simple way of looking at things. In Walker Evans's pictures, as in Antonioni's film (which strike me as comparable), the frontal view amounts to a choice of a low threshold of intensity, of a narrative mode which avoids excitement and relates everything back to a calm, composed style of representation. Unlike, that is, the oblique or foreshortened angle, which always suggests an air of instability, thus introducing expectations that annihilate the simple form of looking, the delay and halt without anxiety.

Antonioni's film ends with such a delay, a frontal view that exploits orthogonal symmetry so as to order our gaze: the girl stands in profile and the man sits on the bench, at dawn, while in the background there is the white curtain of the sky. There is a type of understanding which, here, begins to find its figures, which provokes the sensation of the ineluctable present, the true time of waiting. This ineluctable present, this time that cannot be killed, is the liberation that the film entrusts to us.

If the essence of an era is revealed in the way in which it entrusts itself to time, we must say that our era's essence inheres in the dream of being another era: "more advanced," "future"—this is the continuous dream of the modern view of the world. Thus our era is an era which escapes itself, an era without an era, for its waiting for another time is all crisscrossed by expectations which kill time, which render the present ever more hidden, to the stupefaction of knowledge and culture. To perceive the empty present of an era which dreams of being another era seems then the only way of understanding context—the only kind of understanding that does not depend on the pretensions of culture and that tends to entrust itself once again to time without killing it in advance with expectations.

I started to think about this theme of waiting while looking at a photo by Luigi Ghirri, which can be considered a commentary or a homage to Antonioni. There is the frontal view of a grassy soccer field, one side-line traced by the shadow of great trees that close off the view, and there in the middle, the rectangle of the empty goalposts, in a sort of great silence. Isn't the net of a soccer field the destination of expectancy, here mysteriously suspended in a present without expectation?

In this kind of insight established by Antonioni, all places become observable; there is no longer a difference between beautiful and ugly places. They are all possible places in which to linger; and lingering is the trope of our inhabiting earth, inhabiting the realm of the indeterminate. When we cease to experience a landscape as the realm of the indeterminate, and home of the indescribable, it means that our understanding of the environment has been destroyed.

Last year on a cloudy day I was walking along the banks of the Po toward Porto Tolle, in places unchanged from when they were used as locations for *Il grido,* the film in which Antonioni began to talk to us about our indescribable landscape. A few days later I saw Visconti's *Ossessione* again, which talks about the same landscape, and which is the last Italian film to speak unrestrainedly of death and destiny, of death as our destiny. It was *Ossessione* that caused the spread of notions like "death is the fault of society," "we don't fall ill because we are mortal, but because economic conditions are not what they should be," etc. And what followed was the kind of totalitarian propaganda that dictates that everything in a person's life depends on ideology and social security.

Politicians and administrators and other assassins of the soul, the delirium of advertising—all of these will definitively impose on this country the dream of being another country, and ever more expectations of a "future" which (in any case) will be catastrophic, and ever more machines and spectacles and cultural discourse to kill time.

Filmography and
Bibliography

Antonioni Filmography, 1943–1982

Antonioni's first seven films were short documentaries:

1943–1947 *Gente del Po* (*People of the Po*)
Screenplay by Antonioni.

1948 *N.U.* (*Nettezza urbana*) (*Municipal Sanitation*)
Screenplay by Antonioni.

1948–1949 *L'amorosa menzogna* (*Lies of Love*)
Screenplay by Antonioni.

1949 *Superstizione* (*Superstition*)
Screenplay by Antonioni.

1949 *Sette canne, un vestito* (*Seven Reeds, One Suit*)
Screenplay by Antonioni.

1950 *La villa dei mostri* (*The Villa of the Monsters*)
Screenplay by Antonioni.

1950 *La funivia del Faloria* (*The Funicular of Mount Faloria*)
Screenplay by Antonioni.

Feature films:

1950 *Cronaca di un amore* (*Story of a Love Affair*)
Screenplay by Antonioni, Daniele d'Anza, Silvio Giovaninetti, Francesco Maselli, Piero Tellini.

1952 *I vinti* (*The Vanquished*, or *The Beaten Ones*, or *Youth and Perversion*)
Screenplay by Antonioni, Suso Cecchi D'Amico, Diego Fabbri, Turi Vasile, Giorgio Bassani.

1952–1953 *La signora senza camelie* (*The Lady without Camellias*)
Screenplay by Antonioni, Suso Cecchi D'Amico, Francesco Maselli, P. M. Pasinetti.

1953   "Tentato suicidio" ("Suicide Attempt"), an episode in *Amore in città* (*Love in the City*)
Screenplay by Antonioni, Cesare Zavattini, Aldo Buzzi, Luigi Chiarini, Luigi Malerba, Tullio Pinelli, Vittorio Veltroni

1955   *Le amiche* (*The Girlfriends*)
Screenplay by Antonioni, Suso Cecchi D'Amico, Alba de Cespedes, based on the novella *Tra donne sole*, by Cesare Pavese.

1956   *Il grido* (*The Cry*)
Screenplay by Antonioni, Elio Bartolini, Ennio de Concini, based on a story by Antonioni.

1960   *L'avventura* (*The Adventure*)
Screenplay by Antonioni, Elio Bartolini, Tonino Guerra, based on a story by Antonioni.

1961   *La notte* (*The Night*)
Screenplay by Antonioni, Ennio Flaiano, Tonino Guerra, based on a story by Antonioni.

1962   *L'eclisse* (*The Eclipse*)
Screenplay by Antonioni, Tonino Guerra, Elio Bartolini, Ottiero Ottieri, based on a story by Antonioni.

1964   *Deserto rosso* (*Red Desert*)
Screenplay by Antonioni, Tonino Guerra, based on a story by Antonioni and Guerra.

1965   "Il provino" ("The Screen Test"), preface to *I tre volti* (*The Three Faces*)
Screenplay by Piero Tosi based on his own story.

1966   *Blow-Up*
Screenplay by Antonioni, Tonino Guerra, English dialogue in collaboration with Edward Bond, based on the short story "Las babas del diablo," by Julio Cortázar.

1969   *Zabriskie Point*
Screenplay by Antonioni, Fred Gardner, Sam Shepard, Tonino Guerra, Clare Peploe.

1972   *Chung Kuo Cina* (*China*)
A documentary.

1974   *The Passenger* (in Europe: *Profession: Reporter*)
Screenplay by Antonioni, Mark Peploe, Peter Wollen, based on a story by Mark Peploe.

1980   *Il mistero di Oberwald* (*The Mystery of Oberwald*)
Screenplay by Antonioni and Tonino Guerra, based on the play *L'aigle à deux têtes* (*The Eagle with Two Heads*) by Jean Cocteau.

1982   *Identificazione di una donna* (*Identification of a Woman*)
Screenplay by Antonioni, Gerard Brach, in collaboration with Tonino Guerra, based on a story by Antonioni.

Selected Bibliography

Amerio, Piero. "Antonioni: appunti per una psicologia dell'irrelevant." In *Michelangelo Antonioni,* edited by Carlo di Carlo. Rome: Edizioni di Bianco e nero, 1964.

Andrew, J. Dudley. "The Stature of Objects in Antonioni's Films." *Tri-Quarterly,* no. 11 (Winter 1968), 40–59.

Antonioni, Michelangelo, in collaboration with Elio Bartolini and Tonino Guerra. *L'avventura.* Edited by Tommaso Chiaretti. 2nd ed. Bologna: Cappelli, 1977.

———. "Il 'fatto' e l'immagine." Translated as "One A: The Event and the Image." *Sight and Sound* 33, no. 1 (Winter 1963), 14.

———. *Quel bowling sul Tevere.* Turin: Einaudi, 1983. Translated by William Arrowsmith as *That Bowling Alley on the Tiber.* New York: Oxford University Press, 1985. [A collection of thirty-three stories and ideas for films that never got made.]

———. "La realtà e il cinema-diretto." *Cinema nuovo* 13, no. 167 (January–February 1964), 8–10. Translated as "Reality and Cinéma Verité." *Atlas* 9, no. 2 (February 1965), 122–123. Reprinted in *Blow-Up.* New York: Simon and Schuster, 1971.

———. *Screenplays.* Translated by Roger J. Moore and Louis Brigante. New York: Orion Press, 1963.

———. *Sei Film.* [Includes shooting scripts of *Le amiche, Il grido, L'avventura, La notte, L'eclisse,* and *Deserto rosso* in Italian.] The important introduction by Antonioni was translated as "The

Hollywood Myth Has Fallen," *Popular Photography* (July 1967), 94–97ff.

———. "A Talk with Michelangelo Antonioni on His Work." *Film Culture*, no. 24 (Spring 1962), 45–61 (excerpted in the Grove Press edition of *L'avventura*, pp. 211–234). Translated by Louis Brigante from "La malattia dei sentimenti." *Bianco e nero* 22, nos. 2–3 (February-March 1961), 69–95.

L'avventura: from the filmscript by Michelangelo Antonioni with Elio Bartolini and Tonino Guerra. Reconstructed from the film by David Denby and Jon Swan. Edited by George Amberg and Robert Hughes. New York: Grove Press, 1969. [Contains a translation of Tommaso Chiaretti's account of the making of the film, notes on omitted and variant scenes, interviews with Antonioni, and critiques by Amberg, Penelope Houston, Penelope Gilliatt, Bosley Crowther, John Simon, Dwight Macdonald, Joseph Bennett, and William S. Pechter.]

Cameron, Ian, and Robin Wood. *Antonioni*. Rev. ed. New York: Praeger, 1971.

Chatman, Seymour. *Michelangelo Antonioni, or the Surface of the World*. Berkeley and Los Angeles: University of California Press, 1985.

Cowie, Peter. *Antonioni, Bergman, Resnais*. London: Tantivy Press, 1963.

Cuccu, Lorenzo. *La visione come problema: forme e svolgimento del cinema di Antonioni*. Rome: Bulzoni, 1973.

Di Carlo, Carlo, ed. *Michelangelo Antonioni*. Rome: Edizioni di Bianco e nero, 1963. [A collection of essays on Antonioni, with an extremely full bibliography up to 1963.]

Fink, Guido. "Antonioni e il giallo alla rovescia." *Cinema nuovo* 12, no. 162 (March-April 1963), 100–106. Translated as "Antonioni et le film policier à l'envers," *Etudes cinématographiques*, nos. 36–37 (Winter 1964), 7–16.

Gilman, Richard. "About Nothing—with Precision." *Theatre Arts* 46, no. 7 (July 1962), 10–12.

Godard, Jean-Luc. "La nuit, l'eclipse, l'aurore: Entretien avec Michelangelo Antonioni." *Cahiers du cinéma*, no. 160 (November 1964), 12–16. A translation from a recording of the interview was made by Elizabeth Kingsley-Rowe and appeared as "Jean-Luc Godard Interviews Michelangelo Antonioni." *Movie*, no. 12 (Spring 1965), 31–34. Reprinted in Andrew Sarris, *Interviews with Film Directors*. Indianapolis: Bobbs-Merrill, 1967.

Houston, Penelope. "Michelangelo Antonioni." In *Cinema: A Critical Dictionary,* ed. Richard Roud. London: Martin Secker and Warburg, 1980.

Kauffmann, Stanley. "An Artist for an Age." *The New Republic* (February 26, 1962), 26–27. Reprinted in his *A World on Film.* New York: Dell, 1967.

———. "L'avventura." *Horizon* 14, no. 4 (Autumn 1972), 48–55. Reprinted in altered form in his *Living Images: Film Comment and Criticism.* New York: Harper & Row, 1975.

Leprohon, Pierre. *Michelangelo Antonioni.* 4th ed. Paris: Editions Seghers, 1969. An earlier edition was translated by Scott Sullivan as *Michelangelo Antonioni: An Introduction.* New York: Simon and Schuster, 1963.

Lyons, Robert Joseph. *Michelangelo Antonioni's Neo-Realism: A World View.* New York: Arno Press, 1976.

Manceaux, Michele. "An Interview with Antonioni." *Sight and Sound* 30, no. 1 (Winter 1960), 5–8. Translated from "Entretien avec Michelangelo Antonioni." *L'express* (September 8, 1960), 32–34.

Mitgang, Herbert. "Cinema Concept of a Modern Michelangelo." *The New York Times* (December 2, 1961), Section 2, p. 9. [An interview.]

Perry, Ted, and René Prieto. *Michelangelo Antonioni: A Guide to References and Resources.* Boston: G. K. Hall, 1986. [Contains the most complete and up-to-date bibliography.]

Samuels, Charles Thomas. "An Interview with Antonioni." In his *Encountering Directors.* New York: G. P. Putnam's Sons, 1971.

Strick, Philip. *Michelangelo Antonioni.* A *Motion* monograph, no. 5 (March 1963). London: Motion Publications, 1963.

Young, Vernon. "Nostalgia of the Infinite: Notes on Chirico, Antonioni, and Resnais." *Arts* 37, no. 4 (January 1963), 14–21. Reprinted in *On Film: Unpopular Essays on a Popular Art.* New York: Quadrangle/The New York Times Book Co., 1972.